THE USBORNE
INTERNET-LINKED
WORLD ATLAS

Originally published as *The Usborne Internet-Linked Children's World Atlas*

Stephanie Turnbull and Emma Helbrough
Designers: Stephen Moncrieff and Andrea Slane
Consultant cartographic editor: Craig Asquith

Cartography by European Map Graphics Ltd
Map design by Laura Fearn and Keith Newell
Consultant: Dr. Roger Trend, Senior Lecturer in Earth Science
and Geography Education, University of Exeter

SCHOLASTIC INC.
New York Toronto London Auckland Sydney
Mexico City New Delhi Hong Kong Buenos Aires

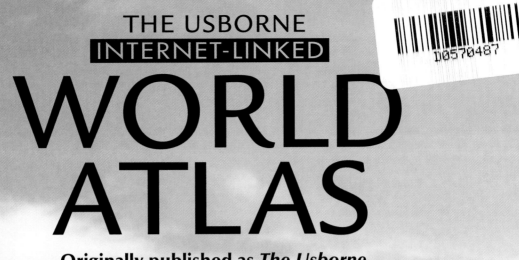

CONTENTS

Here you can see dramatic cloud formations at sunset over a desert in California, U.S.A. Below is a large sandstone arch, shaped by the weather over many years.

INTERNET LINKS

This book contains descriptions of many interesting Web sites where you can find out more about maps and places around the world. For links to these sites, go to the Usborne Quicklinks Web site at **www.usborne-quicklinks.com** and enter the keyword "atlas". There you will find links to take you to all the Web sites.

Site availability

The links on the Usborne Quicklinks Web site will be reviewed and updated regularly. If any sites become unavailable, we will, if possible, replace them with suitable alternatives.

Occasionally, you may get a message saying that a Web site is unavailable. This may be temporary, so try again a few hours later, or even the next day.

> ### Internet links
> For links to all the Web sites described in this book, go to **www.usborne-quicklinks.com** and enter the keyword "atlas".

Help

For general help and advice on using the Internet, go to the Usborne Quicklinks Web site and click on "Net Help".

To find out more about using your Web browser, click on your browser's Help menu and choose "Contents and Index". You'll find a searchable dictionary containing tips on how to find your way around the Internet easily.

What you need

The Web sites described in this book can be accessed using a standard home computer and a Web browser (the software that enables you to display information from the Internet). Here's a list of the basic requirements:

- A PC with Microsoft® Windows® 98 or a later version, or a Macintosh computer with System 9.0 or later

- 64Mb RAM

- A Web browser such as Microsoft® Internet Explorer 5, or Netscape® Navigator 4.7, or later versions

- Connection to the Internet via a modem (preferably 56kbps) or a faster digital or cable line

- An account with an Internet Service Provider (ISP)

- A sound card to hear sound files

> ### Computer not essential
> If you don't have use of the Internet, don't worry. This atlas is a complete, self-contained reference book on its own.

Extras

Some Web sites need additional programs, called plug-ins, to play sounds, or to show videos, animations or 3-D images. If you go to a site and you do not have the necessary plug-in, a message should come up on the screen.

There is usually a button on the site that you can click on to download the plug-in. Alternatively, go to Usborne Quicklinks and click on "Net Help". There you can find links to download plug-ins. Here is a list of plug-ins that you might need:

- **QuickTime** – lets you play video clips.

- **RealPlayer**® – lets you play video clips and sound files.

- **Flash**™ – lets you play animations.

- **Shockwave**® – lets you play animations and enjoy interactive sites.

Computer viruses

A computer virus is a program that can damage your computer. A virus can get into your computer when you download programs from the Internet, or in an attachment (an extra file) that arrives with an e-mail. We strongly recommend that you buy anti-virus software to protect your computer and that you update the software regularly. You can buy anti-virus software at computer stores or download it from the Internet. To find out more about viruses, go to Usborne Quicklinks and click on "Net Help".

Note for parents

The Web sites described in this book are regularly checked and reviewed by Usborne editors and the links in Usborne Quicklinks are updated. However, the content of a Web site may change at any time and Usborne Publishing is not responsible for the content of any Web site other than its own.

We recommend that children are supervised while on the Internet, that they do not use Internet Chat Rooms, and that you use Internet filtering software to block unsuitable material.

Please ensure that your children read and follow the safety guidelines below. For more information, go to the Net Help area on the Usborne Quicklinks Web site at **www.usborne-quicklinks.com**

Internet safety

- Ask your parent's or guardian's permission before you connect to the Internet. They can then stay nearby if they think they should do so.

- If you write a message in a Web site guest book or on a Web site message board, do not include your e-mail address, real name, address or telephone number.

- If a Web site asks you to log in or register by typing your name or e-mail address, ask the permission of an adult first.

- If you receive e-mail from someone you don't know, tell an adult and do not reply to the e-mail.

- Never arrange to meet anyone you have talked to on the Internet.

WHAT IS AN ATLAS?

An atlas is a collection of maps. This atlas helps you explore our world and find out more about its varied landscapes, famous cities and amazing sights.

What maps show

A map is an image that represents an area of the Earth's surface, usually from above. Unlike a photograph, which shows exactly what an area looks like, a map can show features of the area in a clear, simplified way. It can also give different information, such as place names. Symbols are often used to mark features such as volcanoes and waterfalls.

This is a satellite image of part of the Galapagos Islands. Using the map on this page, can you identify the islands shown in the photograph?

Which way is up?

Although the Earth doesn't have a top and a bottom, north is usually at the top of maps. But it is sometimes more convenient to reposition a map, so north might not necessarily be at the top. Some maps have a compass symbol that indicates where north lies.

Wolf volcano

Darwin volcano

San Salvador

Fernandina

Alcedo volcano

La Cumbre volcano

Santa Cruz

Isabela

Sierra Negra volcano

Cerro Azul volcano

This simple map of the central Galapagos Islands names the main islands and their volcanoes.

Floreana

Physical and political

Physical maps indicate natural features such as mountains, deserts, rivers and lakes. Political maps focus on the division of the Earth's surface into different countries. Look on pages 18–19 for a political map of the world, and on pages 20–21 for a physical map. Most of the maps in this atlas show physical features as well as country borders, cities and towns.

Map scales

The size of a map in relation to the area it shows is called its scale. Some maps have a scale bar, which is a rule with measurements. It tells you how many miles or km are represented by a certain distance on the map. Other maps show these relative distances just as numbers. For example, the figure 1:100 means that 1cm on the map represents 100cm on the Earth's surface.

The scale of a map depends on its purpose. A map showing the whole world is on a very small scale, but a town plan is on a much larger scale so that features such as roads can be shown clearly.

1:80,000,000

| 0 | 1,000 | 2,000 | 3,000km |
| 0 | | 1,000 | 2,000 miles |

This map of Europe is on a small scale so that it all fits onto one small map.

1:7,000,000

| 0 | 100 | 200 | 300km |
| 0 | | 100 | 200 miles |

This map of Denmark is on a larger scale to show more detail.

Internet links

For links to the following Web sites, go to **www.usborne-quicklinks.com**

Web site 1 Look at physical and political maps of different countries.

Web site 2 Find street maps of any town or city in the world.

Using this atlas

The maps in this atlas are grouped by continent. There are seven continents, which are (from largest to smallest): Asia, Africa, North America, South America, Antarctica, Europe and Australasia and Oceania. Each map section is accompanied by photographs and satellite images showing some of the continent's most impressive sights. You can look up many of these places on the maps.

This is Mount Rushmore, a huge sculpture of four U.S. presidents, which is one of the most famous sights in the U.S.A. Throughout this atlas you will see pictures of many more well known landmarks from around the world.

THE EARTH FROM SPACE

Modern technology has enabled scientists to make more accurate maps of the world than ever before. Even remote places, such as deserts, ocean floors and mountain ranges, have been mapped in detail, using information from satellites that observe the Earth from space.

What is a satellite?

Artificial satellites are machines that orbit, or travel around, the Earth. They observe the Earth using a technique called remote sensing. Instruments on the satellite monitor the Earth from a distance, and send back pictures of its surface. Satellites also monitor moons and other planets.

This satellite monitors the Earth 24 hours a day. It uses powerful radar that pierces through clouds. This means that the satellite can provide images of the Earth in all weather conditions.

Satellite movement

Some satellites orbit the Earth at a height of between 5km (3 miles) and 1,500km (930 miles), providing views of different parts of the planet. Others stay above the same place all the time, moving at the same speed as the Earth rotates to give a constant view of a particular area. These are called geostationary satellites. They travel at a height of around 36,000km (22,370 miles).

Internet links

For links to the following Web sites, go to **www.usborne-quicklinks.com**

Web site 1 Look at detailed satellite pictures of any part of the world.

Web site 2 See satellite images that show which parts of the Earth are in daylight or darkness at this very moment, plus up-to-date weather conditions across the globe.

This satellite image of Sicily was taken in July 2001. It shows the volcano Mount Etna erupting. You can see smoke from the volcano on the right of the picture.

Satellite uses

Satellite pictures can be used to help predict and monitor natural hazards such as volcanic eruptions. They can also help scientists to observe the effects people have on the environment, for example the destruction of rainforests in South America. Satellite images are often artificially shaded to highlight relevant features, for example forests, so that they are easier to see.

Remote sensing

Satellites use a range of remote sensing techniques. One type is radar, which can provide images of the Earth even when it is dark or cloudy. Radar works by reflecting radio waves off a target object. The time it takes for a wave to bounce back indicates how far away the object is.

Powerful cameras provide pictures of the Earth's surface. Often, infrared cameras are used. Different surfaces reflect infrared rays differently, so infrared images of the Earth are able to show its various types of land surfaces, such as deserts, grasslands and forests.

This satellite image of the Earth is shaded to show different types of land. Deserts and other dry regions are red, and areas with lots of vegetation are orange.

DIVIDING LINES

The Earth is divided up with imaginary lines that help us measure distances and find where places are. There are two sets of lines, called latitude and longitude.

This arctic fox lives in northern Canada, very near the Arctic Circle line of latitude.

Latitude lines

Lines of latitude run around the globe. They are parallel to each other and get shorter the closer they are to the two poles. The latitude line that runs around the middle of the Earth is called the Equator. It is the most important line of latitude as all other lines are measured north or south of it.

Longitude lines

Lines of longitude run from the North Pole to the South Pole. All the lines are the same length, and they all meet at the North and South Poles.

The most important line of longitude is the Prime Meridian Line, which runs through Greenwich, in England. All other lines of longitude are measured east or west of this line.

Other lines

The Equator is not the only named line of latitude. The Tropic of Cancer is a line north of the Equator. The Tropic of Capricorn is at the same distance south of the Equator. Between these lines are the hottest, wettest parts of the world. This region is called the tropics.

The Arctic Circle is a latitude line far north of the Equator. The area north of this includes the North Pole and is called the Arctic. On the other side of the globe is the Antarctic Circle. The area south of this includes the South Pole and is known as the Antarctic.

Latitude lines *Longitude lines*

This drawing of the Earth shows some of the main latitude and longitude lines.

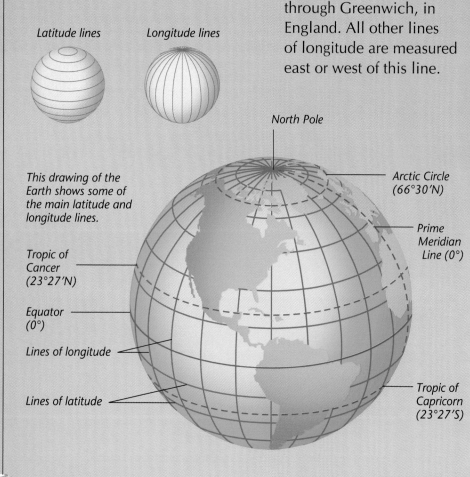

North Pole

Arctic Circle
(66°30'N)

Prime
Meridian
Line (0°)

Tropic of
Cancer
(23°27'N)

Equator
(0°)

Lines of longitude

Lines of latitude

Tropic of
Capricorn
(23°27'S)

Internet links

For a link to a Web site where you can find out more about the Earth's lines of latitude and longitude, and test your knowledge with a great latitude and longitude quiz, go to
www.usborne-quicklinks.com

Using the lines

Lines of latitude and longitude are measured in degrees (°). The positions of places are described according to which lines of latitude and longitude are nearest to them. For example, a place with a location of 50°S and 100°E has a latitude 50 degrees south of the Equator, and a longitude 100 degrees east of the Prime Meridian Line.

Exact locations

The distance between degrees is divided up to give even more precise measurements. Each degree is divided into 60 minutes ('), and each minute is divided into 60 seconds ("). The subdivisions allow us to locate any place on Earth. For example, the city of New York, U.S.A., is at 40°42'51"N and 74°00'23"W.

The steamy rainforests of Malaysia lie near the Equator. Many apes, like the one shown here, live in these rainforests.

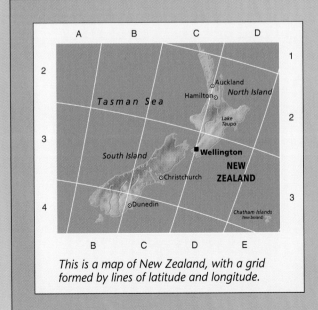

This is a map of New Zealand, with a grid formed by lines of latitude and longitude.

Using a grid

Lines of latitude and longitude form grids on maps. The maps in this book look similar to the one on the left. The columns that run from top to bottom are formed by lines of longitude and marked with letters. The rows running across the page are formed by lines of latitude and are numbered.

All the places listed in the map index on page 130 have a letter and a number reference that tell you where to find them on a particular page. For example, on the map on the left, the city of Christchurch would have a grid reference of C3.

HOW MAPS ARE MADE

The process of making maps is called cartography. Map-makers, or cartographers, compile each map by gathering information about the area and representing it as an image as accurately as possible.

Internet links

For a link to a Web site where you can click on examples of all kinds of map projections, including cylindrical, conical and azimuthal projections, go to
www.usborne-quicklinks.com

Creating maps

Many sources are used to create maps. These include satellite images and aerial photographs. Cartographers often visit the area to be mapped, where they take many extra measurements.

In addition, cartographers use statistics, such as population figures, from censuses and other documents. As the maps are being made, many people check them to make sure they are accurate and up-to-date.

Map projections

Cartographers can't draw maps that show the world exactly as it is, because it is impossible to show a curved surface on a flat map without distorting (stretching or squashing) some areas. A representation of the Earth on a map is called a projection. Projections are worked out using complex mathematics.

There are three basic types of projections – cylindrical, conical and azimuthal, but there are also variations on these. They all distort the Earth's surface in some way, either by altering the shapes or sizes of areas of land or the distance between places.

A cartographer uses an electronic distance measurer to check the measurements of an area of land.

Cylindrical projections

A cylindrical projection is similar to the image created by wrapping a piece of paper around a globe to form a cylinder and then shining a light inside the globe. The shapes of countries would be projected onto the paper. Near the middle they would be accurate, but farther away they would be distorted.

Cartographers often alter the basic cylindrical projection to make the distortion less obvious in certain areas, but they can never make a map that is completely accurate.

This picture of a piece of paper wrapped around a globe illustrates how a cylindrical projection is made.

Below is a type of cylindrical projection called the Mercator projection, which was invented in 1596 by a cartographer named Gerardus Mercator. It makes countries the right shape, but makes those near the poles too big.

This cylindrical projection makes countries the right size in relation to each other, but some parts are too long. The projection was created in 1973 by Arno Peters. It is called the Peters Projection.

Conical projections

A conical projection is similar to the image you would get if you wrapped a cone of paper around part of a globe, then shone a light inside the globe. Where the cone touches the globe, the projection will be most accurate.

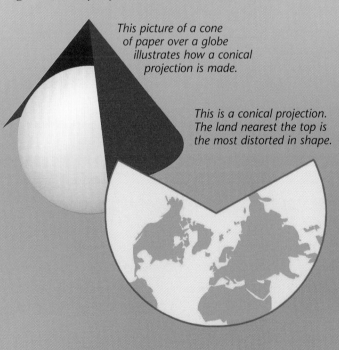

This picture of a cone of paper over a globe illustrates how a conical projection is made.

This is a conical projection. The land nearest the top is the most distorted in shape.

Azimuthal projections

An azimuthal projection is like an image made by holding paper in front of a globe, and shining a light through it. Land projected onto the middle of the paper would be accurate, but areas farther away would be distorted.

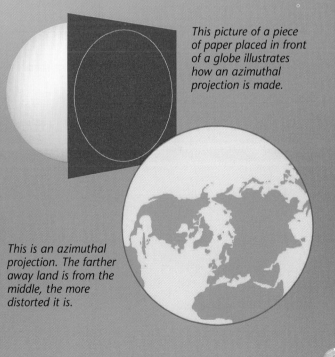

This picture of a piece of paper placed in front of a globe illustrates how an azimuthal projection is made.

This is an azimuthal projection. The farther away land is from the middle, the more distorted it is.

THEMATIC MAPS

Maps that represent information on particular themes, like the ones on these pages, are known as thematic maps. They help you to identify patterns and make comparisons between the features of different areas.

Earth's resources

The Earth contains all kinds of useful resources. Rocks and minerals can be used as building materials, and fuels such as coal, oil and gas contain energy that can be turned into heat and electricity.

Countries with large amounts of natural resources can become very rich. For example, Saudi Arabia, in western Asia, has large oil and gas reserves, which it exports all over the world.

This is an oil field, where oil is extracted from the ground using pumps. It is then piped to refineries and turned into products such as motor fuel.

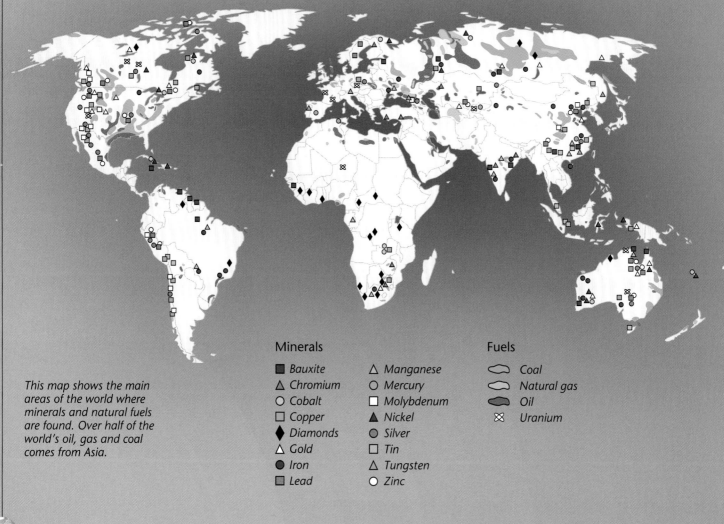

This map shows the main areas of the world where minerals and natural fuels are found. Over half of the world's oil, gas and coal comes from Asia.

Minerals

■ Bauxite	△ Manganese
△ Chromium	○ Mercury
○ Cobalt	□ Molybdenum
□ Copper	▲ Nickel
◆ Diamonds	● Silver
△ Gold	□ Tin
● Iron	△ Tungsten
▣ Lead	○ Zinc

Fuels

◠ Coal
◠ Natural gas
◗ Oil
⊠ Uranium

Different climates

The long-term or typical pattern of weather in a particular area is known as its climate. Climates vary across the world and depend largely on each area's latitude. The hottest parts of the world are those closest to the Equator.

Climate is also affected by other factors, such as wind and the height of the land. Oceans influence climate too – places near the sea normally have a milder, wetter climate than areas farther inland.

In this map, land is divided into five climate types. Dry areas are generally hot, but temperatures there can fall very low too. Some dry places, such as the Gobi Desert in eastern Asia, are extremely cold in winter.

- ☐ Polar
- ☐ Cold
- ☐ Temperate
- ☐ Dry
- ■ Tropical

World population

There are more than six billion people in the world, and the population is still growing. Experts think it may reach more than nine billion by 2050. The number of people living in a given area is known as its population density. Europe and Asia are the most densely populated continents in the world. About a third of the world's population lives in China and India alone.

Internet links

For a link to a Web site where you can discover how many people there were on Earth when you were born, and find out about the effects of population growth, go to **www.usborne-quicklinks.com**

This map shows the average population density by country. The shading indicates the number of people per sq km (0.386 sq miles).

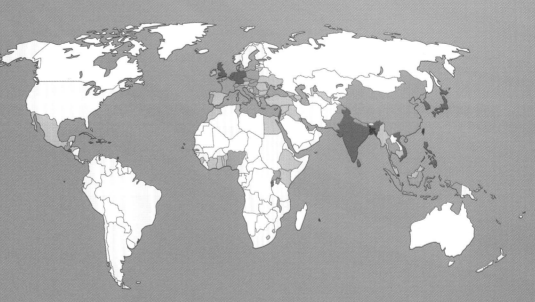

- ■ Over 500 people
- ■ 200–500 people
- ☐ 100–200 people
- ☐ 50–100 people
- ☐ 10–50 people
- ☐ Fewer than 10 people

HOW TO USE THE MAPS

Each continent section in this atlas begins with a political map showing the whole continent. The rest of the maps are larger scale maps showing the various parts of the continent in more detail.

Political maps

The shading on the political maps in this atlas is there to help you see clearly the different countries that make up each continent. The main purpose of these maps is to show country borders and capital cities. Alongside them there are facts and figures about the continents and their features.

This is a section of the political map of South America. You can see the whole map on pages 36–37.

Environmental maps

The majority of the maps in this atlas are environmental maps, like the one on the right. The shading on these maps shows different types of land, or environments, such as desert, mountain or wetland.

The main key on the opposite page shows what the different shading means. It also shows the symbols used to represent towns, cities and other features. There is a smaller key on each environmental map repeating the most important information from this key.

Finding places

To find a particular place or feature on the environmental maps, look up its name in the index on pages 130–143. Its page number and grid reference is given next to the name. You can find out how to use the grid on page 11.

The map on the right is part of the environmental map of the U.S.A. The numbered labels at the top explain some important features of these maps.

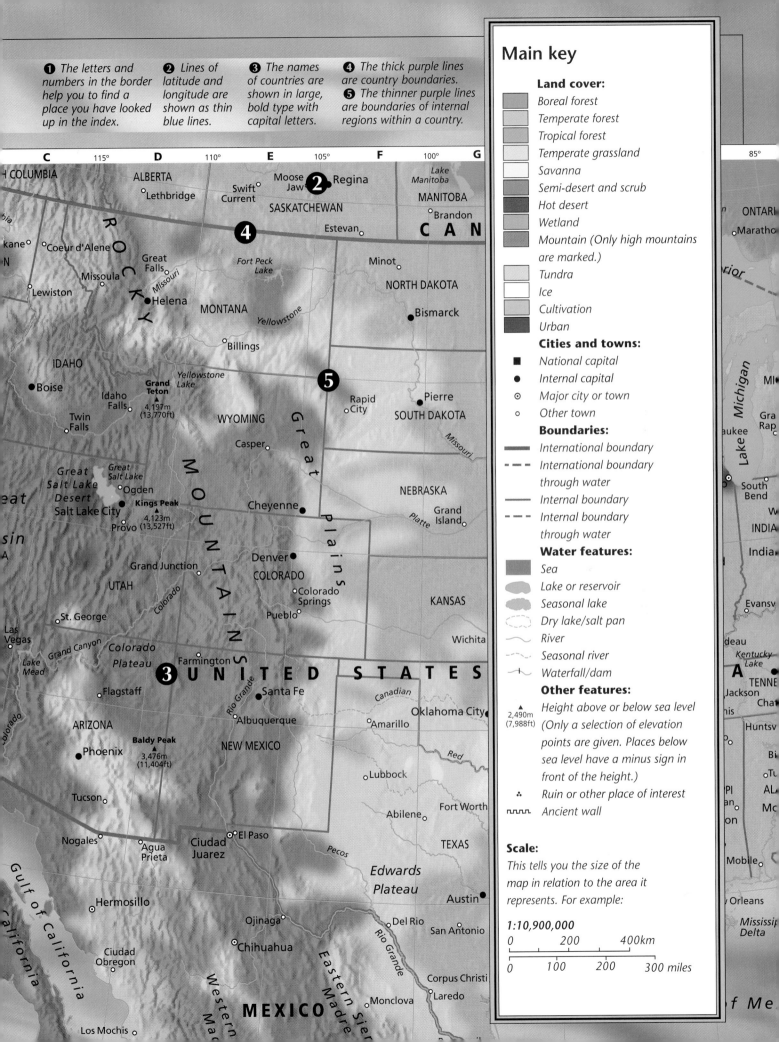

① The letters and numbers in the border help you to find a place you have looked up in the index.

② Lines of latitude and longitude are shown as thin blue lines.

③ The names of countries are shown in large, bold type with capital letters.

④ The thick purple lines are country boundaries.

⑤ The thinner purple lines are boundaries of internal regions within a country.

Main key

Land cover:
- Boreal forest
- Temperate forest
- Tropical forest
- Temperate grassland
- Savanna
- Semi-desert and scrub
- Hot desert
- Wetland
- Mountain (Only high mountains are marked.)
- Tundra
- Ice
- Cultivation
- Urban

Cities and towns:
- ■ National capital
- ● Internal capital
- ⊙ Major city or town
- ○ Other town

Boundaries:
- —— International boundary
- --- International boundary through water
- —— Internal boundary
- --- Internal boundary through water

Water features:
- Sea
- Lake or reservoir
- Seasonal lake
- Dry lake/salt pan
- River
- Seasonal river
- Waterfall/dam

Other features:
- ▲ 2,490m (7,988ft) Height above or below sea level (Only a selection of elevation points are given. Places below sea level have a minus sign in front of the height.)
- ⁂ Ruin or other place of interest
- ⊓⊓⊓ Ancient wall

Scale:
This tells you the size of the map in relation to the area it represents. For example:

1:10,900,000

| 0 | 200 | 400km |

| 0 | 100 | 200 | 300 miles |

WORLD—POLITICAL MAP

80°
160° 140° 120° 100° 80° 60° 40° 20° W 0°

GREENLAND
(Denmark)

ICELAND

NOR

Arctic Circle
ALASKA
(U.S.A.)
60°

CANADA

DENM
UNITED
KINGDOM NE
IRELAND
BELG
SW
FRANC

40°

UNITED STATES
OF AMERICA

SPAIN
PORTUGAL

Azores
(Portugal)

TUN

MOROCCO

Tropic of Cancer

Canary Islands
(Spain)

ALGER

THE BAHAMAS
20°
N

Hawaiian
Islands
(U.S.A.)

MEXICO

WESTERN SAHARA
(Morocco)

CUBA
DOMINICAN
REPUBLIC
HAITI
JAMAICA
BELIZE
GUATEMALA HONDURAS
EL SALVADOR NICARAGUA

DOMINICA

MAURITANIA

MALI
NIG

SENEGAL
THE GAMBIA
GUINEA-BISSAU

CAPE VERDE
BURKINA
FASO

BENIN

COSTA RICA
PANAMA

Caribbean Sea

TRINIDAD AND TOBAGO

VENEZUELA

GUYANA
SURINAM
FRENCH GUIANA
(France)

GUINEA
SIERRA LEONE
LIBERIA

IVORY
COAST

TOGO

NIGE

GHANA
EQUATOR
GUI

PACIFIC

COLOMBIA

SAO TOME AND
PRINCIPE

KIRIBATI

OCEAN

Galapagos Islands
(Ecuador)

ECUADOR

ATLANTIC

Equator
0°

PERU

BRAZIL

OCEAN

Cook
Islands
(New Zealand)

French
Polynesia
(France)

BOLIVIA

20°
S

Tropic of Capricorn

Pitcairn
Islands
(U.K.)

PARAGUAY

CHILE

URUGUAY

ARGENTINA

40°

1:72,700,000
0   1,000   2,000   3,000   4,000   5,000km

0   1,000   2,000   3,000 miles

Falkland Islands
(U.K.)

South Georgia
(U.K.)

60°

Antarctic Circle

Weddell
Sea

80°

160° 140° 120° 100° 80° 60° 40° 20° W 0°

ARCTIC OCEAN

Svalbard
(Norway)

Arctic Circle

RUSSIA

SWEDEN FINLAND

ESTONIA
LATVIA
LITHUANIA
GERMANY BELARUS
POLAND
CZECH REP. UKRAINE
SLOVAKIA MOLDOVA
AUST. HUNGARY
SLOV. ROMANIA
CRO. B.H. YUG. BULGARIA
ITALY MAC.
ALBANIA

KAZAKHSTAN

MONGOLIA

Black Sea
GEORGIA
Caspian
Sea
ARM. AZER.
UZBEKISTAN
KYRGYZSTAN
GREECE TURKEY
TURKMENISTAN
TAJIKISTAN
CYPRUS SYRIA
LEB.
ISRAEL
JORDAN IRAQ IRAN
AFGHANISTAN
PAKISTAN

Mediterranean Sea

KUWAIT

BAHRAIN
QATAR
U.A.E.

NORTH
KOREA
SOUTH
KOREA
JAPAN

CHINA

NEPAL
BHUTAN

BANGLA-
DESH

BURMA
(MYANMAR)

TAIWAN

PACIFIC

OCEAN

Tropic of Cancer

LIBYA EGYPT

SAUDI
ARABIA

OMAN

INDIA

LAOS

THAILAND

Northern
Mariana
Islands
(U.S.A.)

MARSHALL
ISLANDS

CHAD

SUDAN

ERITREA
YEMEN

DJIBOUTI

VIETNAM

CAMBODIA

PHILIPPINES

CENTRAL
AFRICAN
REPUBLIC
CAMEROON

ETHIOPIA

SOMALIA

SRI LANKA

BRUNEI

FEDERATED STATES
OF MICRONESIA

PALAU

Equator

GABON
CONGO
CONGO
(DEMOCRATIC
REPUBLIC)

UGANDA
KENYA
RWANDA
BURUNDI

MALDIVES

MALAYSIA

SINGAPORE

INDONESIA

PAPUA
NEW GUINEA

NAURU

KIRIBATI

SEYCHELLES

SOLOMON
ISLANDS

TUVALU

TANZANIA

COMOROS

INDIAN

OCEAN

Coral Sea
Islands
Territory
(Australia)

VANUATU

SAMOA

ANGOLA

ZAMBIA

MALAWI

New
Caledonia
(France)

FIJI TONGA

ZIMBABWE

MADAGASCAR

MAURITIUS

Tropic of Capricorn

NAMIBIA

BOTSWANA

MOZAMBIQUE

Reunion
(France)

SWAZILAND

AUSTRALIA

LESOTHO

SOUTH AFRICA

NEW
ZEALAND

Kerguelen Islands
(France)

SOUTHERN OCEAN

Antarctic Circle

The shading on this map is there to help
you see the different countries clearly.

ANTARCTICA

Copyright © Usborne Publishing Ltd.

Abbreviations used on map:

ARM.	ARMENIA
AUST.	AUSTRIA
AZER.	AZERBAIJAN
BELG.	BELGIUM
B.H.	BOSNIA AND HERZEGOVINA
CRO.	CROATIA
CZECH REP.	CZECH REPUBLIC
LEB.	LEBANON
LUX.	LUXEMBOURG
MAC.	MACEDONIA
NETH.	NETHERLANDS
SLOV.	SLOVENIA
SWITZ.	SWITZERLAND
U.A.E.	UNITED ARAB EMIRATES
YUG.	YUGOSLAVIA

WORLD – PHYSICAL MAP

80°
160°   140°   120°   100°   80°   60°   40°   20° W   0°

Beaufort
Sea

Ellesmere
Island

Queen
Elizabeth
Islands

Baffin
Island

Baffin
Bay

Greenland

Greenland
Sea

Victoria
Island

Arctic Circle
Alaska
Mount McKinley
▲
6,194m
(20,321ft)

60°

Yukon

Hudson
Bay

Labrador
Sea

Iceland

Nort
Se

Aleutian Islands

Gulf of Alaska

Rocky Mountains

Great plains

**NORTH
AMERICA**

*Great
Lakes*

Newfoundland

British
Isles

40°

Appalachian Mountains

Azores

Mississippi

Atlas Mountain

Tropic of Cancer

Gulf of
Mexico

Canary
Islands

S

20°
N

*Hawaiian
Islands*

Cuba

West Indies

Greater Antilles

Cape Verde
Islands

S

*Caribbean
Sea*

Lesser
Antilles

Guiana
Highlands

Equator

0°

P o l y n e s i a

PACIFIC

Galapagos
Islands

Amazon
Basin

Amazon

ATLANTIC

OCEAN

Selvas

OCEAN

**SOUTH
AMERICA**

Tahiti

A n d e s

20°
S

Tropic of Capricorn

Easter Island

Atacama Desert

40°

Aconcagua
▲
6,959m
(22,831ft)

Pampas

1:72,700,000
0   1,000   2,000   3,000   4,000   5,000km

Patagonia

Falkland Islands

0   1,000   2,000   3,000 miles

Cape Horn

South Georgia

60°

Antarctic Circle

Antarctic
Peninsula

*W e d d e l l
Sea*

80°

160°   140°   120°   100°   80°   60°   40°   20° W   0°

ARCTIC OCEAN

20° E   40°   60°   80°   100°   120°   140°   160°   180°

Svalbard   Novaya   Kara Sea   Severnaya   Laptev Sea   New Siberia   East Siberian Sea
North Cape   Zemlya   Zemlya   Islands

Barents Sea   80°   Arctic Circle

Scandinavia   Siberia   Verkhoyansk Range   60°

North European Plain   Ural Mountains   Yenisey   ASIA   Sea   Kamchatka
Ob   Lake   of   Peninsula
Baikal   Okhotsk

EUROPE   Volga   Aral   Altai Mountains   Hokkaido   40°
Danube   Mount   Sea   Gobi   Sea
Black Sea   Elbrus   Caspian   Desert   Huang He (Yellow)   of
5,642m   Sea   Japan   Honshu
(18,510ft)   Yellow
Mediterranean Sea   Zagros Mountains   Himalayas   Chang Jiang (Yangtze)   Sea   East
China   Taiwan   Tropic of Cancer
Nile   Ganges   Mount Everest   Sea
a r a   Red Sea   Arabian   8,850m   20°
Peninsula   (29,035ft)   N

e l   Arabian   Deccan   Bay   Philippine   Micronesia   PACIFIC
Sea   Plateau   of   Islands
AFRICA   Ethiopian   Bengal   South   OCEAN
Highlands   China   Celebes
Sri Lanka   Sea   Sea
Lake   Borneo   Equator   0°
Victoria   Sumatra
Congo   Kilimanjaro   Seychelles   Greater Sunda Islands   New Guinea   Melanesia
Congo   Basin   5,895m   INDIAN   Java   Mount Wilhelm   Solomon
(19,340ft)   Arafura   4,509m   Islands
Comoro   OCEAN   Lesser Sunda Islands   Sea   (14,793ft)
Islands   New   Fiji
Madagascar   Coral   Caledonia   Islands   20°
Mauritius   Sea   S
Namib   Reunion   Great Sandy   Tropic of Capricorn
Kalahari   Desert
Desert   AUSTRALASIA AND OCEANIA
Rift Valley   Great Victoria   Great Dividing Range   North
Drakensberg   Desert   Tasman   Island
Cape of Good Hope   Sea   40°

Kerguelen   Tasmania   South
Islands   Island

60°

SOUTHERN OCEAN   Antarctic Circle

See page 17 for key.

ANTARCTICA   80°

20° E   40°   60°   80°   100°   120°   140°   160°   180°

NORTH AMERICA

The name "North America" can be used to mean several different things. In this atlas, North America includes Greenland, Canada, the U.S.A., the Caribbean, and the countries of Central America, which run along the narrow strip of land between the U.S.A. and South America. The continent has over 20 countries, including Canada, the second-largest country in the world.

These are columns of rock called hoodoos in Bryce Canyon National Park, U.S.A.

Arctic Circle

ARCTIC OCEAN

Bering
Sea

Beaufort
Sea

Yukon

Victoria
Island

ALASKA
(U.S.A.)

Anchorage

CANADA

Vancouver

PACIFIC

OCEAN

Columbia

Missouri

UNITED STATES

Hawaiian
Islands
(U.S.A.)

Colorado

Los Angeles

Rio Grande

Tropic of Cancer

MEXICO

Mexico City

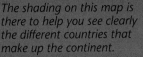

The shading on this map is there to help you see clearly the different countries that make up the continent.

GREENLAND
(Denmark)

Arctic Circle

lesmere
land

*Baffin
Island*

Godthab

Jeen
izabeth
ands

*Hudson
Bay*

Newfoundland

St. Lawrence

*Great
Lakes*

Montreal
Ottawa

Chicago

New York

Washington D.C.

OF AMERICA

ATLANTIC

OCEAN

Mississippi

Houston

Tropic of Cancer

**THE
BAHAMAS**

*Gulf of
Mexico*

Havana
CUBA

Puerto Rico
(U.S.A.)

Guadeloupe
(France)

DOMINICA
Martinique (France)

HAITI   **DOMINICAN
REPUBLIC**

BARBADOS

JAMAICA

**TRINIDAD
AND TOBAGO**

BELIZE   *Caribbean Sea*

GUATEMALA   **HONDURAS**

EL SALVADOR   **NICARAGUA**

COSTA RICA   **PANAMA**

Facts

Total land area 22,656,190 sq km (8,745,289 sq miles)

Total population 487 million

Biggest city Mexico City, Mexico

Biggest country Canada *9,970,610 sq km (3,849,653 sq miles)*

Smallest country Saint Kitts and Nevis *269 sq km (104 sq miles)*

Highest mountain Mount McKinley, Alaska, U.S.A. *6,194m (20,321ft)*

Longest river Mississippi/Missouri, U.S.A. *6,019km (3,741 miles)*

Biggest lake Lake Superior, between the U.S.A. and Canada *82,414 sq km (31,820 sq miles)*

Highest waterfall Yosemite Falls, on the Yosemite Creek, California, U.S.A. *739m (2,425ft)*

Biggest desert Great Basin Desert, U.S.A. *492,000 sq km (190,000 sq miles)*

Biggest island Greenland *2,175,600 sq km (840,000 sq miles)*

Main mineral deposits Silver, gold, copper, lead, zinc, graphite, molybdenum, nickel

Main fuel deposits Oil, coal, natural gas, uranium

The bald eagle is the national bird of the U.S.A. It is not really bald, but has white feathers on its head.

North America covers a huge area, from just south of the North Pole to just north of the Equator. The land in the far north is icy and barren, while southern areas are lush and tropical. The west is dominated by the snow-capped Rocky Mountains.

Enormous parks

North America has many vast national parks. These are specially-protected natural areas where all kinds of animals live. One of the most famous parks is Yellowstone Park in Wyoming, U.S.A., which is home to wolves, black bears and many other animals. The park also has natural hot springs and geysers.

This satellite image of North America shows dry areas in brown, vegetation in green and icy regions in white.

Erupting island

Half of the island of Hawaii is covered by Mauna Loa, the biggest volcano on Earth, and one of the most active. The volcano is monitored constantly to check for impending eruptions. Its biggest eruption was in 1950, when a wide river of red-hot lava flowed 24km (15 miles) to the sea, destroying roads and houses in its path.

This satellite image shows part of Mauna Loa volcano. The dark, round hole at the top is one of the volcano's craters, out of which lava and gases regularly explode.

This huge pool is a natural hot spring in Yellowstone Park, Wyoming, U.S.A. The water heats up under the ground.

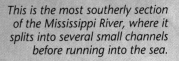

This is the most southerly section of the Mississippi River, where it splits into several small channels before running into the sea.

Mighty Mississippi

The Mississippi/Missouri River is the longest river system in North America and the fourth-longest in the world. The Mississippi flows from Minnesota in northern U.S.A. to the Gulf of Mexico in the south. The Missouri begins in Montana, in the west, and joins the Mississippi in the state of Missouri. The river system is a busy shipping route, and is also vital for wildlife – migratory birds follow it as they fly south in the winter.

The deepest valley

The Grand Canyon, in Arizona, U.S.A., is the world's largest gorge, a deep valley that stretches over 400km (250 miles). In some parts it is 1.6km (1 mile) deep, and up to 29km (18 miles) wide.

The Grand Canyon was carved out by the Colorado River, which eroded the rocky land over many thousands of years. It is possible to hike down the sides of the Canyon, but they are so steep that it takes a whole day to get to the bottom.

Running from top left to bottom right of this satellite image is the jagged Grand Canyon, in the flat, dry state of Arizona, U.S.A. Smaller valleys join the main canyon.

The northern part of North America consists mainly of Canada and the U.S.A. and has many large, dynamic cities as well as forests, deserts and other vast natural spaces.

Huge clouds of spray and mist rise from Horseshoe Falls, one of the two spectacular waterfalls that form Niagara Falls. The falls divide the U.S.A. (left) and Canada (right).

Cold country

Canada has extremely cold, snowy winters, especially in northern and eastern areas. In the city of Montreal, an amazing 1m (40in) of snow once fell in a single day. Not surprisingly, Canada is famous for its many winter sports, such as skiing, ice-skating and ice hockey.

On the border

The border between Canada and the U.S.A. is the longest in the world, covering 6,416km (3,987 miles). In the east, the border runs through several huge lakes, known as the Great Lakes. This section of the border includes Niagara Falls, where water from Lake Erie crashes over two enormous waterfalls.

Big cities

The largest city in the U.S.A. is New York, which is also the country's financial capital. Other big cities include Los Angeles, home of the movie-making area Hollywood, and Las Vegas, which boasts the largest number of hotel rooms of any U.S. city.

At night, the casinos and hotels of Las Vegas are lit up in a blaze of neon lights.

Desert heat

Death Valley in California is the driest place in the U.S.A., and one of the hottest places in the world. The temperature in this vast wilderness has been known to reach a sweltering 57°C (134°F). The desert is generally barren, though when rain does occasionally fall, beautiful wild flowers spring up between the rocks.

In the foreground of this Las Vegas skyline is a replica of the Chrysler Building, a New York skyscraper. It is part of an extravagant hotel that has 12 towers, each in the shape of a famous New York building.

An American alligator lazes in one of Florida's coastal swamps. Alligators eat birds, frogs and other animals – sometimes even small alligators.

The sunshine state

Florida, in southeastern U.S.A., has a hot, tropical climate and is nicknamed "the sunshine state". Southern Florida is covered in swampy wetlands called the Everglades. All kinds of wildlife live there, including Florida panthers and American alligators.

Internet links

For a link to a Web site where you can read profiles of the animals that live in Florida's Everglades National Park and also learn why some of them are in danger of becoming extinct, go to **www.usborne-quicklinks.com**

Central America is dominated by the country of Mexico, with its ancient ruins and crowded cities. Farther south, the countries near the border with South America have beautiful beaches, tropical rainforests and fiery volcanoes.

Here a bright wall mural is being painted in the coastal town of Cancun, one of Mexico's lively tourist spots.

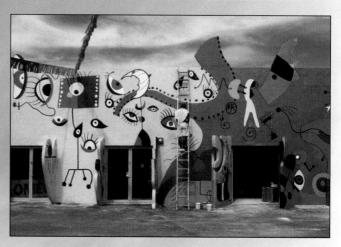

City living

Mexico has a huge population, and also has millions of visitors every year. Its biggest city is the capital, Mexico City, where almost a quarter of Mexico's total population lives. The city is so overcrowded that the air is heavily polluted, and many people have poor living conditions and inadequate water supplies.

These statues are in Tula, Mexico. They were built by the ancient Toltec people, and were probably columns that held up a roof.

Ancient remains

In Mexico and nearby areas there are many remains of ancient cities. These were built by people from ancient civilizations, such as the Maya and the Toltec. The Maya had a powerful empire around AD200–900, while the Toltec ruled from about 900 to 1200. These peoples were excellent builders, and created many impressive temples and elaborately carved statues.

Land of volcanoes

Along the Pacific coast of Central America are more than 40 volcanoes. Lava from volcanic eruptions helps make the soil fertile, which is good for growing crops such as bananas and coffee. The volcanoes erupt regularly, and can be very dangerous. For example, the Arenal volcano in Costa Rica wiped out a whole town in a 1963 eruption, and has produced frequent lava flows ever since.

A white-nosed coati raids a banana tree in Costa Rica. These Central American mammals eat all kinds of fruit.

This is the Arenal volcano during a recent eruption. Lava can flow more than 2km (1.5 miles) from the volcano's base.

Sun and storms

The Caribbean islands have stunning sandy beaches and a hot climate. But their position in the Atlantic Ocean means that they are often hit by tropical storms and hurricanes. Some hurricanes reach wind speeds of 250kph (155mph).

Internet links

For a link to a Web site where you can find out all about Mexico, including useful information about its main cities and amazing ancient sites, go to **www.usborne-quicklinks.com**

Linking oceans

The Panama Canal is one of the world's busiest shipping routes. It cuts through the country of Panama and is a short cut for ships sailing between the Atlantic and Pacific oceans. Before the canal opened, ships had to sail around South America, an extra 12,500km (7,800 miles).

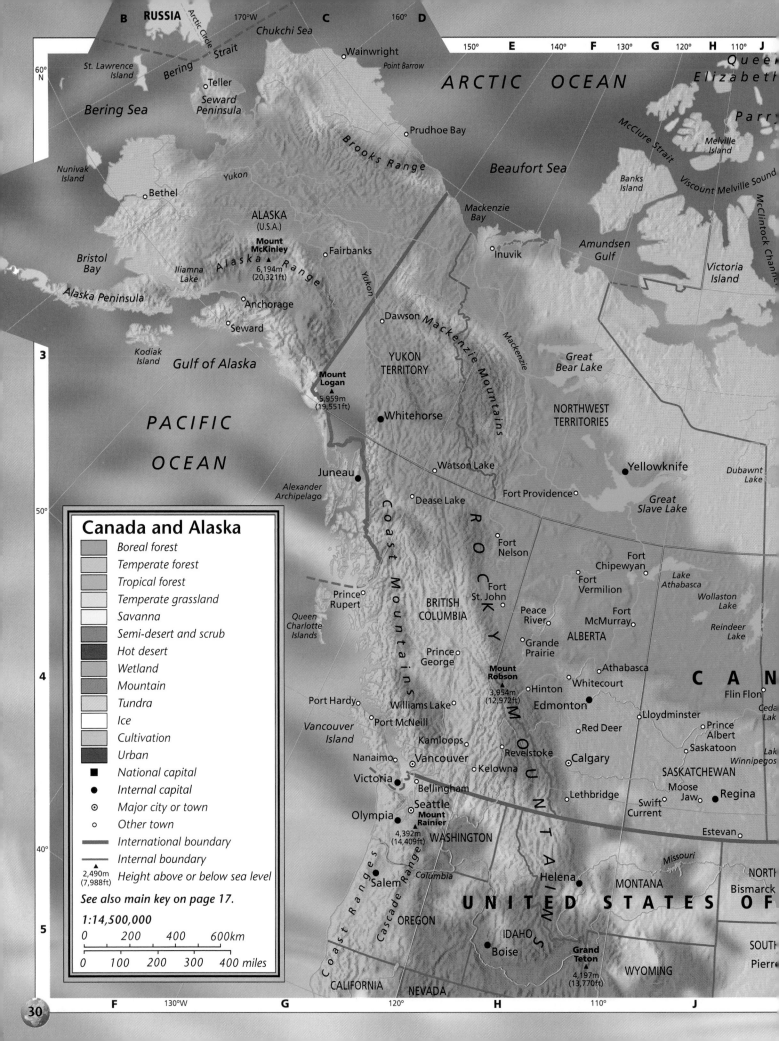

Canada and Alaska

- Boreal forest
- Temperate forest
- Tropical forest
- Temperate grassland
- Savanna
- Semi-desert and scrub
- Hot desert
- Wetland
- Mountain
- Tundra
- Ice
- Cultivation
- Urban
- ■ National capital
- ● Internal capital
- ⊙ Major city or town
- ○ Other town
- ─── International boundary
- ─── Internal boundary
- ▲ 2,490m (7,988ft) Height above or below sea level

See also main key on page 17.

1:14,500,000

0   200   400   600km

0 100 200 300 400 miles

RUSSIA

Chukchi Sea

Wainwright
Point Barrow

ARCTIC OCEAN

Queen Elizabeth

Parry

Arctic Circle

Bering Strait

St. Lawrence Island

Teller

Seward Peninsula

Bering Sea

Prudhoe Bay

Beaufort Sea

McClure Strait

Viscount Melville Sound

Melville Island

Banks Island

McClintock Channel

Nunivak Island

Yukon

Bethel

ALASKA (U.S.A.)

Mount McKinley ▲ 6,194m (20,321ft)

Fairbanks

Mackenzie Bay

Inuvik

Amundsen Gulf

Victoria Island

Bristol Bay

Iliamna Lake

Alaska Range

Yukon

Anchorage

Seward

Dawson

Mackenzie Mountains

Mackenzie

Great Bear Lake

NORTHWEST TERRITORIES

Kodiak Island

Gulf of Alaska

Mount Logan ▲ 5,959m (19,551ft)

YUKON TERRITORY

PACIFIC OCEAN

Whitehorse

Watson Lake

Fort Providence

Yellowknife

Dubawnt Lake

Juneau

Alexander Archipelago

Dease Lake

ROCKY

Great Slave Lake

Fort Nelson

Fort St. John

Fort Chipewyan

Lake Athabasca

Wollaston Lake

Prince Rupert

Coast Mountains

BRITISH COLUMBIA

Peace River

Fort Vermilion

Fort McMurray

Reindeer Lake

Queen Charlotte Islands

Prince George

Grande Prairie

ALBERTA

CAN

Port Hardy

Williams Lake

Mount Robson ▲ 3,954m (12,972ft)

Hinton

Athabasca

Whitecourt

Flin Flon

Vancouver Island

Port McNeill

Kamloops

M O U N T A I N

Edmonton

Lloydminster

Ceda Lak

Nanaimo

Vancouver

Revelstoke

Red Deer

Prince Albert

Kelowna

Calgary

Saskatoon

Lake Winnipegos

Victoria

Bellingham

SASKATCHEWAN

Olympia

Seattle

Mount Rainier ▲ 4,392m (14,409ft)

Lethbridge

Moose Jaw

Swift Current

Regina

WASHINGTON

Estevan

Coast Ranges

Cascade Range

Columbia

Salem

OREGON

Missouri

Helena

MONTANA

NORTH

Bismarck

UNITED STATES OF

CALIFORNIA

NEVADA

Boise

IDAHO

Grand Teton ▲ 4,197m (13,770ft)

WYOMING

SOUTH

Pierr

30

Main map labels (geographic features and places):

Ellesmere Island
Bathurst Island
Devon Island
Lancaster Sound
Somerset Island
Prince of Wales Island
Gulf of Boothia
Boothia Peninsula
King William Island
Baffin Bay
Baffin Island
Cumberland Peninsula
Melville Peninsula
Foxe Basin
Nettilling Lake
Foxe Peninsula
Amadjuak Lake
Iqaluit
NUNAVUT
Southampton Island
Hudson Strait
Ivujivik
Ungava Peninsula
Ungava Bay
Cape Chidley
Davis Strait
Labrador Sea
ATLANTIC OCEAN
GREENLAND (Denmark)
Cape Farewell
Nain
Makkovik
Cartwright
Kuujjuaq
NEWFOUNDLAND
Inukjuak
All islands within Hudson Bay, James Bay and Ungava Bay lie within Nunavut.
Happy Valley-Goose Bay
Smallwood Reservoir
Churchill Falls
Labrador City
Gander
St. John's
Newfoundland
Corner Brook
Churchill
Belcher Islands
La Grande Reservoir
MANITOBA
Thompson
QUEBEC
Manicouagan Reservoir
Anticosti Island
St. Pierre and Miquelon (France)
Sydney
James Bay
Radisson
Gulf of St. Lawrence
CANADA
Lake Winnipeg
Fort Albany
Waskaganish
Baie-Comeau
Gaspe
PRINCE EDWARD ISLAND
Charlottetown
Grand Rapids
Lake Manitoba
Lake Mistassini
Bathurst
Edmundston
NEW BRUNSWICK
Moncton
Halifax
ONTARIO
Chicoutimi
Fredericton
Saint John
NOVA SCOTIA
Winnipeg
Dryden
Lake Nipigon
Kirkland Lake
Val-d'Or
Quebec
St. Lawrence
MAINE
Yarmouth
Brandon
Kenora
Lake of the Woods
Marathon
Trois-Rivieres
Augusta
Thunder Bay
Montreal
Lake Superior
Sudbury
North Bay
Ottawa
Montpelier
Concord
Boston
DAKOTA
MINNESOTA
Sault Ste. Marie
Huntsville
Kingston
Lake Ontario
Albany
MASSACHUSETTS
Providence
RHODE ISLAND
AMERICA
MICHIGAN
Owen Sound
Toronto
NEW YORK
Hartford
CONNECTICUT
St. Paul
WISCONSIN
Hamilton
Niagara Falls
Buffalo
New York
Minneapolis
Mississippi
Madison
Lansing
London
Detroit
Windsor
Lake Huron
Lake Michigan
Lake Erie
Erie
PENNSYLVANIA
Trenton
NEW JERSEY
Cleveland
Harrisburg
Philadelphia
Dover
Chicago
ILLINOIS
INDIANA
OHIO
Pittsburgh
Annapolis
DELAWARE
Columbus
Washington D.C.
VERMONT
NEW HAMPSHIRE
Missouri

Inset map (upper right):

Bering Sea
Aleutian Islands
Attu Island
Near Islands
Rat Islands
Andreanof Islands
Atka Island
Fox Islands
Shishaldin Volcano 2,857m (9,372ft)
Unimak Island
Unalaska Island
Umnak Island
Same scale as main map

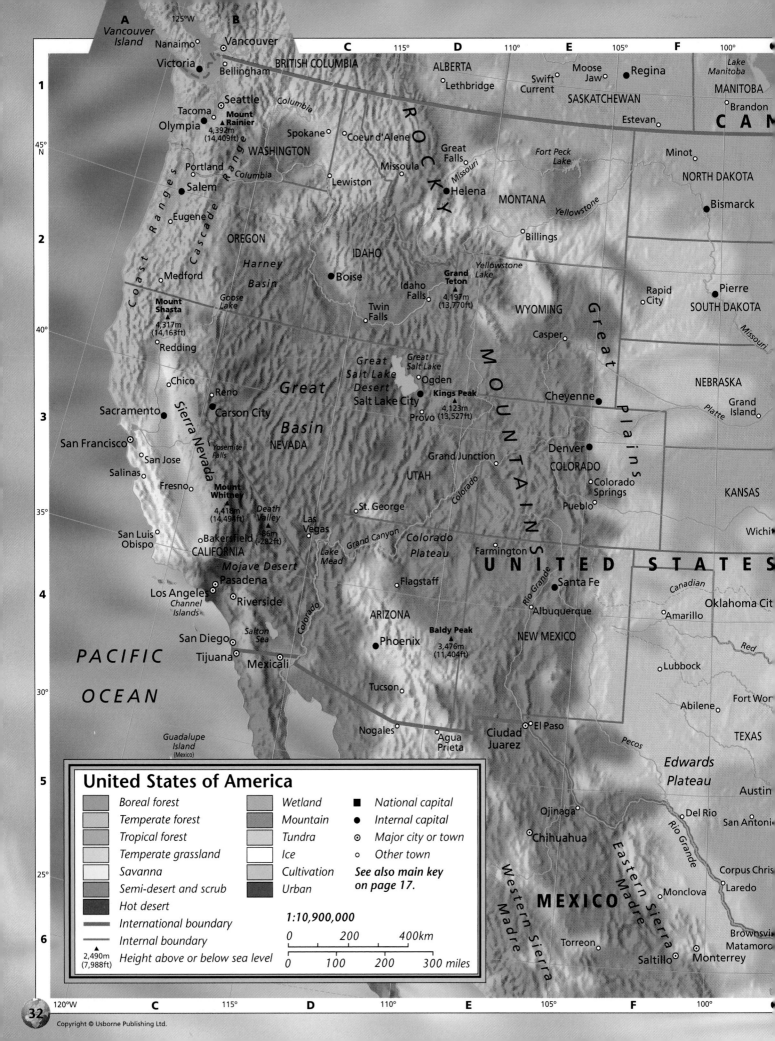

United States of America

Boreal forest
Temperate forest
Tropical forest
Temperate grassland
Savanna
Semi-desert and scrub
Hot desert
International boundary
Internal boundary
▲ 2,490m (7,988ft) Height above or below sea level

Wetland
Mountain
Tundra
Ice
Cultivation
Urban

■ National capital
● Internal capital
◉ Major city or town
○ Other town

See also main key on page 17.

1:10,900,000

0   200   400km
0 100 200 300 miles

Map labels

Vancouver Island
Nanaimo
Victoria
Bellingham
BRITISH COLUMBIA
ALBERTA
Lethbridge
Swift Current
Moose Jaw
Regina
SASKATCHEWAN
Lake Manitoba
MANITOBA
Brandon
CANADA
Estevan
Seattle
Tacoma
Olympia
Mount Rainier 4,392m (14,409ft)
Columbia
Spokane
Coeur d'Alene
Great Falls
Fort Peck Lake
Minot
NORTH DAKOTA
Bismarck
Portland
Salem
WASHINGTON
Missoula
Helena
MONTANA
Billings
Yellowstone
Eugene
OREGON
IDAHO
Medford
Harney Basin
Boise
Idaho Falls
Grand Teton 4,197m (13,770ft)
Yellowstone Lake
WYOMING
Rapid City
Pierre
SOUTH DAKOTA
Mount Shasta 4,317m (14,163ft)
Goose Lake
Twin Falls
Redding
Chico
Reno
Great Salt Lake Desert
Great Salt Lake
Ogden
Kings Peak 4,123m (13,527ft)
Casper
Cheyenne
NEBRASKA
Grand Island
Sacramento
Carson City
Salt Lake City
Provo
Great Basin
San Francisco
San Jose
Salinas
Fresno
Sierra Nevada
NEVADA
Yosemite Falls
UTAH
Grand Junction
Colorado
Denver
COLORADO
Colorado Springs
KANSAS
Wichita
Mount Whitney 4,418m (14,494ft)
Death Valley -86m (-282ft)
Las Vegas
St. George
Pueblo
San Luis Obispo
Bakersfield
CALIFORNIA
Mojave Desert
Lake Mead
Grand Canyon
Colorado Plateau
Farmington
UNITED STATES
Pasadena
Los Angeles
Channel Islands
Riverside
Flagstaff
Santa Fe
Albuquerque
Rio Grande
Canadian
Oklahoma City
Amarillo
San Diego
Tijuana
Salton Sea
Mexicali
ARIZONA
Phoenix
Baldy Peak 3,476m (11,404ft)
NEW MEXICO
Red
Lubbock
PACIFIC OCEAN
Tucson
Colorado
Abilene
Fort Worth
TEXAS
Guadalupe Island (Mexico)
Nogales
Agua Prieta
Ciudad Juarez
El Paso
Pecos
Edwards Plateau
Austin
Ojinaga
Del Rio
San Antonio
Chihuahua
Rio Grande
Corpus Christi
Western Sierra Madre
Eastern Sierra Madre
Monclova
Laredo
MEXICO
Torreon
Brownsville
Matamoros
Saltillo
Monterrey

125°W 115° 110° 105° 100°
120°W 115° 110° 105° 100°
45°N 40° 35° 30° 25°

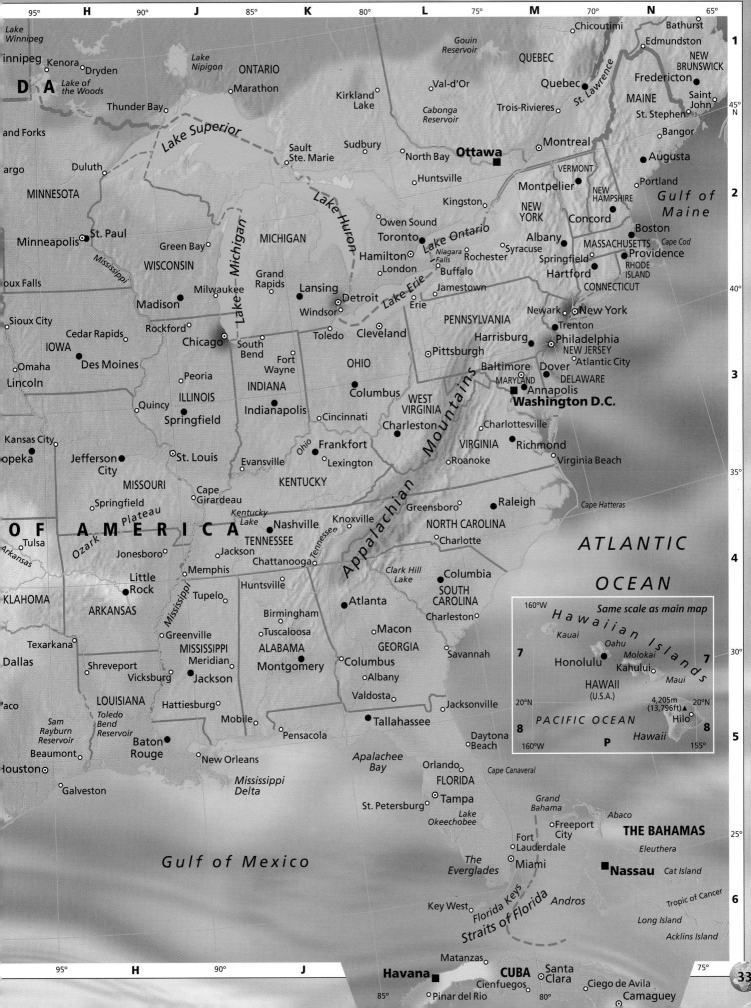

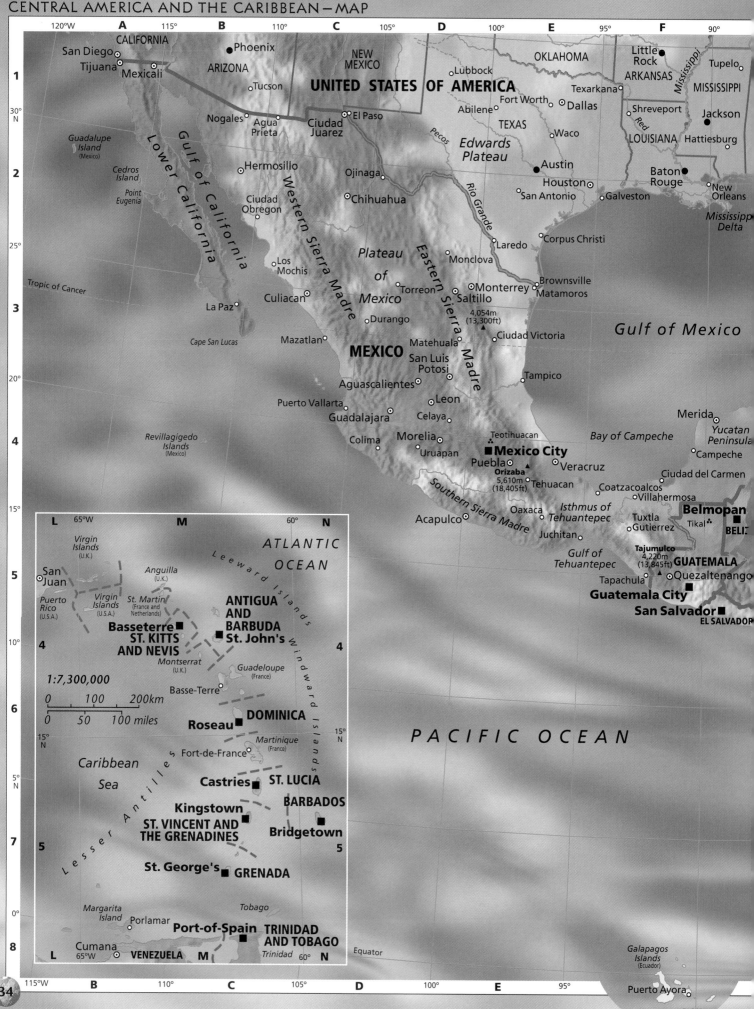

120°W   A   115°   B   110°   C   105°   D   100°   E   95°   F   90°

UNITED STATES OF AMERICA

San Diego
Tijuana
Mexicali
CALIFORNIA
Phoenix
ARIZONA
Tucson
Nogales
Agua Prieta
Ciudad Juarez
El Paso
NEW MEXICO
OKLAHOMA
Lubbock
Texarkana
Little Rock
ARKANSAS
Tupelo
MISSISSIPPI
Shreveport
Jackson
Hattiesburg
LOUISIANA
Abilene
Fort Worth
Dallas
Waco
TEXAS
Austin
San Antonio
Houston
Baton Rouge
New Orleans
Galveston
Corpus Christi
Brownsville
Matamoros

Guadalupe Island (Mexico)
Cedros Island
Point Eugenia
Lower California
Gulf of California
Western Sierra Madre

Hermosillo
Ciudad Obregon
Los Mochis
Culiacan
La Paz
Cape San Lucas
Mazatlan
Durango

Plateau of Mexico
Eastern Sierra Madre
MEXICO

Tropic of Cancer

Edwards Plateau
Pecos
Rio Grande
Ojinaga
Chihuahua
Monclova
Saltillo
Torreon
Monterrey
4,054m (13,300ft)
Ciudad Victoria
Tampico

Gulf of Mexico
Mississippi Delta

Revillagigedo Islands (Mexico)

Matehuala
San Luis Potosi
Aguascalientes
Leon
Celaya
Guadalajara
Puerto Vallarta
Morelia
Colima
Uruapan
Mexico City
Puebla
Orizaba 5,610m (18,405ft)
Teotihuacan
Tehuacan
Veracruz
Oaxaca
Acapulco
Southern Sierra Madre
Juchitan
Isthmus of Tehuantepec
Coatzacoalcos
Villahermosa
Bay of Campeche
Merida
Yucatan Peninsula
Campeche
Ciudad del Carmen
Tuxtla Gutierrez
Belmopan
BELIZE
Tikal
Gulf of Tehuantepec
Tapachula
Quezaltenango
Tajumulco 4,220m (13,845ft)
GUATEMALA
Guatemala City
San Salvador
EL SALVADOR

PACIFIC OCEAN

Galapagos Islands (Ecuador)
Puerto Ayora

Inset map

1:7,300,000

L   65°W   M   60°   N

Virgin Islands (U.K.)
Anguilla (U.K.)
ATLANTIC OCEAN
Leeward Islands
San Juan
Puerto Rico (U.S.A.)
Virgin Islands (U.S.A.)
St. Martin (France and Netherlands)
ANTIGUA AND BARBUDA
St. John's
Basseterre
ST. KITTS AND NEVIS
Montserrat (U.K.)
Guadeloupe (France)
Basse-Terre
Windward Islands
Roseau
DOMINICA
Martinique (France)
Fort-de-France
Caribbean Sea
Lesser Antilles
Castries
ST. LUCIA
Kingstown
ST. VINCENT AND THE GRENADINES
BARBADOS
Bridgetown
St. George's
GRENADA
Margarita Island
Porlamar
Tobago
Cumana
VENEZUELA
Port-of-Spain
TRINIDAD AND TOBAGO
Trinidad
Equator

0   100   200km
0   50   100 miles

115°W   B   110°   C   105°   D   100°   E   95°

Central America and the Caribbean

Key:
- Boreal forest
- Temperate forest
- Tropical forest
- Temperate grassland
- Savanna
- Semi-desert and scrub
- Hot desert
- ⎯⎯ International boundary
- ⎯⎯ Internal boundary
- ▲ 2,490m (7,988ft) Height above or below sea level
- Wetland
- Mountain
- Tundra
- Ice
- Cultivation
- Urban
- ■ National capital
- ● Internal capital
- ⊙ Major city or town
- ○ Other town

See also main key on page 17.

1:14,500,000

0 200 400 600km
0 100 200 300 400 miles

United States (Southeast)

mingham · Atlanta
GEORGIA · Columbia · SOUTH CAROLINA
Macon · NORTH CAROLINA
ABAMA · Columbus · Charleston
ontgomery · Savannah
Albany
nsacola · Tallahassee
FLORIDA · Daytona Beach
Apalachee Bay · Orlando · Cape Canaveral
St. Petersburg · Tampa
Lake Okeechobee
The Everglades · Miami
Key West · Florida Keys · Straits of Florida

THE BAHAMAS

Grand Bahama
Freeport City
Abaco
Eleuthera
■ Nassau
Cat Island
Andros
Long Island
Acklins Island
Great Inagua
Turks and Caicos Islands (U.K.)

ATLANTIC OCEAN

Tropic of Cancer

CUBA

Havana ■
Pinar del Rio
Matanzas
Santa Clara
Cienfuegos
Camaguey
Holguin
Bayamo · Guantanamo
Santiago de Cuba
Cayman Islands (U.K.)
Isle of Youth
Cancun
Montego Bay
Swan Islands (Honduras)
Gulf of onduras

JAMAICA
Kingston ■

Greater Antilles
Windward Passage
Gonaives
Les Cayes
HAITI
Port-au-Prince ■
Cap-Haitien
Hispaniola
Santiago
DOMINICAN REPUBLIC
Santo Domingo ■
La Romana
Ponce
Puerto Rico (U.S.A.)
San Juan
Virgin Islands (U.K.)

Leeward Islands
ANTIGUA AND BARBUDA
Guadeloupe (France)
ST. KITTS AND NEVIS
DOMINICA
Martinique (France)
ST. LUCIA
BARBADOS
ST. VINCENT AND THE GRENADINES
GRENADA
Lesser Antilles

Caribbean Sea

HONDURAS
egucigalpa
Puerto Cabezas
Matagalpa
Leon · **NICARAGUA**
Managua ■
Rivas
Lake Nicaragua
Liberia
Puntarenas
COSTA RICA · San Jose ■
Limon
Almirante
PANAMA
David
Santiago
Coiba Island
Colon
Gulf of Mosquitos
Panama City ■
Panama Canal
La Palma
Gulf of Panama
Cocos Island (Costa Rica)

San Andres Island (Colombia)
Cape Gallinas
Aruba (Netherlands)
Netherlands Antilles (Netherlands)
Willemstad
Margarita Island
Cumana
Port-of-Spain ■
TRINIDAD AND TOBAGO
Maturin
Orinoco Delta

Riohacha
Gulf of Venezuela
Paraguaipoa
Santa Marta
Barranquilla
Cristobal Colon ▲ 5,775m (18,947ft)
Cartagena
Maracaibo
Lake Maracaibo
Valera
Caracas ■
Valencia
Maracay
Barcelona
Barquisimeto
VENEZUELA
Ciudad Bolivar
Ciudad Guayana
Georgetown ■
GUYANA

Sincelejo
Colon
Gulf of Darien
Bolivar Peak ▲ 5,007m (16,427ft)
Cucuta
San Cristobal
San Fernando de Apure
Orinoco
Puerto Paez
Angel Falls
Mount Roraima ▲ 2,810m (9,219ft)
Santa Elena

Dabeiba
Pamplona
Bucaramanga
Medellin
Tunja
Quibdo
Western Cordillera
Cordillera
Manizales
Pereira
Ibague
Bogota ■
Eastern Cordillera
COLOMBIA
Llanos
Guaviare
Puerto Inirida
Guiana Highlands
Boa Vista

Buenaventura
Cali
Neiva ▲ 5,750m (18,865ft)
Popayan
San Jose del Guaviare
Orinoco
Negro
BRAZIL

Tumaco
Esmeraldas
Pasto
Florencia
Puerto Leguizamo
Equator

ECUADOR
Quito ■
Ibarra
Ipiales

Malpelo Island (Colombia)

SOUTH AMERICA

South America is made up of 12 independent countries, along with French Guiana, which belongs to France. The continent's biggest and most industrialized country is Brazil, which covers about half of the total land. Brazil is also home to half of South America's population.

This is a guanaco. Guanacos are members of the camel family that live in South America. Guanaco hair is used to make textiles.

Caribbean Sea

Caracas

VENEZUELA

Medellin°   ■ **Bogota**

Orinoco

COLOMBIA

Equator   **Quito** ■

Galapagos
Islands
(Ecuador)   **ECUADOR**

Guayaquil°

Mana

PERU

Lima ■

BOLIVIA
■ **La Paz**

■ **Sucre**

Tropic of Capricorn

CHILE

PACIFIC

OCEAN

Santiago ■   °Mendoza

ARGENTIN

Cape Horn

Drake Passage

The shading on this map is there to help you see clearly the different countries that make up the continent.

Georgetown
Paramaribo
UYANA   Cayenne
SURINAM FRENCH
         GUIANA
         (France)

Amazon

Equator

°Recife

B R A Z I L

■ Brasilia

Parana

°Belo Horizonte

ARAGUAY   °Rio de Janeiro
   Sao Paulo°

■ Asuncion

Tropic of Capricorn

°Porto Alegre

ATLANTIC

URUGUAY

OCEAN

■ Montevideo

Buenos Aires

Falkland Islands
(U.K.)

This is a red-eyed tree frog. These frogs live in rainforests in South and Central America.

Facts

Total land area 17,866,130 sq km (6,898,113 sq miles)

Total population 346 million

Biggest city Sao Paulo, Brazil

Biggest country Brazil *8,547,400 sq km (3,300,151 sq miles)*

Smallest country Surinam *163,270 sq km (63,039 sq miles)*

Highest mountain Aconcagua, Argentina *6,959m (22,831ft)*

Longest river Amazon, mainly in Brazil *6,440km (4,000 miles)*

Biggest lake Lake Maracaibo, Venezuela *13,312 sq km (5,140 sq miles)*

Highest waterfall Angel Falls, on the Churun River, Venezuela *979m (3,212ft)*

Biggest desert Patagonian Desert, Argentina *673,000 sq km (260,000 sq miles)*

Biggest island Tierra del Fuego *46,360 sq km (17,900 sq miles)*

Main mineral deposits Copper, tin, molybdenum, bauxite, emeralds

Main fuel deposits Oil, coal

South America has a varied and dramatic landscape. In the north there are lush, tropical rainforests, and in central areas are grassy plains, called pampas. In the far south there are glaciers, which are huge, slow-moving masses of ice.

The big picture

The Andes mountain range stretches more than 7,250km (4,500 miles) down the whole length of western South America. It is the longest chain of mountains on Earth.

South America also has the second-longest river in the world, the Amazon. It snakes through the northern half of the continent, from the Andes in Peru to the coast of Brazil, and carries around one-fifth of the world's fresh water.

On this satellite image of South America the Andes mountains are clearly visible in the west. The range contains many active volcanoes.

This flock of large birds, called scarlet ibises, is flying over lush forest in Venezuela.

Icy lands

The southern tip of South America is near Antarctica, which means that the climate is extremely cold. There are glaciers in the mountainous regions, and icebergs in the area's many lakes. South America's most southerly point is Cape Horn. The seas around it are rough and stormy, which can make sailing around Cape Horn very dangerous.

The bluish-white shape in the middle of this image is part of a huge glacier. Melting ice gradually flows into Lake Viedma, shown in the bottom right.

Internet links

For a link to a Web site where you can test your knowledge of the world's deserts, including the Atacama Desert of South America, go to **www.usborne-quicklinks.com**

Water source

On the border of Brazil and Paraguay is a vast expanse of water, about 1,350 sq km (520 sq miles) in size. This is the Itaipu reservoir, a man-made water source which provides water for homes, farms and factories in many areas of Brazil and Paraguay. In the past there had been many droughts, so the reservoir was built to provide a reliable supply of water.

This large blue area is part of the huge Itaipu reservoir, which forms part of the border between Paraguay (left) and Brazil (right).

The river running down the lower part of this image is the Parana River. It flows southward on the eastern side of South America.

This is a mountainous part of the Atacama Desert. In the middle are two snow-capped volcanoes, and on the right are white areas of salt from evaporated salt lakes.

The driest desert

Running down the western coast of Chile is the Atacama Desert, the driest place on Earth. Many areas of the desert go for decades without rain and in some parts rainfall has never been recorded.

Vast areas of the desert are covered in salt, which is all that is left of evaporated saltwater lakes. The rocky landscape looks like the Moon's surface, and NASA vehicles have been tested there in preparation for crossing the Moon's rugged terrain.

One of South America's main features is the Amazon rainforest. This is the largest rainforest in the world, covering an area nearly the size of Europe. The continent also has fascinating cities, both ancient and modern.

Parrot snakes live in trees in the Amazon rainforest. They often open their mouths wide like this to scare off predators.

Machu Picchu

High in the Andes Mountains of Peru lies the ancient, ruined city of Machu Picchu. It was built by the Incas, the South American people who ruled the western part of the continent from about 1400 to 1530. The city contains the ruins of many stone buildings, such as temples, palaces and storerooms, which were built around large central courtyards.

This is Machu Picchu, in the Andes. The city's buildings were constructed on wide steps cut into the sloping ground.

Amazing Amazon

The Amazon rainforest spreads across northern South America and is home to one-third of all the world's animal species. The rainforest contains over 100 species of snakes, from rare boa constrictors to common green parrot snakes.

Here is part of the wealthy, crowded financial district in Santiago, Chile.

City sprawl

South America has many huge cities, such as Sao Paulo in Brazil and Santiago in Chile. The growth of business and industry in these cities has led to the creation of towering skyscrapers, but also causes extra traffic and pollution. The cities are so overcrowded that many people live in poor, run-down suburbs.

Island animals

The Galapagos Islands are a cluster of small, rocky islands that lie in the Pacific Ocean, about 1,000km (600 miles) off the coast of Ecuador.

The islands are home to all kinds of unusual animals, such as giant tortoises. These enormous creatures weigh up to 250kg (550lb), and can live for more than a hundred years. Many tropical birds live on the islands too, including Galapagos penguins and frigate birds.

Fantastic falls

South America's mountainous landscape has led to the formation of many waterfalls, including Angel Falls in Venezuela, which is the world's biggest waterfall. It is 979m (3,212ft) high, more than twice the height of the tallest building in the world.

A male frigate bird puffs out his bright red pouch to attract females. Frigate birds live on many of the Galapagos Islands.

Internet links

For a link to a Web site where you can discover the sights and sounds of the Amazon rainforest, including howling monkeys and squawking macaws, go to **www.usborne-quicklinks.com**

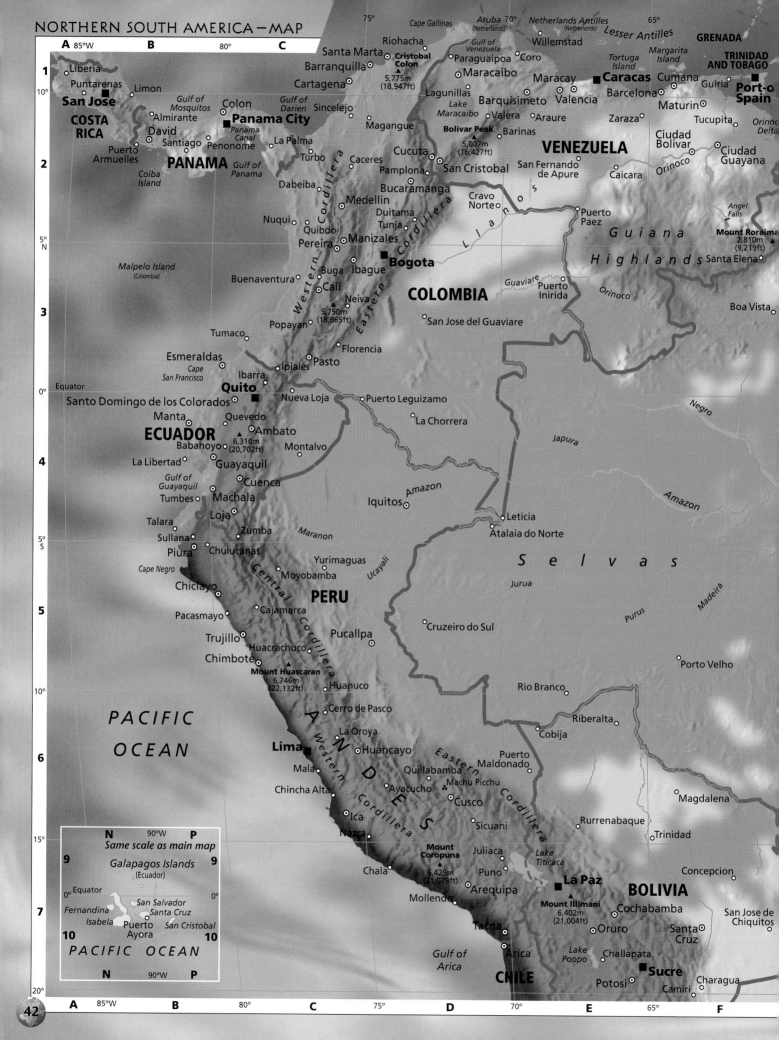

A 85°W B 80° C

1

Liberia
Puntarenas
Limon
San Jose
COSTA
RICA

2

Gulf of
Mosquitos
Almirante
David
Santiago Penonome
Puerto
Armuelles
PANAMA
Coiba
Island
Gulf of
Panama

Colon
Panama City
Panama
Canal
La Palma
La Palma

Cape Gallinas

Cristobal
Colon
5,775m
(18,947ft)

Santa Marta
Barranquilla
Cartagena

Sincelejo
Turbo
Caceres
Dabeiba
Medellin
Quibdo
Pereira Manizales
Buenaventura Buga Ibague
Cali
Neiva
5,750m
(18,865ft)
Popayan

Magangue

Pamplona
Bucaramanga
Duitama
Tunja
Bogota

COLOMBIA

Riohacha
Paraguaipoa
Maracaibo
Lagunillas
Lake
Maracaibo
Valera
San Cristobal

Gulf of
Venezuela
Coro
Barquisimeto
Araure
Barinas

Aruba 70°
(Netherlands)
Netherlands Antilles
(Netherlands)
Willemstad
Lesser Antilles
65°
GRENADA

Maracay
Valencia
Zaraza

Caracas
Barcelona

Bolivar Peak
5,007m
(16,427ft)
San Fernando
de Apure

VENEZUELA

Tortuga
Island
Margarita
Island
Cumana
Maturin

TRINIDAD
AND TOBAGO
Port-o
Spain
Guiria
Tucupita

Ciudad
Bolivar
Ciudad
Guayana
Orino
Delta

Cucuta

Caicara
Orinoco

Cravo
Norte
Llanos
Puerto
Paez

Guaviare
Puerto
Inirida

Guiana
Highlands

Angel
Falls
Mount Roraima
2,810m
(9,219ft)
Santa Elena

5°N

Florencia

San Jose del Guaviare

Orinoco

Boa Vista

3

Tumaco
Esmeraldas
Cape
San Francisco
Ibarra
Quito
Santo Domingo de los Colorados
Manta
Quevedo
ECUADOR
6,310m
(20,702ft)
Babahoyo
La Libertad
Guayaquil
Gulf of
Guayaquil Cuenca
Tumbes Machala
Loja

Ipiales Pasto

Nueva Loja

Puerto Leguizamo

La Chorrera

Japura

Negro

Equator

0°

Ambato
Montalvo

Iquitos
Amazon

Leticia
Atalaia do Norte

Amazon

4

Talara
Sullana
Piura
Cape Negro

Zumba
Maranon
Chulucanas

Yurimaguas
Moyobamba
Ucayali

Selvas

Jurua

Madeira

5°S

5

Chiclayo
Pacasmayo
Trujillo Cajamarca
Chimbote Huacrachuco
Mount Huascaran
6,746m
(22,132ft)

PERU

Pucallpa

Cruzeiro do Sul

Purus

Porto Velho

6

PACIFIC

OCEAN

Huanuco
Cerro de Pasco
La Oroya
Lima Huancayo
Mala
Chincha Alta
Ica
Nazca

Quillabamba
Ayacucho
Machu Picchu
Cusco

Sicuani

A
N
D
E
S
Western
Cordillera
Eastern
Cordillera

Rio Branco

Cobija
Riberalta

Puerto
Maldonado

Rurrenabaque

Magdalena

Trinidad

7

Chala

Mount
Coropuna
6,425m
(21,079ft)

Mollendo

Juliaca
Puno
Arequipa

Lake
Titicaca

La Paz
Mount Illimani
6,402m
(21,004ft)

BOLIVIA
Cochabamba
Oruro
Santa
Cruz

Concepcion

San Jose de
Chiquitos

Tacna

Arica
Gulf of
Arica

CHILE

Lake
Poopo
Challapata

Potosi
Sucre

Charagua
Camiri

20°

N 90°W P
9 Same scale as main map 9
Galapagos Islands
(Ecuador)
0° Equator
Fernandina
Isabela
San Salvador
Santa Cruz
Puerto
Ayora
San Cristobal
10 10
PACIFIC OCEAN
N 90°W P

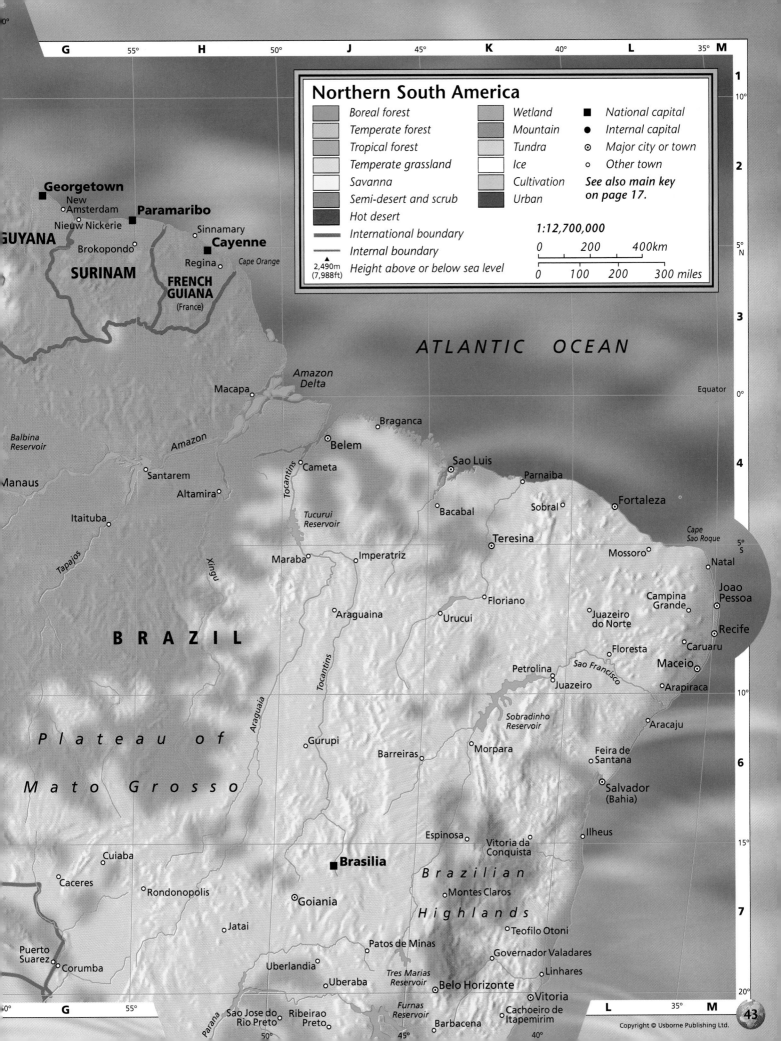

Northern South America

Key:
- Boreal forest
- Temperate forest
- Tropical forest
- Temperate grassland
- Savanna
- Semi-desert and scrub
- Hot desert
- Wetland
- Mountain
- Tundra
- Ice
- Cultivation
- Urban
- ■ National capital
- ● Internal capital
- ⊙ Major city or town
- ○ Other town

See also main key on page 17.

International boundary
Internal boundary

2,490m (7,988ft) ▲ Height above or below sea level

1:12,700,000

0   200   400km
0   100   200   300 miles

Coordinate grid labels (top): G 55° H 50° J 45° K 40° L 35° M
Right margin: 10° (1), (2), 5°N, 0° Equator, 5°S, 10° (6), 15° (7), 20°

Georgetown
New Amsterdam
Nieuw Nickerie
Brokopondo
GUYANA
SURINAM
Paramaribo
Sinnamary
Regina
Cayenne
FRENCH GUIANA (France)
Cape Orange

ATLANTIC OCEAN

Macapa
Amazon Delta
Balbina Reservoir
Amazon
Manaus
Santarem
Altamira
Itaituba
Tapajos
Xingu
Braganca
Belem
Cameta
Tocantins
Tucurui Reservoir
Maraba
Imperatriz
Araguaia
Sao Luis
Parnaiba
Bacabal
Sobral
Teresina
Floriano
Urucui
Juazeiro do Norte
Fortaleza
Cape Sao Roque
Mossoro
Natal
Joao Pessoa
Campina Grande
Recife
Caruaru
Floresta
Maceio
Arapiraca

B R A Z I L

Araguaia
Gurupi
Barreiras
Morpara
Petrolina
Juazeiro
Sao Francisco
Sobradinho Reservoir
Aracaju
Feira de Santana
Salvador (Bahia)

P l a t e a u   o f
M a t o   G r o s s o

Cuiaba
Caceres
Rondonopolis
Jatai
Puerto Suarez
Corumba
Goiania
Brasilia
Espinosa
Vitoria da Conquista
Ilheus
B r a z i l i a n
Montes Claros
H i g h l a n d s
Teofilo Otoni
Patos de Minas
Governador Valadares
Uberlandia
Linhares
Uberaba
Tres Marias Reservoir
Belo Horizonte
Vitoria
Parana
Sao Jose do Rio Preto
Ribeirao Preto
Furnas Reservoir
Barbacena
Cachoeiro de Itapemirim

Coordinate grid labels (bottom): G 55° L 35° M, 45°, 50°, 40°, 20°

SOUTHERN SOUTH AMERICA—MAP

1 10°S

L

40°

Sobradinho
Reservoir

Morpara

Feira de Santana

Ilheus

Vitoria da
Conquista

Espinosa

Teofilo Otoni

Montes Claros

Governador
Valadares

Linhares

Vitoria

Cachoeiro
de Itapemirim

Campos

Macae

Nova Iguacu

Rio de Janeiro

Tropic of Capricorn

Belo Horizonte

Barbacena

Juiz
de Fora

B r a z i l i a n

H i g h l a n d s

Barreiras

Patos de Minas

*Tres Marias
Reservoir*

*Furnas
Reservoir*

Mount
Aguilhas
Negras
▲ 2,787m
(9,144ft)

Sao Paulo

Brasilia

Goiania

Uberaba

Ribeirao
Preto

Pocos de
Caldas

Campinas

Araraquara

Marilia

Itapetininga

Curitiba

Paranagua

Itajai

Florianopolis

Tocantins

B R A Z I L

Gurupi

Sao Jose do Rio Preto

Presidente
Prudente

Londrina

Cascavel

Guarapuava

Passo Fundo

Caxias do Sul

Porto Alegre

*Patos
Lagoon*

Rio Grande

Araguaia

Jatai

Parana

Foz do Iguacu

*Iguacu
Falls*

Eldorado

Santa Maria

Bage

Pelotas

Melo

*Mirim
Lake*

P l a t e a u   o f

M a t o   G r o s s o

Rondonopolis

Cuiaba

Caceres

Campo Grande

Dourados

Ponta Pora

Pedro Juan
Caballero

Concepcion

PARAGUAY

Ciudad
del
Este

Posadas

Uruguaiana

URUGUAY

Rivera

Tacuarembo

Durazno

Minas

Trinidad

Magdalena

San Jose de
Chiquitos

Puerto Suarez

Corumba

Concepcion

Paraguay

Asuncion

Villarrica

Encarnacion

Reconquista

Concordia

Salto

Paysandu

Gualeguaychu

Rurrenabaque

BOLIVIA

Santa Cruz

Camiri

Charagua

Formosa

Corrientes

Santa Fe

San Nicolas
de los Arroyos

Rivera

Gran Chaco

Pilcomayo

Tartagal

San Miguel de Tucuman

Santiago del Estero

Salado

San Francisco

Villa Maria

Rufino

Venado
Tuerto

Rosario

**Buenos
Aires**

Chacabuco

Cobija

Riberalta

Rio Branco

Puerto
Maldonado

PERU

Juliaca

Puno

*Lake
Titicaca*

La Paz

Mount
Illimani
▲ 6,402m
(21,004ft)

Cochabamba

Sucre

Oruro

*Lake
Poopo*

Challapata

Potosi

Tarija

San Salvador
de Jujuy

A

Catamarca

La Rioja

San Juan

Mendoza

San Luis

Merlo

Villa Mercedes

San
Rafael

Tacna

Arica

Iquique

Pica

Uyuni

Ollague

Calama

San Pedro de Atacama

Salta

N

D

Cordoba

Rio Cuarto

Aconcagua
▲ 6,959m
(22,831ft)

E

S

Atacama Desert

Antofagasta

Taltal

Chanaral

Copiapo

Mount
Ojos del Salado
▲ 6,908m
(22,664ft)

Vallenar

Coquimbo

San Juan

San Luis

C

H

I

L

E

Ovalle

Illapel

Valparaiso

Santiago

Rancagua

San Fernando

Coquimbo

Tropic of Capricorn

44

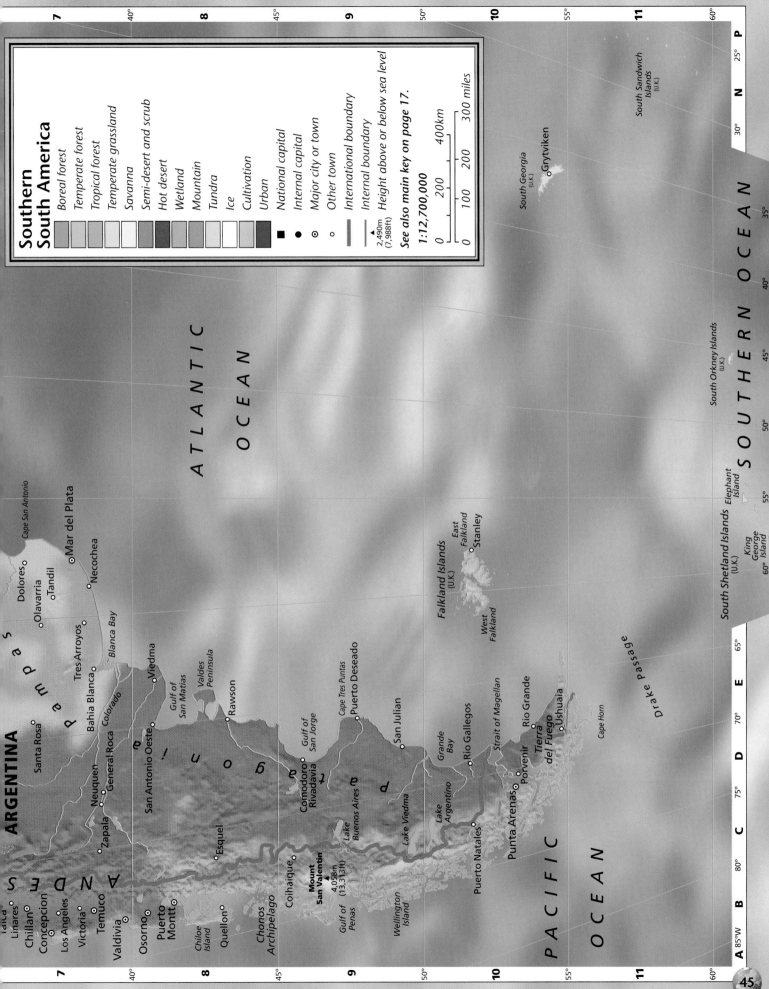

Southern South America

Key

- Boreal forest
- Temperate forest
- Tropical forest
- Temperate grassland
- Savanna
- Semi-desert and scrub
- Hot desert
- Wetland
- Mountain
- Tundra
- Ice
- Cultivation
- Urban

- ■ National capital
- ● Internal capital
- ◉ Major city or town
- ○ Other town

- International boundary
- Internal boundary
- ▲ 2,490m (7,988ft) Height above or below sea level

See also main key on page 17.

1:12,700,000

0 100 200 300 400km
0 100 200 300 miles

ARGENTINA

Pampas

Linares
Chillán
Concepcion
Los Angeles
Victoria
Temuco
Valdivia
Osorno
Puerto Montt
Quellon
Chiloe Island
Chonos Archipelago
Coihaique
Esquel
Mount San Valentín 4,058m (13,313ft)
Gulf of Penas
Wellington Island
Puerto Natales
Punta Arenas
Porvenir
Tierra del Fuego
Ushuaia
Río Grande
Río Gallegos
Lake Argentino
Lake Viedma
Lake Buenos Aires
Comodoro Rivadavia
Gulf of San Jorge
Cape Tres Puntas
Puerto Deseado
San Julián
Grande Bay
Strait of Magellan

Santa Rosa
Neuquen
Zapala
General Roca
Colorado
Bahia Blanca
San Antonio Oeste
Viedma
Gulf of San Matias
Valdes Peninsula
Rawson
Tres Arroyos
Olavarria
Dolores
Tandil
Necochea
Mar del Plata
Cape San Antonio
Blanca Bay

ANDES

Patagonia

ATLANTIC OCEAN

PACIFIC OCEAN

Cape Horn
Drake Passage

SOUTHERN OCEAN

Falkland Islands (U.K.)
West Falkland
East Falkland
Stanley

South Shetland Islands (U.K.)
Elephant Island
King George Island

South Orkney Islands (U.K.)

South Georgia (U.K.)
Grytviken

South Sandwich Islands (U.K.)

45

AUSTRALASIA AND OCEANIA

Australasia is made up of Australia, New Zealand and Papua New Guinea. Oceania is a collection of over 20,000 islands stretching out into the Pacific Ocean.

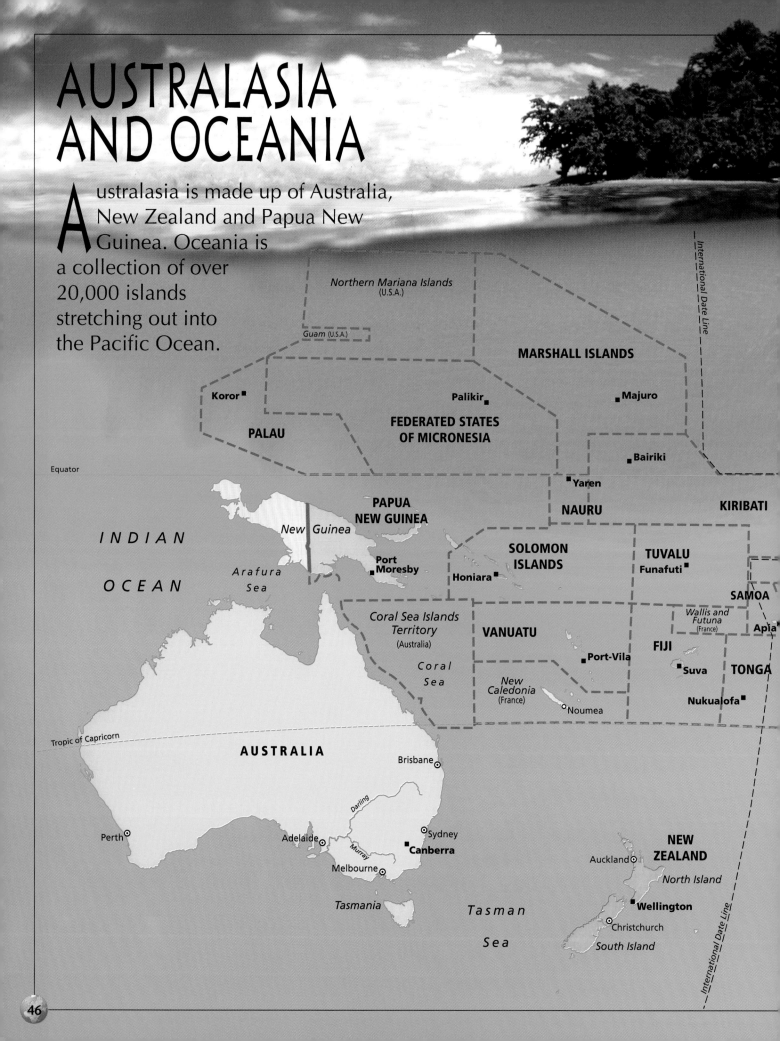

International Date Line

Northern Mariana Islands
(U.S.A.)

Guam (U.S.A.)

MARSHALL ISLANDS

Koror ■

Palikir ■

■ Majuro

PALAU

**FEDERATED STATES
OF MICRONESIA**

■ Bairiki

Equator

■ Yaren

**PAPUA
NEW GUINEA**

NAURU

KIRIBATI

New Guinea

INDIAN

*Arafura
Sea*

Port
■ Moresby

**SOLOMON
ISLANDS**

TUVALU
Funafuti ■

OCEAN

Honiara ■

SAMOA

*Wallis and
Futuna
(France)*

Apia ○

Coral Sea Islands
Territory
(Australia)

VANUATU

FIJI

*Coral
Sea*

Port-Vila ■

■ Suva

TONGA

*New
Caledonia
(France)*

○ Noumea

Nukualofa ■

Tropic of Capricorn

AUSTRALIA

Brisbane ◉

Darling

Perth ○

Adelaide ◉

Sydney ○

Murray

■ **Canberra**

Melbourne ○

**NEW
ZEALAND**

Auckland ◉

North Island

Tasmania

Tasman

■ **Wellington**

Christchurch ○

Sea

South Island

International Date Line

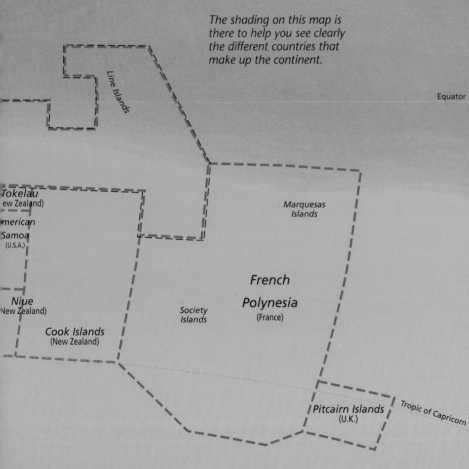

This small island belongs to Papua New Guinea.

PACIFIC OCEAN

The shading on this map is there to help you see clearly the different countries that make up the continent.

Line Islands

Equator

Tokelau
(New Zealand)

American Samoa
(U.S.A.)

Niue
(New Zealand)

Cook Islands
(New Zealand)

Society Islands

Marquesas Islands

French Polynesia
(France)

Pitcairn Islands
(U.K.)

Tropic of Capricorn

Facts

Total land area 8,564,400 sq km (3,306,715 sq miles)

Total population 31 million

Biggest city Sydney, Australia

Biggest country Australia 7,686,850 sq km (2,967,124 sq miles)

Smallest country Nauru 21 sq km (8 sq miles)

Highest mountain Mount Wilhelm, Papua New Guinea 4,509m (14,793ft)

Longest river Murray/Darling River, Australia 3,718km (2,310 miles)

Biggest lake Lake Eyre, Australia 9,000 sq km (3,470 sq miles)

Highest waterfall Sutherland Falls, on the Arthur River, New Zealand 580m (1,904ft)

Biggest desert Great Victoria Desert, Australia 388,500 sq km (150,000 sq miles)

Biggest island New Guinea 800,000 sq km (309,000 sq miles) (Australia is counted as a continental land mass and not as an island.)

Main mineral deposits Iron, nickel, precious stones, lead, bauxite

Main fuel deposits Oil, coal, uranium

The Moorish idol fish is found in shallow waters throughout the Pacific. It has very bold stripes and a long, distinctive snout.

Australasia and Oceania's climate is generally very hot. New Zealand and Papua New Guinea are both lush, while Australia is mostly barren. The tiny tropical islands that make up Oceania are surrounded by vast areas of open sea.

This image shows a section of the Southern Alps of South Island, New Zealand. The two turquoise patches are Lake Pukaki and Lake Tekapo.

In this satellite view of Australasia and Oceania, areas of vegetation are green and desert areas are yellow.

Milky waters

New Zealand has two main islands, North Island and South Island, and several smaller ones. On South Island there is a mountain range called the Southern Alps, which has some dramatic milky-turquoise lakes. Their cloudy appearance is caused by rock dust, which is collected, finely ground and then deposited in the lake by glaciers. The rock dust is so fine, it stays suspended in the water, instead of sinking.

Land of bushfires

Most of Australia is hot, dry desert and the country suffers badly from bushfires almost every year. The fires are usually caused by lightning striking dry vegetation. Some species of trees found in Australia have adapted to cope with the constant outbreaks of fire. Eucalyptus trees can withstand fire, and some types of banksia trees actually need fire to open their seed pods.

Internet links

For a link to a Web site where you can find out how eucalyptus trees have become fire resistant, go to **www.usborne-quicklinks.com**

These are the Palau Rock Islands of Micronesia, Oceania. There are over 200 rock islands in total. Each one is made of limestone rock and covered with thick forest.

Tropical islands

Lots of the small islands in the South Pacific are volcanoes. Coral reefs (dense colonies of tentacled sea animals) often grow in shallow waters around the islands. They form barriers which trap water between the reef and the island's coast. The trapped water is known as a lagoon.

Many of the volcanoes are inactive, and are slowly sinking back into the sea. Sometimes, a volcano sinks entirely into the sea, leaving behind a shallow lagoon surrounded by a coral reef. This is called an atoll.

This is Bora Bora Island, a volcanic island in the South Pacific. Vegetation is green, deep water is black and shallow water is pale blue.

The coral reef is the thin, white line around the edge.

This is Lake Eyre in Australia. It wasn't completely dry when this picture was taken – dry areas are pale pink and wet areas are dark pink.

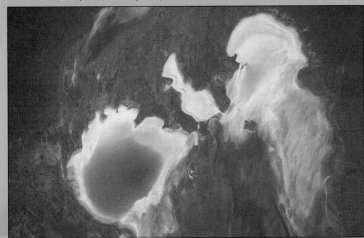

A vanishing lake

Australia's largest salt lake, Lake Eyre, is in the dry, central part of the country. Most of the year it is virtually dry, and you can see a glistening sheet of white salt on the lake bed. When the lake fills, it spreads out over 9,500 sq km (3,670 sq miles), but this usually only happens about once every eight years. The lake has two main sections, Lake Eyre North and Lake Eyre South, which are joined by a channel called the Goyder Channel.

Australasia and Oceania's attractions include a group of huge stone carvings, a strange tree formation and animals equipped with their own baby-carriers.

Great Barrier Reef

Around the coast of Queensland, Australia, lies the Great Barrier Reef, an enormous coral reef structure. It is made up of over 2,800 coral reefs, covering 345,000 sq km (133,200 sq miles) and is home to more than 1,500 species of fish.

Coral reefs are very fragile. They are found in clear, shallow waters with a constant, warm temperature. Global warming might make the sea too hot for coral reefs to survive, and the Great Barrier Reef could die out.

Easter Island

Easter Island is a remote island, far east of Australia, famous for its large stone carvings of human figures with large heads. The carvings are thought to be between 400 and 1,000 years old, and are believed to represent the spirits of important chiefs and ancestors of the island. A Dutch navigator named Jacob Roggeveen gave Easter Island its name when he first visited it on Easter day in 1722.

These sculptures on Easter Island were carved out of volcanic rock. They are about 4m (13ft) tall, and some are partly buried.

Internet links

For a link to a Web site where you can explore interactive pictures of Easter Island go to **www.usborne-quicklinks.com**

The Olgas

In Uluru National Park, in Australia's Northern Territory, there is a group of 36 enormous rocks known as the Olgas. The rocks are a type of sandstone, which means they were formed by loose sand that has become hardened and folded by the Earth's movements to produce layered rocks. The rocks were gradually eroded by wind and rain into the rounded hills we see today. The sand grains that make up the sandstone are mostly made of a pink mineral called feldspar.

These rounded rocks are the Olgas. The aboriginals, who were the first people to settle in Australia, named the site "Kata Tjunta" meaning "many heads".

This is a tree kangaroo, a type of animal only found in Queensland, Australia, and Papua New Guinea. Tree kangaroos can leap great distances from tree to tree.

The seven-in-one tree

On the island of Rarotonga, in the Cook Islands, there is a group of seven coconut trees which have grown naturally in a perfect circle. A legend tells that the seven trees grew from one seed, so they are known as the "seven-in-one tree", but they probably grew from seven separate seeds.

Marsupials

Australasia and Oceania are home to lots of unusual animals, including a group of mammals called marsupials. As soon as marsupials are born, they crawl into a pouch of skin on their mother's tummy. They stay inside the pouch for the first few months of their lives. Kangaroos, koalas, wombats and possums are all marsupials.

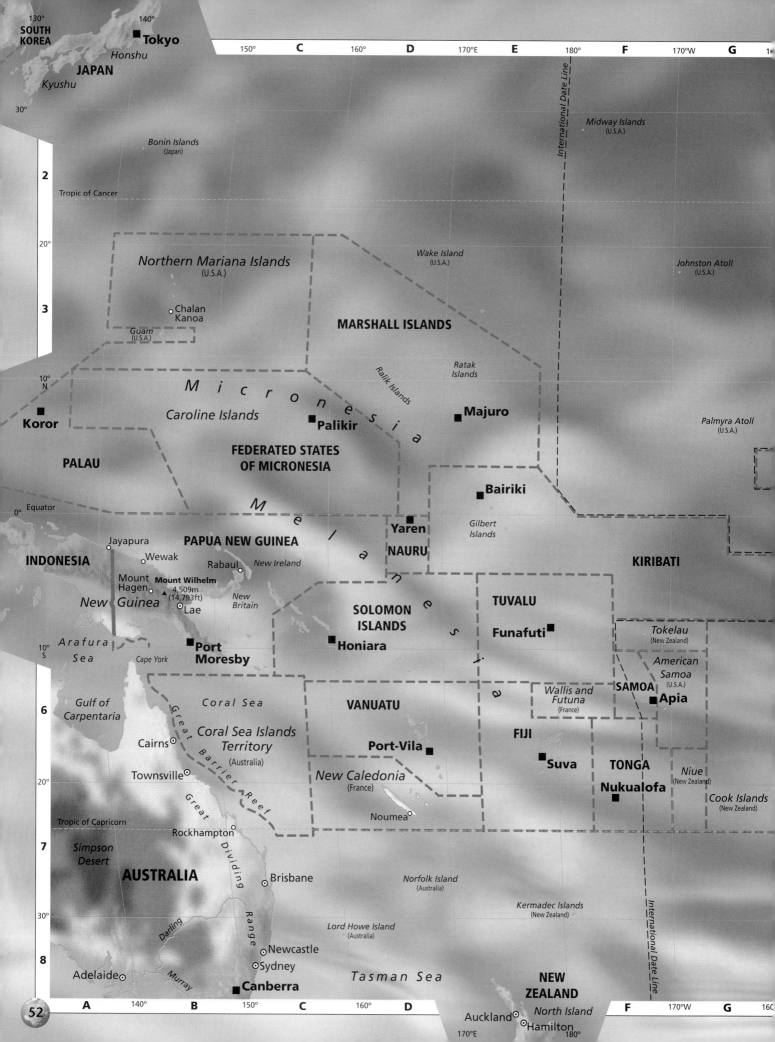

Tokyo

JAPAN

Honshu

Kyushu

30°

2

Bonin Islands
(Japan)

Tropic of Cancer

20°

3

Midway Islands
(U.S.A.)

Wake Island
(U.S.A.)

Johnston Atoll
(U.S.A.)

Northern Mariana Islands
(U.S.A.)

Chalan
Kanoa

Guam
(U.S.A.)

MARSHALL ISLANDS

Ratak
Islands

10°
N

M i c r o n e s i a

Caroline Islands

Ralik Islands

Majuro

Koror

Palmyra Atoll
(U.S.A.)

PALAU

Palikir

FEDERATED STATES
OF MICRONESIA

Bairiki

0°   Equator

M e l

Gilbert
Islands

Jayapura

PAPUA NEW GUINEA

a

Yaren

KIRIBATI

INDONESIA

Wewak

Rabaul

New Ireland

n

NAURU

Mount
Hagen

Mount Wilhelm
▲ 4,509m
(14,793ft)

New Guinea

Lae

New
Britain

e

s

TUVALU

Tokelau
(New Zealand)

10°
S

Arafura
Sea

Cape York

Port
Moresby

SOLOMON
ISLANDS

Honiara

i

Funafuti

American
Samoa
(U.S.A.)

SAMOA

Apia

Gulf of
Carpentaria

Coral Sea

a

Wallis and
Futuna
(France)

6

Cairns

Coral Sea Islands
Territory
(Australia)

VANUATU

FIJI

Niue
(New Zealand)

Townsville

Port-Vila

Suva

TONGA

20°

New Caledonia
(France)

Nukualofa

Cook Islands
(New Zealand)

Tropic of Capricorn

Rockhampton

Noumea

7

Simpson
Desert

Norfolk Island
(Australia)

AUSTRALIA

Brisbane

Kermadec Islands
(New Zealand)

30°

Darling

Range

Lord Howe Island
(Australia)

8

Newcastle

Adelaide

Murray

Sydney

Tasman Sea

NEW
ZEALAND

Canberra

Auckland   *North Island*

Hamilton

170°E   180°

International Date Line

Great Barrier Reef

Great Dividing

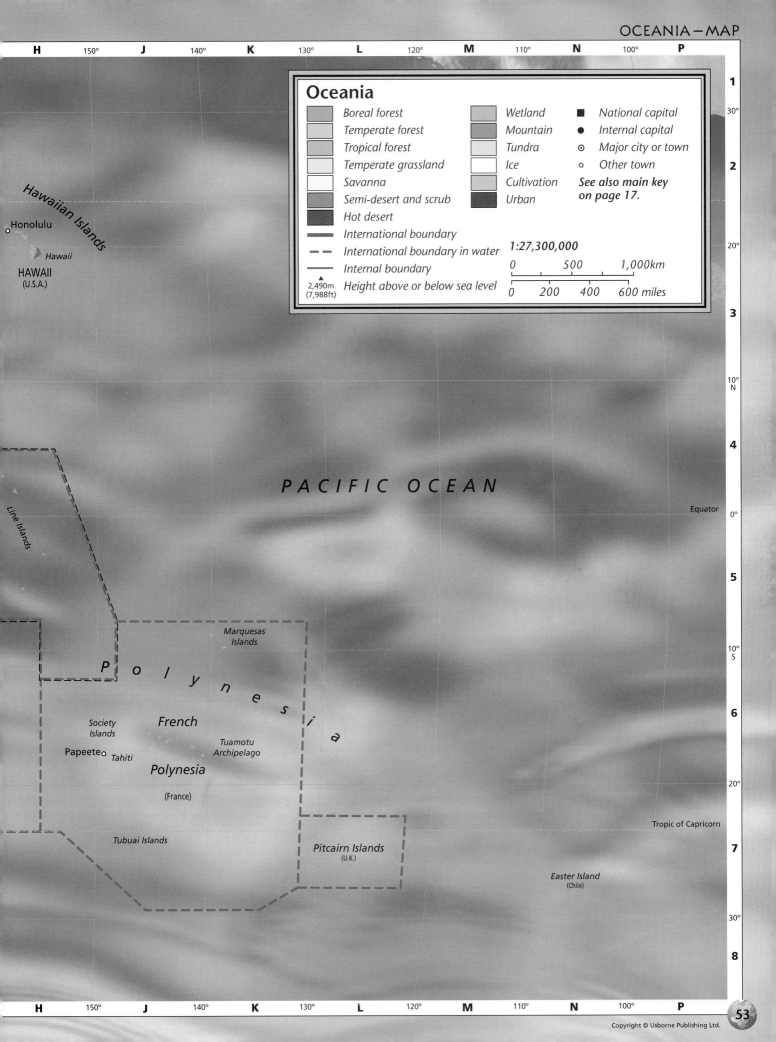

Oceania

Boreal forest	Wetland	■ National capital
Temperate forest	Mountain	● Internal capital
Tropical forest	Tundra	⊙ Major city or town
Temperate grassland	Ice	○ Other town
Savanna	Cultivation	**See also main key**
Semi-desert and scrub	Urban	**on page 17.**
Hot desert		

International boundary
International boundary in water
Internal boundary
▲ 2,490m (7,988ft) Height above or below sea level

1:27,300,000

0   500   1,000km

0   200   400   600 miles

H 150° J 140° K 130° L 120° M 110° N 100° P

30°
20°
10° N
Equator 0°
10° S
20°
Tropic of Capricorn
30°

1
2
3
4
5
6
7
8

Hawaiian Islands

○ Honolulu

Hawaii

HAWAII
(U.S.A.)

Line Islands

PACIFIC OCEAN

Marquesas Islands

P o l y n e s i a

Society Islands

French

Papeete ○ Tahiti

Polynesia

Tuamotu Archipelago

(France)

Tubuai Islands

Pitcairn Islands
(U.K.)

Easter Island
(Chile)

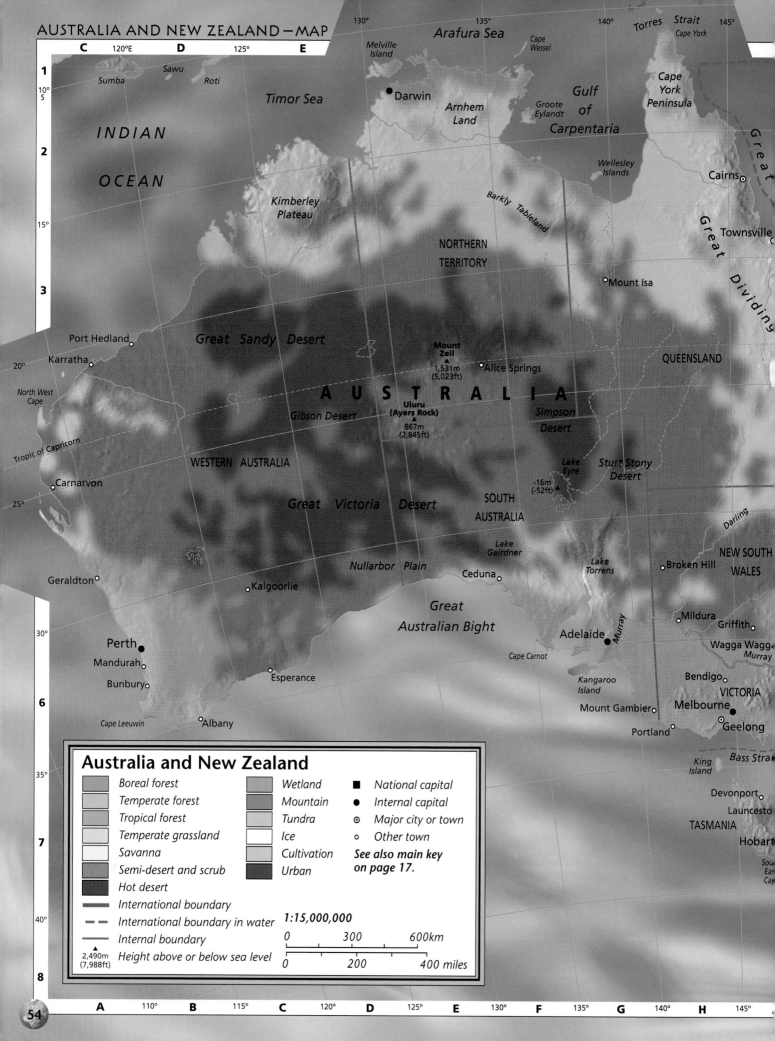

Australia and New Zealand

Boreal forest	Wetland	■	National capital
Temperate forest	Mountain	●	Internal capital
Tropical forest	Tundra	◉	Major city or town
Temperate grassland	Ice	○	Other town
Savanna	Cultivation		
Semi-desert and scrub	Urban	**See also main key on page 17.**	
Hot desert			

International boundary
International boundary in water
Internal boundary
▲ 2,490m (7,988ft) Height above or below sea level

1:15,000,000

0   300   600km
0   200   400 miles

1

Coral Sea

Rennell Island **SOLOMON ISLANDS** *Santa Cruz Islands*

10°S

TUVALU

2

Coral Sea Islands Territory (Australia)

Banks Islands

Espiritu Santo ○Luganville

VANUATU

Malakula

15°

FIJI

Vanua Levu

Lautoka○

Viti Levu ■**Suva**

○Mackay

Chesterfield Islands

Efate ■**Port-Vila**

Barrier Reef

○ckhampton

○Gladstone

New Caledonia (France)

Noumea○ *Loyalty Islands*

20°

○Bundaberg

Fraser Island

○Gympie

4

Tropic of Capricorn

Toowoomba○ ●Brisbane
○Gold Coast

PACIFIC OCEAN

○Moree

○Grafton

Norfolk Island (Australia)

25°

Great Dividing Range

○Armidale

Lord Howe Island (Australia)

Dubbo○ ○Port Macquarie

5

○Newcastle

●Sydney
○Wollongong

Kermadec Islands (New Zealand)

30°

■**Canberra**
AUSTRALIAN CAPITAL TERRITORY
▲**Mount Kosciuszko**
2,229m
7,313ft)

North Cape

6

Tasman Sea

○Whangarei

Flinders Island

○Auckland

North Island

Hamilton○

35°

New Plymouth○ ○Rotorua
Lake Taupo

Cape Farewell

○Napier

7

Nelson○

■**Wellington**

South Island

NEW ZEALAND

Aoraki
(Mount Cook)
▲
3,754m
(12,316ft)

○Christchurch

Sutherland Falls

40°

Cape Providence

○Dunedin

Invercargill○

Chatham Islands (New Zealand)

Stewart Island

South West Cape

8

ASIA

Asia is the largest continent and has over 40 countries, including Russia, the biggest country in the world. As well as large land masses, it has thousands of islands and inlets, giving it over 160,000km (100,000 miles) of coastline. Turkey and Russia are partly in Europe and partly in Asia, but both are shown in full on the map on the right.

The shading on this map is there to help you see clearly the different countries that make up the continent.

ARCTIC OCEAN

Franz Josef Land

Novaya Zemlya

Barents Sea

Kara Sea

Ob

Yenisey

■ Moscow

R U S S

Volga

Black Sea

■ Ankara

TURKEY

GEORGIA

Caspian Sea

Astana ■

KAZAKHSTAN

CYPRUS

ARMENIA

AZERBAIJAN

Aral Sea

UZBEKISTAN

LEBANON

SYRIA

■ Bishkek

Beirut ■ ■ Damascus

TURKMENISTAN

Tashkent ■

KYRGYZSTAN

Jerusalem ■ ■ Amman

Ashgabat ■

ISRAEL

JORDAN

■ Baghdad

Dushanbe ■

TAJIKISTAN

IRAQ

■ Tehran

IRAN

KUWAIT

Kabul ■

Islamabad ■

AFGHANISTAN

SAUDI ARABIA

BAHRAIN

QATAR

PAKISTAN

Riyadh ■

■ Doha

Indus

New Delhi ■

NEPAL

Kathmandu ■

■ Abu Dhabi

UNITED ARAB EMIRATES

■ Muscat

Ganges

Thimphu

BANGLADESH

■ Sana

OMAN

Arabian Sea

INDIA

YEMEN

Tropic of Cancer

Socotra (Yemen)

Bay of Bengal

INDIAN OCEAN

Equator

Sri Jayewardenepura Kotte ■

SRI LANKA

■ Colombo

MALDIVES

■ Male

This is a type of Chinese boat called a junk, sailing in the sea off Singapore.

Wrangel Island

Bering Sea

East Siberian Sea

New Siberia Islands

Severnaya Zemlya

Laptev Sea

A

Lena

Sea of Okhotsk

Lake Baikal

Hokkaido

Ulan Bator ■

MONGOLIA

Sea of Japan

NORTH KOREA

JAPAN

■ **Tokyo**

Pyongyang ■

Seoul

Beijing ■

SOUTH KOREA

Honshu

Huang He (Yellow)

East China Sea

C H I N A

Chang Jiang (Yangtze)

Tropic of Cancer

Taipei

TAIWAN

UTAN

Irrawaddy

haka

BURMA (MYANMAR)

LAOS

Hanoi ■

South China Sea

PHILIPPINES

P A C I F I C

O C E A N

angoon

Vientiane ■

THAILAND

Mekong

VIETNAM

Manila ■

Philippine Sea

Bangkok ■

CAMBODIA

Andaman Islands (India)

Phnom Penh ■

Nicobar Islands (India)

BRUNEI

MALAYSIA

Equator

Kuala Lumpur ■

New Guinea

SINGAPORE

Borneo

Celebes

Sumatra

I N D O N E S I A

Dili ■ **EAST TIMOR**

Arafura Sea

Jakarta ■

Java

Facts

Total land area 44,537,920 sq km (17,196,090 sq miles)

Total population 3.8 billion (including all of Russia)

Biggest city Tokyo, Japan

Biggest country Russia *Total area: 17,075,200 sq km (6,592,735 sq miles) Area of Asiatic Russia: 12,780,800 sq km (4,934,667 sq miles)*

Smallest country Maldives *300 sq km (116 sq miles)*

Highest mountain Mount Everest, Nepal/China border *8,850m (29,035ft)*

Longest river Chang Jiang (Yangtze), China *6,380km (3,964 miles)*

Biggest lake Caspian Sea, western Asia *370,999 sq km (143,243 sq miles)*

Highest waterfall Jog Falls, on the Sharavati River, India *253m (830ft)*

Biggest desert Arabian Desert, in and around Saudi Arabia *2,230,000 sq km (900,000 sq miles)*

Biggest island Borneo *751,100 sq km (290,000 sq miles)*

Main mineral deposits Zinc, mica, tin, chromium, iron, nickel

Main fuel deposits Oil, coal, uranium, natural gas

These are lotus flowers, a type of water lily. In China they are associated with purity and for Buddhists they are sacred.

57

Asia is made up of all kinds of rugged terrain. In the far north are vast, frozen plains, and farther south are dry deserts. Asia also has enormous mountain ranges, including the Himalayas, the world's highest range. Most of Asia's population lives in the far south, which is hot and humid, with lush rainforests.

The white areas in the middle of this satellite image of Asia are mountain ranges, which include the Himalayas.

Empty land

Southern Saudi Arabia has a sandy desert that covers an area about the size of France. It is called Rub al Khali, and is often nicknamed the Empty Quarter as it has hardly any plants or animals and no permanent human settlements. Strong winds blow the sand into mounds that can be more than 330m (1,000ft) high, taller than the Eiffel Tower in Paris.

This view of Rub al Khali in Saudi Arabia shows how the wind has blown sand into long, high ridges.

This photograph shows a section of the Great Wall of China, which winds across northern China. The wall can be seen from space as a long, thin line.

This satellite image shows several volcanoes in Kamchatka, Russia. Red areas indicate snow. The pale streaks down the craters' sides are mudflows of ash and melting snow.

Russian wilderness

Kamchatka, in the far east of Russia, is one of the world's most remote areas. Its one main town is accessible only by air or sea. Much of the land is mountainous, with more than 300 volcanoes. Some of these are active, and they regularly eject boiling rivers of mud and great plumes of steam from their rocky craters.

Internet links

For a link to a Web site where you can discover more about the Great Wall of China and see a photograph of it taken from space, go to **www.usborne-quicklinks.com**

A sacred river

The River Ganges begins in the Himalayas and flows through India and Bangladesh to the Indian Ocean. The river is regarded as holy by followers of the Hindu religion. Every day thousands of Hindus bathe in the Ganges, which they believe washes away their sins. People often worship the river by throwing flowers into it or floating oil lamps on its surface.

Here is the Ganges Delta in India, where the River Ganges flows into the Bay of Bengal (bottom).

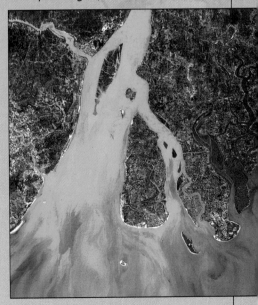

Much of central and southern Asia is densely populated, so there are many large cities, including Tokyo, the world's most populous city. There are beautiful natural areas too, such as the forests and mountain ranges of China.

A panda climbs a tree in China. Pandas are good climbers, and often rest or sleep high in trees.

Pandas of China

Wild pandas live in the mountainous forests of China. Pandas depend on the bamboo that grows there, as their diet consists almost exclusively of bamboo shoots. But forests are being cut down, so pandas are losing their habitat and food source. There may be as few as 1,000 wild pandas left.

A floating market

Near Bangkok, in Thailand, there is a famous floating market which is held on a canal. Farmers go there daily with fresh fruit and vegetables piled high on narrow boats. Customers weave their way along the busy canal in similar boats, looking for bargains. They must come early, though, as the market begins at about 8 a.m., and everything is sold by 11 a.m.

These women have brought fruit and vegetables to sell at Bangkok's floating market.

Enormous department stores with glaring neon signs line a street in central Tokyo.

Japanese capital

One of Asia's most vibrant cities is Tokyo, the capital of Japan. This big, sprawling city has been rebuilt twice, first in the 1920s when an earthquake destroyed vast areas, and then after the Second World War, when bombs devastated the city. Modern Tokyo is a mixture of a few old streets and many new, towering skyscrapers.

Forbidden City

In the middle of the city of Beijing, in China, is an ancient, walled city. For hundreds of years it was the palace of China's kings, or emperors. It was known as the Forbidden City because no one but the emperor, his family and guests was allowed in its grounds.

China no longer has a royal family, and the Forbidden City is a popular tourist attraction. The city has 800 buildings, including huge temples and elaborate arches, decorated with ornate carvings and grand bronze statues.

Internet links

For a link to a Web site where you can take a tour of the Forbidden City's most famous buildings, go to **www.usborne-quicklinks.com**

This bronze tortoise stands in Beijing's Forbidden City. According to ancient Chinese beliefs, tortoises were divine animals, and tortoise statues were said to bring good luck.

The countries of western Asia are full of important cultural and historical sights, such as places of worship and the remains of ancient civilizations. The Asian part of Russia stretches far across the continent. It is dominated by the region of Siberia, where the climate is so harsh that most of the land is uninhabited.

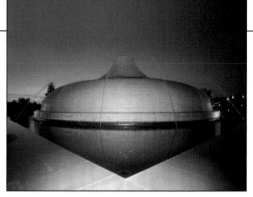

This museum in Jerusalem, Israel, houses ancient manuscripts known as the Dead Sea Scrolls.

The Dead Sea

The Dead Sea, in Israel, gets its name because it is so salty that nothing can live in it. However, many people swim in the sea, as its water contains health-giving minerals.

The Dead Sea is also famous for the Dead Sea Scrolls. These are 2,000-year-old Jewish handwritten papers that were discovered in caves by the sea. The scrolls cover mainly religious topics, and have helped historians to learn what life was like in ancient times.

Homes of rock

The region of Cappadocia, near Ankara in central Turkey, has a strange landscape of rocky cones, made of soft volcanic rock. Many hundreds of years ago, people carved caves in the rock, creating whole towns and villages that included houses, stables and even churches. They also built an amazing network of underground tunnels that linked the houses.

These rocky peaks in Cappadocia, Turkey, were carved out to create rock houses. Today, they are crumbling away.

Holy places

Many different religions are followed in Asia, and their various places of worship and study, such as Muslim mosques and Hindu temples, are found in towns and cities all over the continent. Many of these buildings are intricately decorated, for example with huge domes covered in thousands of patterned tiles.

This elaborate, domed building in Esfahan, Iran, is a school for Muslim students.

This is the Trans-Siberian Express in Siberia. The train runs from Moscow to Vladivostok, stopping at other stations on the way.

Russian train trip

Crossing the enormous country of Russia is the Trans-Siberian rail line. This is the longest rail line in the world, running more than 9,000km (5,600 miles) between Moscow in the west and Vladivostok in the east. The line passes through the plains of Siberia, which freeze over in winter. The fastest train trip along the line takes about seven days.

Reindeers

Siberia is home to many reindeers. They have thick fur that keeps them warm in winter, and also have such a good sense of smell that they can sniff out plants to eat that are buried deep under the snow.

Internet links

For a link to a Web site where you can read a fascinating account of a reindeer-herding journey in Siberia, go to **www.usborne-quicklinks.com**

These reindeers are being driven by Siberian herders through western Siberia. Reindeers can easily pull heavy, loaded sleds.

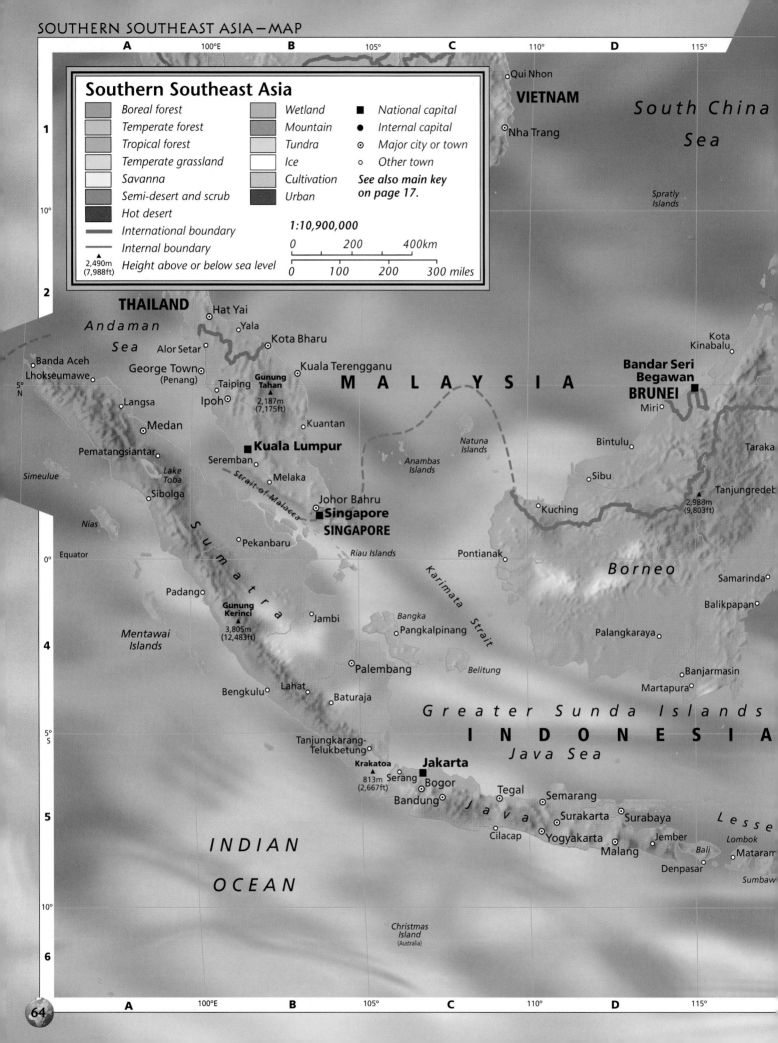

Southern Southeast Asia

▨	Boreal forest	
▨	Temperate forest	
▨	Tropical forest	
▨	Temperate grassland	
▨	Savanna	
▨	Semi-desert and scrub	
▨	Hot desert	
—	International boundary	
—	Internal boundary	
▲ 2,490m (7,988ft)	Height above or below sea level	

▨	Wetland
▨	Mountain
▨	Tundra
▨	Ice
▨	Cultivation
▨	Urban

■	National capital
●	Internal capital
⊙	Major city or town
○	Other town

See also main key on page 17.

1:10,900,000

0   200   400km
0 100 200 300 miles

VIETNAM

South China Sea

Qui Nhon

Nha Trang

Spratly Islands

THAILAND

Andaman Sea

Hat Yai
Yala
Alor Setar
Kota Bharu
Kuala Terengganu

George Town (Penang)
Banda Aceh
Lhokseumawe
Taiping
Gunung Tahan ▲ 2,187m (7,175ft)
Ipoh
Langsa
Kuantan

Medan

Pematangsiantar

Simeulue

Lake Toba
Sibolga

Nias

Padang

MALAYSIA

Kuala Lumpur
Seremban
Melaka
Strait of Malacca

Johor Bahru
Singapore
SINGAPORE

Pekanbaru

Anambas Islands

Natuna Islands

Riau Islands

Kota Kinabalu

Bandar Seri Begawan
BRUNEI
Miri

Bintulu

Sibu

Kuching

Taraka

Tanjungredeb
▲ 2,988m (9,803ft)

Borneo

Pontianak

Samarinda

Balikpapan

Palangkaraya

S u m a t r a

Gunung Kerinci ▲ 3,805m (12,483ft)

Mentawai Islands

Jambi

Palembang

Bengkulu
Lahat
Baturaja

Bangka
Pangkalpinang

Belitung

Karimata Strait

Banjarmasin
Martapura

G r e a t e r   S u n d a   I s l a n d s

I N D O N E S I A

Java Sea

Tanjungkarang-Telukbetung

Krakatoa ▲ 813m (2,667ft)
Serang
Jakarta
Bogor
Bandung

J a v a

Tegal
Cilacap
Semarang
Surakarta
Yogyakarta
Surabaya
Malang
Jember

Bali
Denpasar

Lombok
Mataram

L e s s e

Sumbaw

INDIAN

OCEAN

Christmas Island (Australia)

0° Equator

5° N

5° S

10°

A 100°E B 105° C 110° D 115°

PHILIPPINES

120° Cabanatuan
Luzon
Olongapo ● Quezon City
Manila ■
Lucena
Calapan Naga
Mindoro Legaspi
Calamian Masbate Calbayog
Group *Masbate* *Samar*
Panay Roxas Tacloban
Taytay Iloilo Bacolod
Cebu

Philippine

Sea

Negros Bohol Surigao
Puerto Princesa Dumaguete Butuan
Palawan Cagayan de Oro
Pagadian Iligan
Mindanao
Sulu Sea Zamboanga Davao
Jolo
andakan General Santos
Sulu
Archipelago
awu

Celebes Sea *Talaud*
Islands

Sangihe
Islands Morotai

PACIFIC **PALAU**

OCEAN

Manado
Molucca Ternate *Halmahera*
Gorontalo
Sea
Makassar Strait Palu Sorong *Biak*
Peleng Obi
Celebes *Misool* *Yapen*
Palopo *Sula* *Ceram Sea*
Islands *Ceram* Fakfak
Parepare Kendari *Buru* Ambon
Watampone *Maoke Range*
Buton Puncak Jaya *New*
Ujung Pandang ▲ *Guinea*
Banda Sea 5,030m
(16,502ft)

Flores Sea *Aru*
Islands *Dolak*

Wetar
Tanimbar
unda Islands *Islands*
Flores ■ **Dili**
Ende **EAST TIMOR** *Arafura Sea* *Torres Strait*
Sumba *Timor* 10°
Sawu Sea
Sawu Kupang
Roti *Timor Sea* **AUSTRALIA**

● Darwin **NORTHERN TERRITORY**

120° F 125° G 130° H 135° J 140°

Inset map

J 140°E K 145° L 150° M Equator 155° N 0°
PACIFIC
Admiralty **OCEAN**
Islands
Jayapura Wewak *Bismarck Sea* *New Ireland*
5° **Mount Wilhelm** Madang Rabaul
S 4,509m
(14,793ft) *New Britain*
Mount Hagen Lae **PAPUA NEW GUINEA**
New Guinea *Solomon Sea*
Kerema *D'Entrecasteaux*
Islands
10° *Gulf of*
Papua ■ **Port**
Torres Strait **Moresby** **1:16,400,000**
Cape York
Cape York 0 400km
AUSTRALIA 0 200 miles
Peninsula
J 140°E K 145° L 150° M 155° N

Jayapura

Pacific
Sea

5°N

Equator 0°

5°S

10°

6

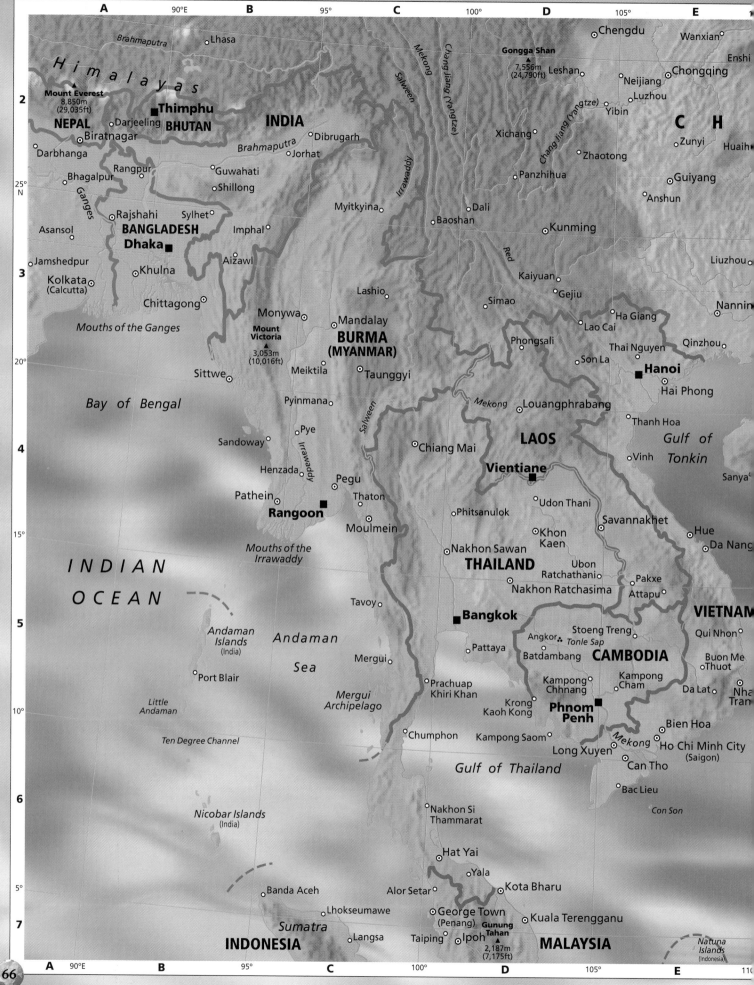

A 90°E B 95° C 100° D 105° E

Brahmaputra Lhasa

H i m a l a y a s

Mount Everest
8,850m
(29,035ft)

Chengdu Wanxian

Gongga Shan
7,556m
(24,790ft) Leshan Chongqing Enshi

NEPAL Darjeeling BHUTAN
Biratnagar Thimphu

INDIA Neijiang
Xichang Luzhou C H

Darbhanga Dibrugarh Zhaotong Yibin
Jorhat Zunyi Huaih
Bhagalpur Rangpur Guwahati
Asansol Shillong Panzhihua Guiyang
Rajshahi Sylhet Anshun
BANGLADESH Imphal Dali Kunming Liuzhou
Jamshedpur Dhaka Aizawl Nannin

Khulna Myitkyina Baoshan

Kolkata
(Calcutta) Kaiyuan Simao Gejiu
Chittagong Lashio Ha Giang Qinzhou
Monywa Phongsali Lao Cai
Mouths of the Ganges Mandalay Son La Thai Nguyen
Mount
Victoria
3,053m
(10,016ft) BURMA
(MYANMAR) Taunggyi Hanoi
Sittwe Meiktila Louangphrabang Hai Phong
Pyinmana Thanh Hoa
Bay of Bengal Pye Chiang Mai LAOS Vinh *Gulf of Tonkin*
Sandoway Vientiane Sanya
Henzada Udon Thani
Pegu Phitsanulok Savannakhet Hue
Pathein Thaton Khon
Kaen Da Nang
Rangoon Moulmein Nakhon Sawan Ubon
Ratchathani Pakxe
THAILAND Nakhon Ratchasima Attapu VIETNAM

INDIAN

OCEAN Tavoy Bangkok Stoeng Treng Qui Nhon
Andaman
Islands
(India) *Andaman*
Sea Pattaya Angkor *Tonle Sap* CAMBODIA Buon Me
Thuot
Batdambang
Mergui Da Lat Nha
Tran
Port Blair Kampong
Chhnang Kampong
Cham
Little
Andaman *Mergui*
Archipelago Prachuap
Khiri Khan Krong
Kaoh Kong Phnom
Penh Bien Hoa
Chumphon Kampong Saom Long Xuyen Ho Chi Minh City
(Saigon)
Ten Degree Channel Mekong Can Tho
Gulf of Thailand Bac Lieu
Nakhon Si
Thammarat *Con Son*
Nicobar Islands
(India)
Hat Yai
Yala
Sumatra Alor Setar Kota Bharu
Banda Aceh George Town
(Penang) Gunung
Tahan Kuala Terengganu
Lhokseumawe INDONESIA Langsa Taiping Ipoh MALAYSIA 2,187m
(7,175ft) *Natuna*
Islands
(Indonesia)

A 90°E B 95° C 100° D 105° E 110

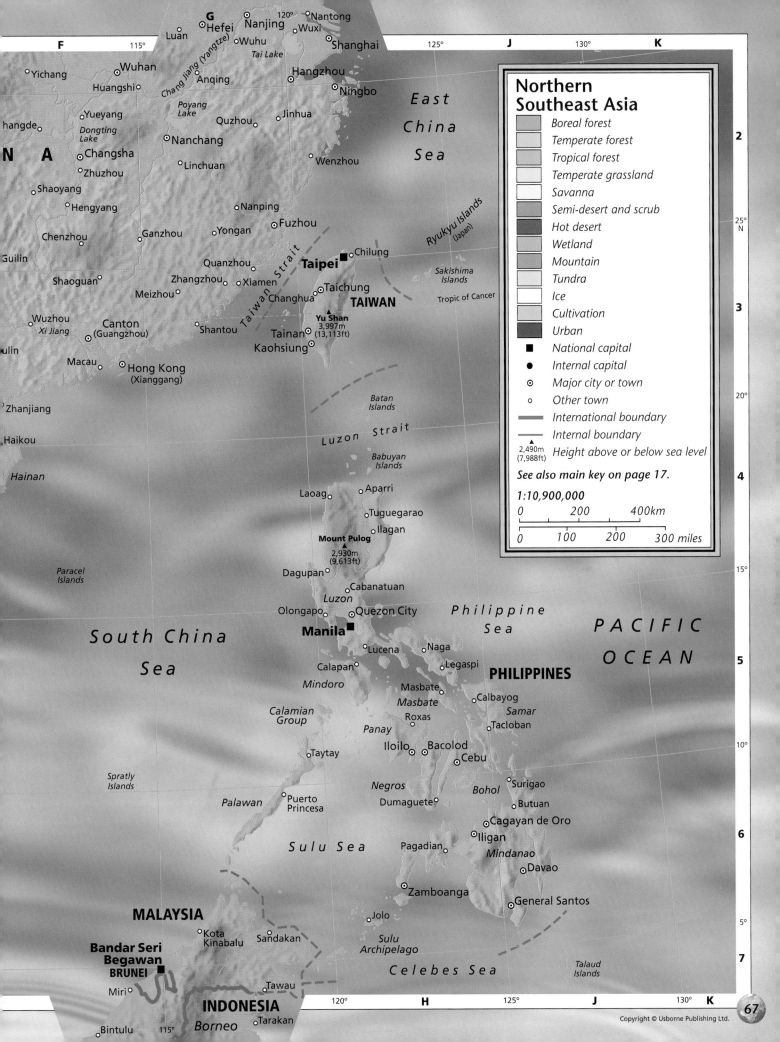

F · 115° · G · 120° · J · 125° · 130° · K

East China Sea

Yichang
Huangshi
Wuhan
hangde
Yueyang
Dongting Lake
Changsha
Zhuzhou
Shaoyang
Hengyang
Chenzhou
Ganzhou
uilin
Shaoguan
Meizhou
Wuzhou
Canton (Guangzhou)
Xi Jiang
ulin
Macau
Hong Kong (Xianggang)
Zhanjiang
Haikou
Hainan

N A

Luan
Hefei
Nanjing
Nantong
Wuxi
Wuhu
Shanghai
Chang Jiang (Yangtze)
Anqing
Tai Lake
Hangzhou
Poyang Lake
Ningbo
Nanchang
Quzhou
Jinhua
Linchuan
Wenzhou
Nanping
Fuzhou
Yongan
Quanzhou
Zhangzhou
Xiamen
Taipei
Chilung
Taiwan Strait
Taichung
Changhua
TAIWAN
Shantou
Tainan
Yu Shan 3,997m (13,113ft)
Kaohsiung

Ryukyu Islands (Japan)

Sakishima Islands

Tropic of Cancer

25° N

3

20°

Batan Islands

Luzon Strait

Babuyan Islands

Laoag
Aparri
Tuguegarao
Ilagan
Mount Pulog 2,930m (9,613ft)
Dagupan
Cabanatuan
Luzon
Olongapo
Quezon City
Manila
Lucena
Naga
Calapan
Legaspi
Mindoro
Masbate
Masbate
Roxas
Calamian Group
Panay
Taytay
Iloilo
Bacolod
Cebu
Negros
Surigao
Bohol
Puerto Princesa
Dumaguete
Butuan
Palawan
Cagayan de Oro
Iligan
Pagadian
Mindanao
Davao
Zamboanga
General Santos
Jolo
Sulu Archipelago
Talaud Islands

South China Sea

Paracel Islands

Spratly Islands

Sulu Sea

PHILIPPINES

Philippine Sea

PACIFIC OCEAN

4

15°

5

10°

6

5°

7

MALAYSIA

Bandar Seri Begawan
BRUNEI
Miri
Kota Kinabalu
Sandakan
Tawau
INDONESIA
Borneo
Bintulu
Tarakan

Celebes Sea

120° · H · 125° · J · 130° · K

Northern Southeast Asia

	Boreal forest
	Temperate forest
	Tropical forest
	Temperate grassland
	Savanna
	Semi-desert and scrub
	Hot desert
	Wetland
	Mountain
	Tundra
	Ice
	Cultivation
	Urban
■	National capital
●	Internal capital
◉	Major city or town
○	Other town
━━	International boundary
──	Internal boundary
▲ 2,490m (7,988ft)	Height above or below sea level

See also main key on page 17.

1:10,900,000

0 — 200 — 400km
0 — 100 — 200 — 300 miles

67

A 80°E B 85° C 90° D 95° E 100° F 105° G 110°

KAZAKHSTAN

Bulgan

Karamay

■ Ulan Bator

2 Almaty

Yining

Dzungarian
Basin

MONGOLIA

Lake
Issyk

Kuytun

Altay

KYRGYZSTAN

Shihezi

▲ Pik Pobedy
7,439m
(24,406ft)

Urumqi

40°
N

Aksu

Turpan

Tien Shan

Erenhot

Korla

Bosten
Lake

-154m
(-505ft)

Turpan
Depression

Hami

Gobi   Desert

3

Tarim Basin

Lop Lake

Hotan

Taklimakan
Desert

Mogao Caves

Baotou

Hohhot

Altun Mountains

Yumen

The Great Wall of China

Wuhai

35°

Kunlun Mountains

5,547m
(18,199ft)

Yinchuan

Taiyu

Qaidam
Basin

Golmud

Qinghai
Lake

Xining

Lanzhou

4

Plateau of Tibet

CHINA

Huang He (Yellow)

Siling Lake

Baoji

Mount Li
(Terracotta Arm

30°

TIBET

Yushu

Xian

Himalayas

Nam Lake

Brahmaputra

Lhasa

Salween

Chang Jiang (Yangtze)

Shiyan

Xiangfan

NEPAL

Kathmandu ▲

Chengdu

Yichang

5

Darbhanga

Mount Everest
8,850m
(29,035ft)

Darjeeling

Thimphu

Gongga Shan
7,556m
(24,790ft)

Leshan

Chongqing

Patna

Biratnagar

BHUTAN

Chang Jiang (Yangtze)

Changde

25°

Bhagalpur

Rangpur

Brahmaputra

Dibrugarh

Xichang

Luzhou

Zunyi

Huaihua

INDIA

Guwahati

Panzhihua

Guiyang

Hengyan

Ranchi

Asansol

Rajshahi

Shillong

Sylhet

Dali

6

Tropic of Cancer

BANGLADESH

Imphal

Myitkyina

Kunming

Guilin

Dhaka ■

Aizawl

Kolkata
(Calcutta)

Khulna

Liuzhou

Chittagong

Lashio

Red

Gejiu

Wuzhou

Cuttack

Mouths of the
Ganges

Monywa

Mandalay

Simao

Nanning

Xi

Bay of Bengal

Mount
Victoria
3,053m
(10,016ft)

BURMA
(MYANMAR)

Lao Cai

Yulin

Sittwe

Taunggyi

Phongsali

Son La

Thai
Nguyen

7

INDIAN

Pyinmana

Hanoi ■

Zhanjiang

OCEAN

Sandoway

Pye

Salween

Mekong

Louangphrabang

Hai
Phong

Gulf of
Tonkin

Haikou

Henzada

Irrawaddy

Chiang
Mai

Thanh Hoa

Hainan

THAILAND

LAOS

VIETNAM

Pathein

Pegu

Vientiane ■

Vinh

Sanya

Rangoon ■

Udon Thani

C 90°E D
Mouths of the
Irrawaddy
95°

Moulmein

F 100° G 105° 110°

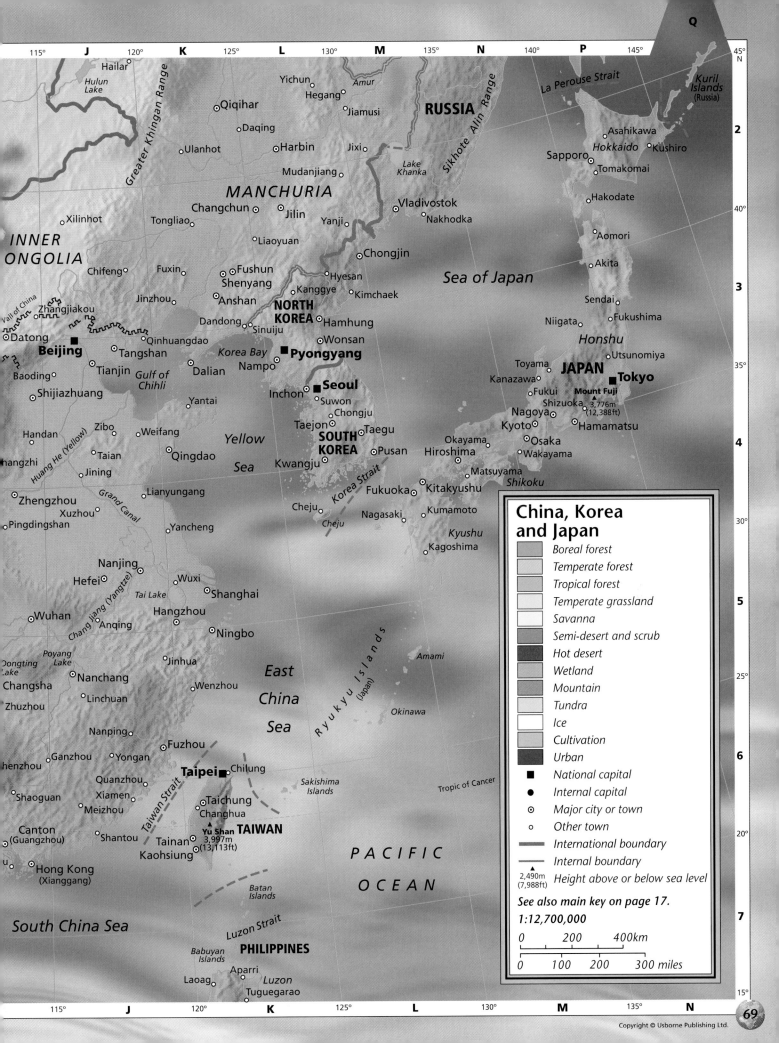

Map labels

Coordinates (top): 115° J 120° K 125° L 130° M 135° N 140° P 145°

Coordinates (right): 45° N · 2 · 40° · 3 · 35° · 4 · 30° · 25° · 6 · 20° · 7 · 15°

Hailar
Hulun Lake
Greater Khingan Range
Yichun
Hegang
Amur
Jiamusi
RUSSIA
La Perouse Strait
Kuril Islands (Russia)
Qiqihar
Daqing
Harbin
Jixi
Sikhote Alin Range
Asahikawa
Hokkaido
Kushiro
Sapporo
Tomakomai
Ulanhot
Mudanjiang
Lake Khanka
Hakodate
MANCHURIA
Xilinhot
Changchun
Jilin
Vladivostok
Nakhodka
Aomori
INNER MONGOLIA
Tongliao
Yanji
Sea of Japan
Akita
Liaoyuan
Chongjin
Chifeng
Fuxin
Fushun
Shenyang
Hyesan
Sendai
Niigata
Fukushima
Honshu
Wall of China
Zhangjiakou
Jinzhou
Anshan
Kanggye
Kimchaek
NORTH KOREA
Hamhung
Utsunomiya
Toyama
Datong
Dandong
Sinuiju
Wonsan
JAPAN
Tokyo
Beijing
Qinhuangdao
Korea Bay
Pyongyang
Kanazawa
Mount Fuji
Baoding
Tangshan
Nampo
Fukui
3,776m (12,388ft)
Tianjin
Gulf of Chihli
Dalian
Shizuoka
Hamamatsu
Shijiazhuang
Yantai
Seoul
Nagoya
Inchon
Suwon
Kyoto
Handan
Zibo
Weifang
Chongju
Taejon
Taegu
Osaka
Wakayama
Hangzhi
Taian
Qingdao
Yellow
SOUTH KOREA
Pusan
Okayama
Hiroshima
Matsuyama
Huang He (Yellow)
Jining
Sea
Kwangju
Shikoku
Zhengzhou
Lianyungang
Kuma moto
Fukuoka
Kitakyushu
Xuzhou
Grand Canal
Cheju
Nagasaki
Pingdingshan
Yancheng
Cheju
Kyushu
Kagoshima
Nanjing
Hefei
Wuxi
Tai Lake
Shanghai
Wuhan
Anqing
Chang Jiang (Yangtze)
Hangzhou
Poyang Lake
Ningbo
Dongting Lake
Nanchang
Jinhua
East
Changsha
Linchuan
Wenzhou
China
Amami
Zhuzhou
Nanping
Sea
Ganzhou
Yongan
Fuzhou
Ryukyu Islands (Japan)
Okinawa
henzhou
Quanzhou
Taipei
Chilung
Shaoguan
Xiamen
Taichung
Sakishima Islands
Tropic of Cancer
Meizhou
Changhua
Taiwan Strait
Canton (Guangzhou)
Shantou
Tainan
TAIWAN
Yu Shan 3,997m (13,113ft)
u
Hong Kong (Xianggang)
Kaohsiung
PACIFIC
Batan Islands
OCEAN
South China Sea
Luzon Strait
PHILIPPINES
Babuyan Islands
Laoag
Aparri
Luzon
Tuguegarao

Legend

China, Korea and Japan

- Boreal forest
- Temperate forest
- Tropical forest
- Temperate grassland
- Savanna
- Semi-desert and scrub
- Hot desert
- Wetland
- Mountain
- Tundra
- Ice
- Cultivation
- Urban
- ■ National capital
- ● Internal capital
- ⊙ Major city or town
- ○ Other town
- ── International boundary
- ── Internal boundary
- ▲ 2,490m (7,988ft) Height above or below sea level

See also main key on page 17.

1:12,700,000

0   200   400km

0   100   200   300 miles

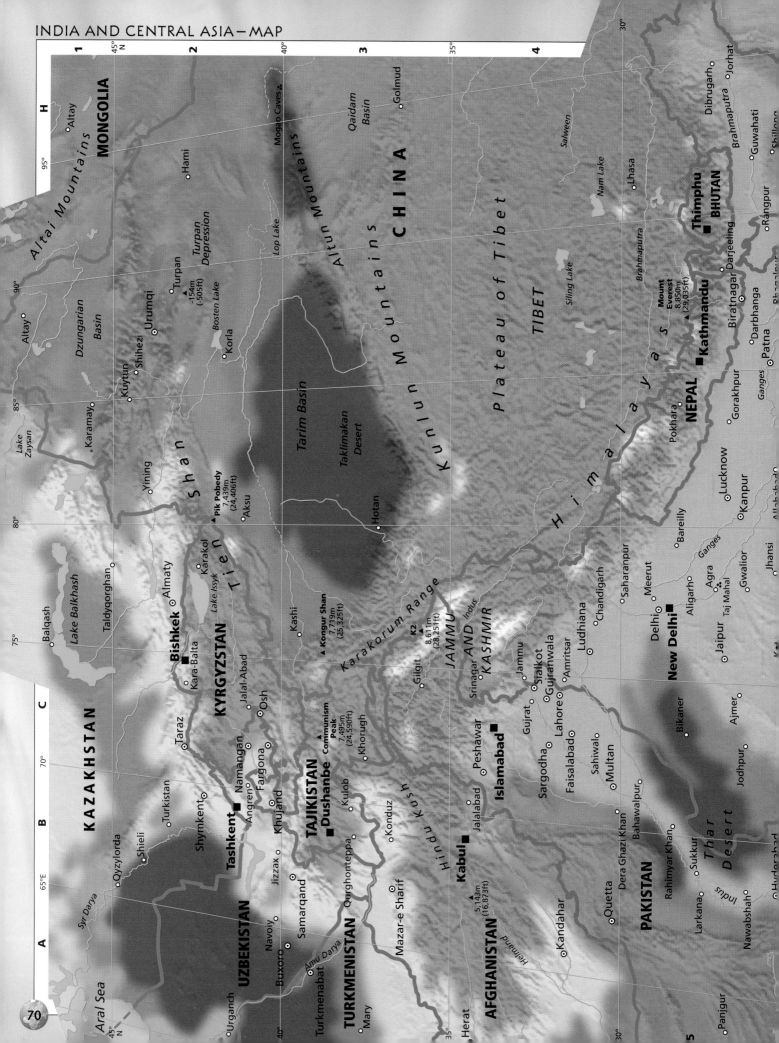

1   2   3   4

H

95°   90°   85°   80°   75°   70°   65°E   45°N

MONGOLIA

Altai Mountains

Altay
Altay

KAZAKHSTAN

Lake
Zaysan
Balqash
Lake Balkhash

Karamay

Qyzylorda
Shieli
Turkistan
Shymkent
Taraz
Taldyqorghan
Kuytun
Shihezi
Urumqi
Yining
Karamay

Dzungarian
Basin

Hami

Turpan
Turpan
Depression
-154m
(-505ft)

Mogo Caves

Lop Lake
Bosten Lake
Korla

CHINA

Golmud

Qaidam
Basin

Altun Mountains

T i e n   S h a n

▲ Pik Pobedy
7,439m
(24,406ft)
Aksu
Kashi

Tarim Basin

Taklimakan
Desert

Hotan

Kunlun   Mountains

Plateau of Tibet

TIBET

Nam Lake
Lhasa
Salween
Silling Lake
Brahmaputra

Mount
Everest
8,850m
(29,035ft) ▲

Dibrugarh
Jorhat
Brahmaputra
Guwahati
Rangpur
Shillong

Thimphu ■
BHUTAN

Darjeeling
Biratnagar
Darbhanga
Patna

NEPAL
Pokhara
■ Kathmandu

Gorakhpur
Lucknow
Kanpur
Bareilly
Ganges

Saharanpur
Meerut
Chandigarh
Ludhiana
Aligarh
Agra
Taj Mahal
Gwalior
Jhansi

Delhi
New Delhi ■
Jaipur
Ajmer
Bikaner

Jodhpur

Balqash

KYRGYZSTAN
Bishkek ●
Kara-Balta
Lake Issyk
Karakol
Almaty
Jalal-Abad
Osh
Namangan
Fargona
Angren
Jizzax

**Communism
Peak ▲**
7,495m
(24,590ft)

Kongur Shan ▲
7,719m
(25,325ft)

K2 ▲
8,611m
(28,251ft)
Gilgit

Karakorum   Range

Indus

**JAMMU   AND
KASHMIR**

Srinagar
Jammu
Sialkot
Gujranwala
Amritsar

TAJIKISTAN
■ Dushanbe
Kulob
Khorugh
Konduz
Ourghonteppa

Hindu Kush

Peshawar
Islamabad ■
Jalalabad

UZBEKISTAN
■ Tashkent
Turkistan
Khujand

Taraz

Syr Darya

Navoiy
Buxoro
Samarqand

TURKMENISTAN
Turkmenabat
Mary

Amu Darya

Mazar-e Sharif

AFGHANISTAN
5,143m
(16,873ft) ▲

Kabul ■

Helmand
Kandahar
Herat
Quetta

PAKISTAN
Gujrat
Lahore
Sargodha
Faisalabad
Sahiwal
Multan
Bahawalpur
Dera Ghazi Khan
Rahimyar Khan
Sukkur
Larkana
Nawabshah
Hyderabad
Panjgur

Thar
Desert

Indus

Aral Sea
Urganch
45°N

40°   35°   30°

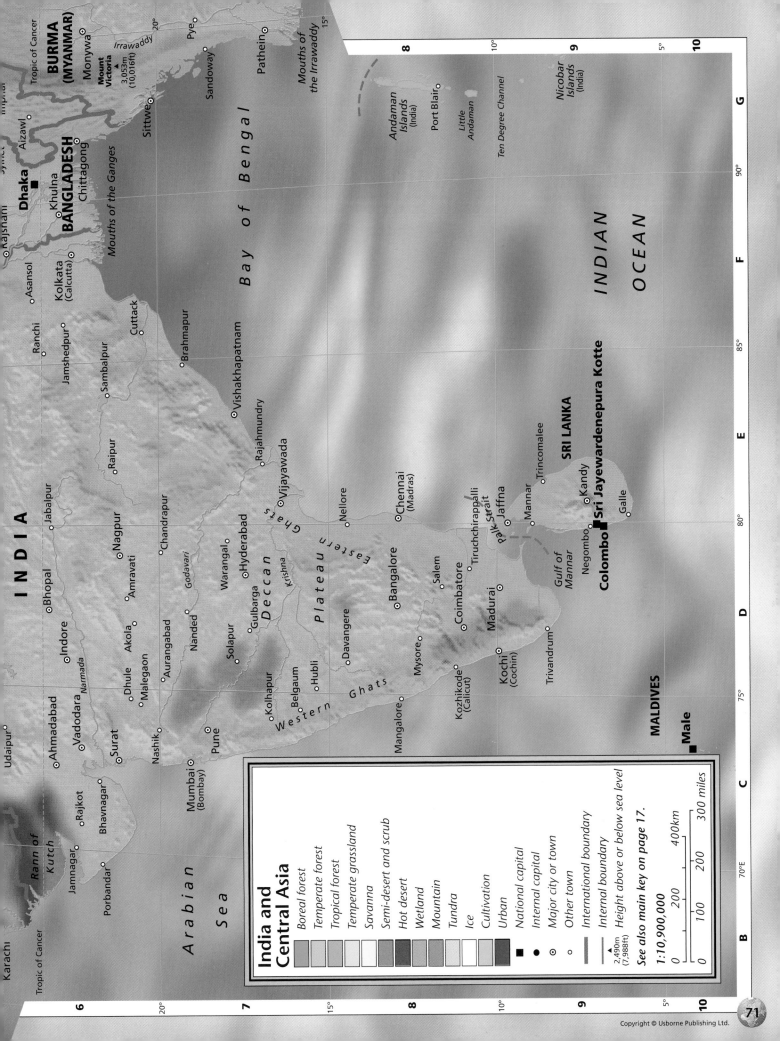

Karachi

Tropic of Cancer

**BURMA
(MYANMAR)**

Monywa ○ Pye ○

Irrawaddy

Aizawl ○

Mount
Victoria ▲
3,053m
(10,016ft)

20°

15°

Sandoway ○

Pathein ○

Sittwe ○

*Mouths of
the Irrawaddy*

Rajshahi ○

Dhaka ■
Khulna ○
BANGLADESH

Chittagong ○

Mouths of the Ganges

○ Asansol

Kolkata
(Calcutta) ○

Cuttack ○

Ranchi ○

Jamshedpur ○

Sambalpur ○

Brahmapur ○

B a y   o f   B e n g a l

I N D I A

Udaipur ○

Ahmadabad ○

Rajkot ○

*Rann of
Kutch*

Jamnagar ○

Bhavnagar ○

Porbandar ○

Jabalpur ○
Bhopal ○

Indore ○

Vadodara ○

Narmada

Surat ○

Dhule ○
Malegaon ○

Nashik ○

Nagpur ○
Amravati ○
Akola ○

Aurangabad ○

Godavari

Chandrapur ○

Nanded ○

Raipur ○

Rajahmundry ○

Vishakhapatnam ○

Eastern Ghats

Vijayawada ○

Warangal ○
Hyderabad ○

Gulbarga ○

Krishna

Nellore ○

Chennai
(Madras) ○

D e c c a n   P l a t e a u

Mumbai
(Bombay) ○

Pune ○

Solapur ○

Kolhapur ○
Belgaum ○

Hubli ○

Davangere ○

Bangalore ○

Salem ○

Tiruchchirappalli ○

Western Ghats

Mangalore ○

Mysore ○

Coimbatore ○

Kozhikode
(Calicut) ○

Kochi
(Cochin) ○

Madurai ○

Trivandrum ○

*A r a b i a n
S e a*

MALDIVES

■ **Male**

Palk Strait

Jaffna ○

Mannar ○

*Gulf of
Mannar*

Negombo ○
Colombo ■

Kandy ○

Sri Jayewardenepura Kotte ■

Galle ○

Trincomalee ○

SRI LANKA

*I N D I A N
O C E A N*

*Andaman
Islands
(India)*

Port Blair ○

*Little
Andaman*

Ten Degree Channel

*Nicobar
Islands
(India)*

90° 85° 80° 75° 70°E

F E D C B

India and
Central Asia

Boreal forest
Temperate forest
Tropical forest
Temperate grassland
Savanna
Semi-desert and scrub
Hot desert
Wetland
Mountain
Tundra
Ice
Cultivation
Urban

■ National capital
● Internal capital
⊙ Major city or town
○ Other town

International boundary
Internal boundary

▲ 2,490m
(7,988ft) Height above or below sea level

See also main key on page 17.

1:10,900,000

0 100 200 300 400km
0 100 200 300 miles

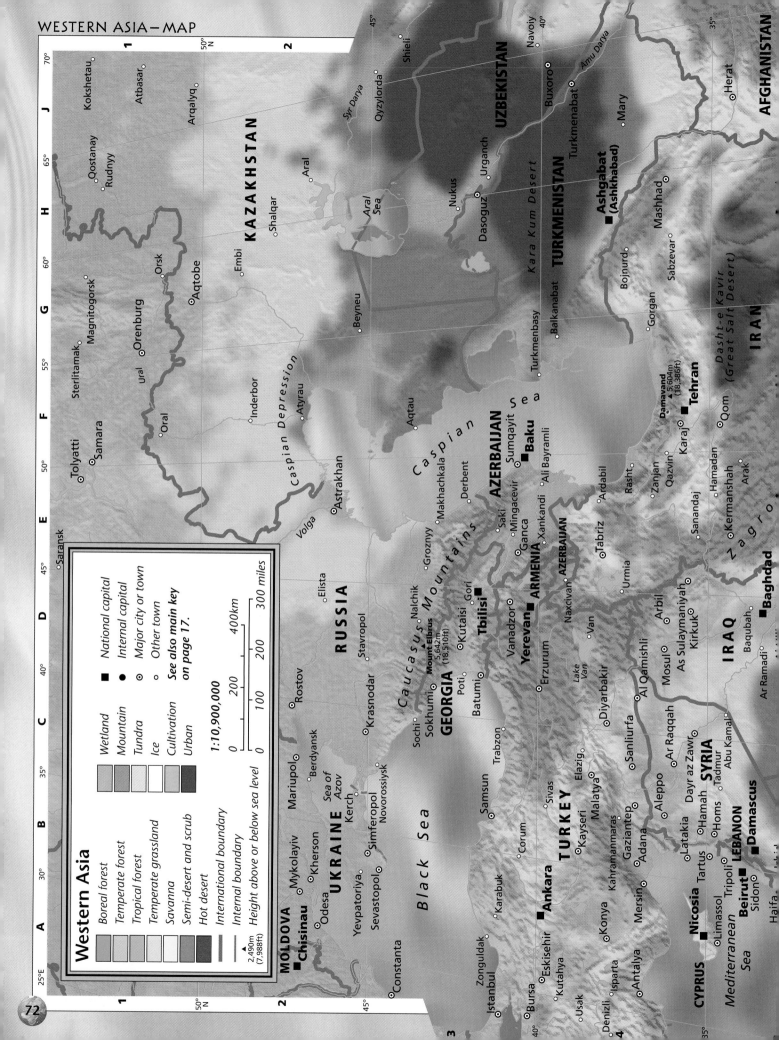

Western Asia

Boreal forest	■	National capital
Temperate forest	●	Internal capital
Tropical forest	◉	Major city or town
Temperate grassland	○	Other town
Savanna		*See also main key*
Semi-desert and scrub		*on page 17.*
Hot desert		
Wetland		International boundary
Mountain		Internal boundary
Tundra		
Ice		▲ 2,490m
Cultivation		(7,988ft)
Urban		Height above or below sea level

1:10,900,000

0   100   200   300 miles
0   200   400km

KAZAKHSTAN

Kokshetau
Atbasar
Arqalyq
Qostanay
Rudnyy
Shieli
Qyzylorda
Syr Darya
Aral
Aral Sea
Shalqar
Nukus
Dasoguz
Urganch
Buxoro
Navoiy
Mary
Herat

UZBEKISTAN
TURKMENISTAN
AFGHANISTAN

Amu Darya
Kara Kum Desert
Turkmenabat
Ashgabat
(Ashkhabad)
Mashhad
Sabzevar
Bojnurd

Magnitogorsk
Sterlitamak
Orenburg
Ural
Orsk
Aqtobe
Embi
Beyneu
Inderbor
Atyrau

Tolyatti
Samara
Oral
Astrakhan
Volga

Caspian Depression

Aqtau

Caspian Sea

Turkmenbasy
Balkanabat
Gorgan

IRAN

Dasht-e Kavir
(Great Salt Desert)

Damavand
5,604m
(18,386ft)
Tehran
Qom
Karaj
Qazvin
Zanjan
Hamadan
Arak

Saransk
RUSSIA
Elista
Rostov
Stavropol
Krasnodar
Novorossiysk

Makhachkala
Derbent
Grozny
Nalchik

AZERBAIJAN
Sumqayit
Baku
Ali Bayramli
Mingacevir
Ganca
Xankandi
AZERBAIJAN
Naxcivan

Saki
ARMENIA
Yerevan
Vanadzor

Ardabil
Rasht
Tabriz
Urmia
Zagros

Sochi
Sokhumi
Batumi
Poti
Kutaisi
Gori
Tbilisi
GEORGIA
Mount Elbrus
5,642m
(18,510ft)
Caucasus Mountains

Erzurum
Naxcivan

Sanandaj
Kermanshah
Baghdad
IRAQ
Arbil
Mosul
Kirkuk
As Sulaymaniyah
Al Qamishli
Baqubah
Ar Ramadi

Mariupol
Berdyansk
Sea of Azov
Kerch

Trabzon
Samsun
Sivas
Diyarbakir

Van
Lake Van

Mykolayiv
Kherson
UKRAINE
Odesa
Yevpatoriya
Simferopol
Sevastopol

Black Sea

Zonguldak
Istanbul
Bursa
Eskisehir
Karabuk
Corum
TURKEY
Ankara
Kayseri
Malatya
Elazig
Sanliurfa
Ar Raqqah
Dayr az Zawr
Abu Kamal
Tadmur

MOLDOVA
Chisinau
Constanta

Kutahya
Usak
Denizli
Isparta
Antalya
Konya
Karaman
Mersin
Adana
Gaziantep
Kahramanmaras

Aleppo
Hamah
Homs
Latakia
Tartus
Tripoli
Beirut
Sidon
LEBANON
Damascus
SYRIA

CYPRUS
Nicosia
Limassol

Mediterranean Sea
Haifa

50°N
70°
65°
60°
55°
50°
45°
40°
35°
30°
25°E

J
H
G
F
E
D
C
B
A
50°N
45°

1
2
3
4

72

PAKISTAN

Helmand
Zabol
Zahedan
Kerman
Iranshahr
Panjgur
Turbat

30°
25°

Yazd
Persepolis
Shiraz
Bandar-e Abbas
Sirjan
Bushehr

M o u n t a i n s

Ahvaz
Abadan
Basra

Al Kut
Al Amarah
An Nasiriyah
Euphrates
Tigris

S y r i a n   D e s e r t

Tel Aviv-Yafo
Jerusalem
Gaza
Beer Sheva
ISRAEL
Amman
Az Zarqa
JORDAN
Maan
Al Aqabah
Petra
Tabuk

Cairo
Port Said
Ismailia
Suez Canal
El Mansura
Suez
Sinai
Sharm el Sheikh
Beni Suef
Pyramids of Giza
El Minya
Asyut
Sohag
Qena
Luxor
Valley of
the Kings
Aswan
Aswan High Dam
Tropic of Cancer
Lake
Nasser
Nile

Mount
Sinai
2,285m
(7,497ft)
Elat
Hurghada

A r a b i a n   D e s e r t

Nile
Delta

EGYPT

Hejaz

Medina

Mecca
At Taif

Jedda

Port Sudan

Nubian Desert

SUDAN
Nile
Atbarah

Kassala
Gedaref
Wad Medani

Karora

Teseney

ERITREA
Keren
Asmara
Massawa

Gonder
Bahir Dar
Lake Tana

Strait of Hormuz
OMAN
Dubai
Sharjah
Al Ayn

Sur
Gulf of Oman
Tropic of Cancer
Muscat
Suhar

OMAN

Masirah Island

Arabian Sea

Salalah

Socotra
(Yemen)

INDIAN
OCEAN

Cape Guardafui

UNITED ARAB
EMIRATES
Abu Dhabi
QATAR
Doha
BAHRAIN
Manama

Persian Gulf
(The Gulf)
Kuwait City
KUWAIT
Ad Dammam
Al Mubarrez

Haradh

Riyadh

SAUDI ARABIA

A r a b i a n
P e n i n s u l a

R u b   a l   K h a l i
(E m p t y   Q u a r t e r)

Burҩydah

Hail

A s i r
3,133m
(10,279ft)
Abha

YEMEN
Marib
Najran
Sadah
Sana
3,760m
(12,336ft)
Dhamar
Ibb
Taizz
Al Mukalla
Hadhramaut

Al Hudaydah

Farasan
Islands

Dahlak
Archipelago

Red   Sea

Bab al Mandab
Assab
Kobar
Sink
-116m
(-381ft)
Aden
Gulf of Aden
DJIBOUTI
Djibouti
Dikhil

ETHIOPIA
Mekele
Ras Dashen
4,620m
(15,157ft)
Ethiopian
Highlands
Blue Nile
Dese
Dire Dawa

SOMALIA
Berbera
Hargeysa

45°
40°
35°E

50°
55°
60°

7
8
9

20°
15°

H
G
F

73

Copyright © Usborne Publishing Ltd.

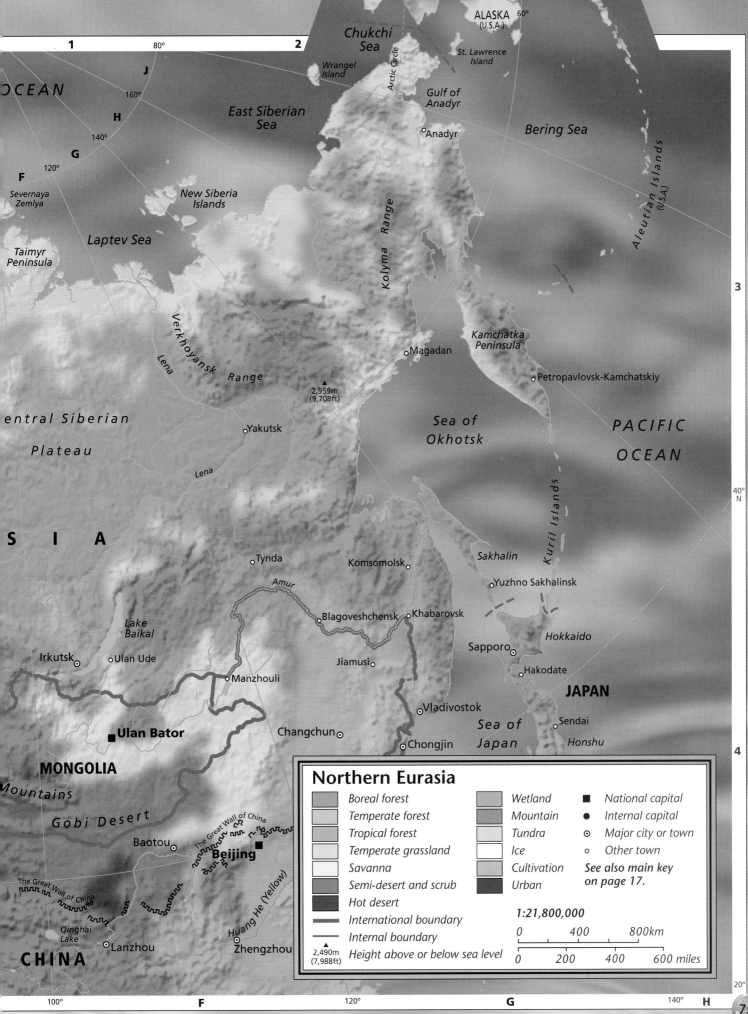

ALASKA 60°
(U.S.A.)

Chukchi
Sea

St. Lawrence
Island

Wrangel
Island

Arctic Circle

Gulf of
Anadyr

Bering Sea

OCEAN

J

160°

H

140°

East Siberian
Sea

Anadyr

G

120°

F

Severnaya
Zemlya

New Siberia
Islands

Kolyma Range

Aleutian Islands
(U.S.A.)

Taimyr
Peninsula

Laptev Sea

3

Verkhoyansk Range

Lena

2,959m
(9,708ft)

Magadan

Kamchatka
Peninsula

PACIFIC

entral Siberian

Plateau

Yakutsk

Lena

Petropavlovsk-Kamchatskiy

Sea of
Okhotsk

OCEAN

40°
N

S I A

Tynda

Komsomolsk

Sakhalin

Kuril Islands

Amur

Yuzhno Sakhalinsk

Lake
Baikal

Blagoveshchensk

Khabarovsk

Hokkaido

Sapporo

Irkutsk

Ulan Ude

Jiamusi

Hakodate

Manzhouli

JAPAN

Vladivostok

Sendai

■ **Ulan Bator**

Changchun

Sea of
Japan

Honshu

MONGOLIA

Chongjin

ountains

G o b i   D e s e r t

The Great Wall of China

Baotou

The Great Wall of China

■
Beijing

Huang He (Yellow)

Qinghai
Lake

Lanzhou

Zhengzhou

CHINA

Northern Eurasia

Boreal forest	Wetland
Temperate forest	Mountain
Tropical forest	Tundra
Temperate grassland	Ice
Savanna	Cultivation
Semi-desert and scrub	Urban
Hot desert	
▬▬ International boundary	■ National capital
— Internal boundary	● Internal capital
▲ 2,490m (7,988ft) Height above or below sea level	⊙ Major city or town
	○ Other town

See also main key
on page 17.

1:21,800,000

0   400   800km

0   200   400   600 miles

1
80°

2

100°
F

120°
G

140°
H

20°

EUROPE

Europe is a small continent, packed with over 40 countries and more than 700 million people. Russia is an enormous country, spanning two continents. Its western part is in Europe, while its eastern part is in Asia. The European part of Russia is larger than any other country in Europe.

The shading on this map is there to help you see clearly the different countries that make up the continent.

Arctic Circle

ARCTIC OCEAN

Reykjavik
ICELAND

Norwegian
Sea

Faroe Islands
(Denmark)

SWEDEN

Shetland
Islands

NORWAY

Oslo

Orkney
Islands

Stockholm

North
Sea

DENMARK
Copenhagen

Baltic
Sea

IRELAND
Dublin

UNITED
KINGDOM

London

The
Hague

Amsterdam
NETHERLANDS

Berlin

POLAND

Brussels
BELGIUM

GERMANY

Paris

LUXEMBOURG
Luxembourg

Prague

CZECH
REPUBLIC

Rhine

Vienna
Bratislava

Bay
of
Biscay

FRANCE

SWITZERLAND

LIECHTENSTEIN
Bern Vaduz

AUSTRIA

Budapest

HUNGARY

SLOVENIA
Ljubljana

Zagreb
CROATIA

ATLANTIC

OCEAN

PORTUGAL

Lisbon

Madrid

SPAIN

ANDORRA

Andorra
la Vella

MONACO

SAN MARINO

Corsica

ITALY

VATICAN CITY
Rome

BOSNIA AND
HERZEGOVINA
Sarajevo

ALBANIA
Tirana

Balearic
Islands

Sardinia

Mediterranean Sea

Sicily

MALTA
Valletta

Barents Sea

Arctic Circle

Murmansk

Arkhangelsk

FINLAND

elsinki

St. Petersburg

Tallinn
ESTONIA

R U S S I A

Nizhniy Novgorod   Kazan

Riga LATVIA   Moscow

LITHUANIA
Vilnius
SSIA

Minsk

BELARUS

Volga

Warsaw

Kiev

Volgograd

Dnieper

UKRAINE

OVAKIA

MOLDOVA

Chisinau

ROMANIA

elgrade

Bucharest   Black Sea

Danube

GOSLAVIA

BULGARIA
Sofia

Skopje
ACEDONIA   TURKEY

REECE

Athens

Crete

Facts

Total land area 10,205,720 sq km (3,940,428 sq miles) (including European Russia)

Total population 727 million (including all of Russia)

Biggest city Moscow, Russia

Biggest country Russia *Total area: 17,075,200 sq km (6,592,735 sq miles) Area of European Russia: 4,294,400 sq km (1,658,068 sq miles)*

Smallest country Vatican City *0.44 sq km (0.17 sq miles)*

Highest mountain Elbrus, Russia *5,642m (18,510ft)*

Longest river Volga *3,700km (2,298 miles)*

Biggest lake Lake Ladoga, Russia *17,700 sq km (6,834 sq miles)*

Highest waterfall Utigard, on the Jostedal Glacier, Norway *800m (2,625ft)*

Biggest desert No deserts in Europe

Biggest island Great Britain *234,410 sq km (90,506 sq miles)*

Main mineral deposits Bauxite, zinc, iron, potash, fluorspar

Main fuel deposits Oil, coal, natural gas, peat, uranium

A cow in Devon, in the south of England

77

Europe has lots of islands and many of its countries are largely surrounded by sea. The Alps, one of Europe's principal mountain ranges, lies in the west, and is the source of many of its major rivers, including the Rhine and the Rhone.

Europe by night

Satellite pictures taken at night show how much light is being generated in different areas. Highly populated areas, such as Europe, where there are many big cities, light up brightly at night. This is because when many people live in one area, the combined lights of all the buildings at night are so bright they show up as a dot.

This is a satellite image of Mount Vesuvius, a volcano in southern Italy. The black dot in the middle is the crater.

Mount Vesuvius

Mount Vesuvius is a volcano near the city of Naples in southern Italy. It is famous for its eruption in AD79, which buried the towns of Pompeii and Herculaneum in around 30m (100ft) of ash, mud and stones. The towns remained buried until the 18th century when they were rediscovered.

Vesuvius is monitored very carefully today, as it is close to the city of Naples and more than two million people live nearby. It has had over 50 minor eruptions since the one in AD79.

This satellite image of Europe was taken at night, but the land and water have been falsely-shaded, so you can see their outlines clearly. Each blue dot represents a highly populated area that is lit up.

Internet links

For a link to a Web site where you can find out more about Mount Vesuvius' famous eruption, go to **www.usborne-quicklinks.com**

This area of the Alps is in Switzerland. Over 70% of Switzerland is mountainous.

The Rhine River

The Rhine River carries more traffic than any other river in the world. It is 1,320km (820 miles) long and winds through the west of Europe, flowing from the Alps in Switzerland, along the Swiss-Austrian border, through Germany and France to the Netherlands. Many cities lie along its banks, including Strasbourg, in France, and Cologne, in Germany.

This is a section of the Rhine River running through west Germany. The river is black, vegetation is blue and buildings are brown. The patchwork of rectangles to the east of the river is farmland.

Norwegian fjords

Norway's dramatic coastline is a mixture of steep mountains and long, thin inlets of water, called fjords. The fjords were formed by glaciers. When glacier ice builds up at the top of a mountain, it becomes heavy and starts to slide down the slopes, carving out a deep channel in the rock. When the glacier melts, the water fills the channel, making a fjord.

The satellite image below shows an area of Norway's coastline. The long, thin blue strips are inlets of water, called fjords.

Eastern Europe stretches as far as the Ural Mountains, which separate European Russia from Asian Russia. Northern Europe is made up of Iceland and the Scandinavian countries, including Norway and Sweden.

Onion-shaped domes

Early Russian churches have an easily recognizable style, with high walls, very few doors and windows, and steeply-sloped roofs topped with onion-shaped domes. This style became popular during the 11th century. Many of these early churches were built from wood, as it was a building material widely available from Russia's dense forests.

This is the Church of the Intercession on Kizhi Island in northern Russia. It was built almost entirely from wood in 1764.

This is a Viking helmet. It was discovered in a grave in Uppland, Sweden.

Viking lands

During the 9th to the 11th centuries, the Vikings, a group of master ship builders and sea traders from Scandinavia, dominated northern Europe. Viking heritage can still be seen today. The Vikings carved stories and pictures into large stones, called rune stones. Many of these stones have survived and give clues to how they lived. The Viking Ship Museum in Oslo, Norway, has three well-preserved Viking ships, and in Sweden, a Viking festival is held each year in a reconstructed Viking village.

In this dramatic image of Budapest you can see the Chain Bridge, which links Buda and Pest across the Danube River.

Internet links

For a link to a Web site where you can go on a virtual Viking quest, go to **www.usborne-quicklinks.com**

Danube River

The Danube River flows from the west to the east of Europe, through many major cities, including Bratislava, the capital of Slovakia, and Budapest, the capital of Hungary. The river splits Budapest into two parts, Buda and Pest. The Royal Palace, is in Buda, on the west bank, while Hungary's parliament building is in Pest, on the east bank.

Atlantic puffins

One type of bird common throughout northern Europe is the Atlantic puffin. Atlantic puffins are sea birds that live in the cold waters around the coasts of the North Atlantic Ocean.

Atlantic puffins are very skilled at diving underwater to catch fish to eat. They only come ashore once a year to nest on rocky cliff tops and grassy islands. Iceland has the largest puffin population in the world at around nine million.

These are Atlantic puffins. They are about 18cm (10in) tall and have yellow, orange and blue beaks, which is why they are also known as sea parrots.

The west of Europe stretches as far as Portugal on the Atlantic coast, while southern Europe reaches down to the many small islands in the Mediterranean Sea, where the climate is famously sunny, warm and dry.

Sights of London

There are many famous sights in London, from the huge clock tower of Big Ben, to Buckingham Palace, the official residency of the Queen.

One of the city's most recent additions is the London Eye, the world's largest Ferris wheel, which was constructed to mark the millennium. The top of the wheel is 135m (443ft) high, giving an impressive view of the city.

The London Eye sits on the south bank of the River Thames. Big Ben sits on the opposite bank.

Internet links

For a link to a Web site where you can explore the Tower of London, where the Crown Jewels are kept, go to **www.usborne-quicklinks.com**

Eiffel Tower

The Eiffel Tower in Paris, France, was opened in 1889, and has since had over 200 million visitors. It was built for an international exhibition celebrating the scientific and engineering achievements of the time. The iron structure is around 300m (980ft) tall and has three levels with many shops and restaurants.

There are over 350 electric lamps fitted to the outside of the Eiffel Tower, lighting it up dramatically at night.

The Leaning Tower

One of Italy's most famous sights is the Leaning Tower of Pisa. The 55m (180ft) tall bell tower is part of Pisa Cathedral. Building work began on it in 1173, and the tower started to lean while it was being built. It leans because the ground beneath it is a mixture of sand and clay, which are easily compressed. The huge weight of the tower compressed the ground more in some areas than others, so the tower began to lean.

This marble statue of a discus thrower is a copy of a bronze statue from 5th-century Greece. The statue, housed in the National Museum in Rome, Italy, is a symbol of the Olympic games.

Home of the Olympics

Athletes from all over the world compete in the Olympic games every four years. The first Olympic games were held in celebration of the Greek God Zeus in Olympia, Greece, in 776BC. Today, some of the foundations, steps and pillars of the original stadium, which seated around 30,000 spectactors, remain. The start and finish lines of the running track, and the judges' seats, have also survived.

20°E

Baltic Sea

Hameenlinna
Turku
Lahti
Kouvola
Lappeenranta
FINLAND
Mikkeli
Paijanne Lake
Pihlaja Lake
25°
30°
Espoo
Helsinki
Kotka
Vyborg
Saimaa Lake

Aland Islands

Gulf of Finland
Zelenogorsk
St. Petersburg
Lake Ladoga
Lake Onega
Konosha

Hiiumaa
Tallinn
Kohtla-Jarve
Kingisepp
Gatchina
Pushkin
Volkhov
White Lake

Haapsalu
Narva
Tikhvin

Kuressaare
ESTONIA
Kirishi

Saaremaa
Parnu

2
Ventspils
Gulf of Riga
Tartu
Lake Peipus
Novgorod
Lake Ilmen
Borovichi
Cherepovets
Vologda

Jurmala
Voru
Lake Pskov
Vyshniy Volochek
Rybinsk Reservoir
Rybinsk

Jelgava
Riga
Cesis
Pskov
Opochka
Valdai Hills
343m (1,125ft)
Tver
Yaroslavl
Kostroma
Volga

LATVIA
Aluksne
North
Rzhev
Kineshma
Volga

Siauliai
Jekabpils
Ludza
Velikiye Luki
Ivanovo
Gorki Reservoir

Panevezys
Daugavpils
European
Sergiyev Posad
Semenov

55°N
LITHUANIA
Navapolatsk
Polatsk
Zelenograd
Vladimir
Nizhniy Novgorod

Kaunas
Western Dvina
Plain
Podolsk
Moscow
Murom
Arzamas

Marijampole
Vitsyebsk
Oka

Alytus
Vilnius
Maladzyechna
Orsha
Dnieper
Smolensk
Obninsk
Kolomna

Hrodna
Lida
Barysaw
Kaluga
Serpukhov
Ryazan
Saransk

Minsk
Zhodzina
Mahilyow
Roslavl
Oka
Tula

3
Baranavichy
Oka

Slutsk
Babruysk
293m (961ft)
Michurinsk
Kamenka
Penza

Salihorsk
Zhlobin
Klintsy
Bryansk
Central
Yelets
Lipetsk
Tambov

Pripet Marshes
Svyetlahorsk
Orel

Pinsk
Pripet
Homyel
Rechytsa
Staryy Oskol
Voronezh

Mazyr
Desna
Kursk
Russian

Lutsk
Chernihiv

Rivne
Korosten
Sumy

Shepetivka
Kievske Reservoir
Kharkiv
Uplands
Kamyshin

50°
Zhytomyr
Kiev
Lubny
Slovyansk
Lysychansk

417m (1,368ft)
Bila Tserkva
Poltava
Kramatorsk
Luhansk
Volgograd

Khmelnytskyy
Dnieper
Kremenchukske Reservoir
Donets
Horlivka

Vinnytsya
Cherkasy
Kremenchuk
UKRAINE
Dnipropetrovsk
Donetsk

Kamyanets-Podilskyy
Uman
Kirovohrad
Oleksandriya
Dniprodzerzhynsk
Zaporizhzhya
Novocherkassk

4
Botosani
Balti
Dniester
Kryvyy Rih
Nikopol
Don
Tsimlyansk Reservoir

Rabnita
Yuzhnoukrayinsk
Mariupol
Volgodonsk

Iasi
MOLDOVA
Tighina
Tiraspol
Mykolayiv
Kakhovske Reservoir
Melitopol
Rostov

ROMANIA
Chisinau
Dnieper
Kherson
Berdyansk

Bilhorod Dnistrovskyy
Odesa
Black Sea
Sea of Azov

Galati
Braila
Tulcea
Mouths of the Danube

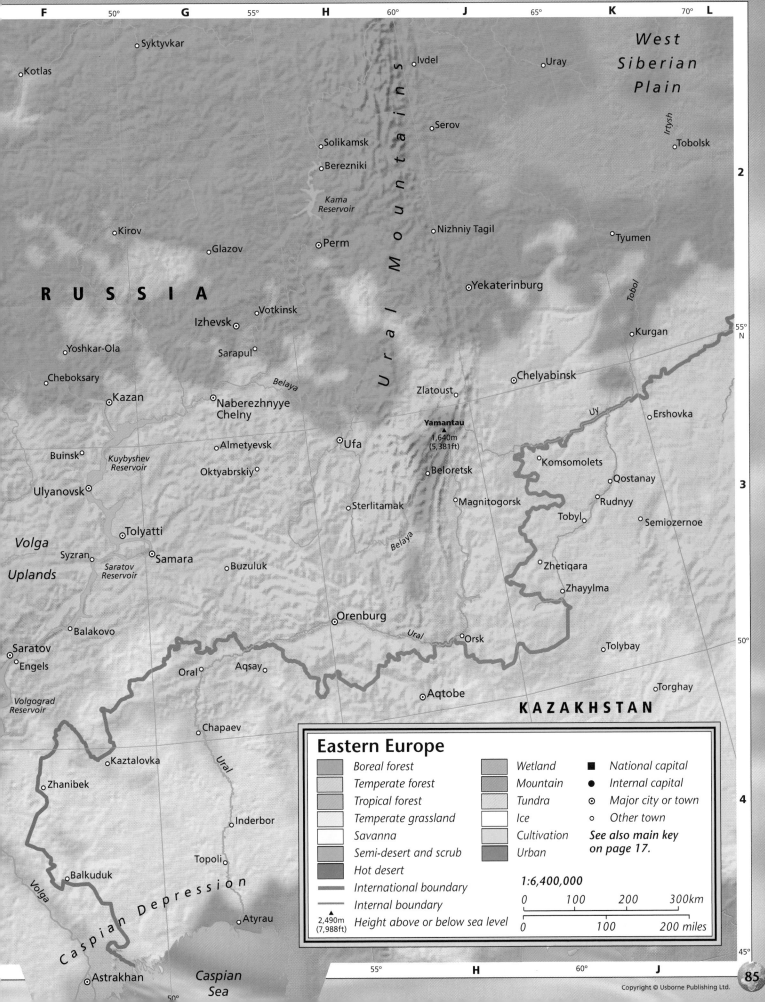

F 50° **G** 55° **H** 60° **J** 65° **K** 70° **L**

West Siberian Plain

Syktyvkar

Kotlas

Ivdel

Uray

Solikamsk

Serov

Berezniki

Irtysh

Tobolsk

Kama Reservoir

2

Kirov

Nizhniy Tagil

Tyumen

Glazov

Perm

U r a l   M o u n t a i n s

R U S S I A

Yekaterinburg

Votkinsk

Izhevsk

Yoshkar-Ola

Sarapul

Belaya

Kurgan

55° N

Cheboksary

Chelyabinsk

Tobol

Kazan

Zlatoust

Ershovka

Naberezhnyye Chelny

Uy

Buinsk

Almetyevsk

Yamantau ▲ 1,640m (5,381ft)

Komsomolets

Qostanay

Ulyanovsk

Oktyabrskiy

Beloretsk

Rudnyy

3

Kuybyshev Reservoir

Magnitogorsk

Tobyl

Semiozernoe

Sterlitamak

Ufa

Belaya

Tolyatti

Volga

Syzran

Samara

Buzuluk

Zhetiqara

Uplands

Saratov Reservoir

Zhayylma

Balakovo

Orenburg

Ural

Orsk

Tolybay

50°

Saratov

Engels

Oral

Aqsay

Torghay

Volgograd Reservoir

Aqtobe

K A Z A K H S T A N

Chapaev

Ural

4

Kaztalovka

Zhanibek

Inderbor

Topoli

Balkuduk

Volga

C a s p i a n   D e p r e s s i o n

Atyrau

Caspian Sea

Astrakhan

50°

Eastern Europe

- Boreal forest
- Temperate forest
- Tropical forest
- Temperate grassland
- Savanna
- Semi-desert and scrub
- Hot desert
- International boundary
- Internal boundary
- ▲ 2,490m (7,988ft) Height above or below sea level

- Wetland
- Mountain
- Tundra
- Ice
- Cultivation
- Urban

1:6,400,000

- ■ National capital
- ● Internal capital
- ⊙ Major city or town
- ○ Other town

See also main key on page 17.

0   100   200   300km

0   100   200 miles

55° **H** 60° **J** 45°

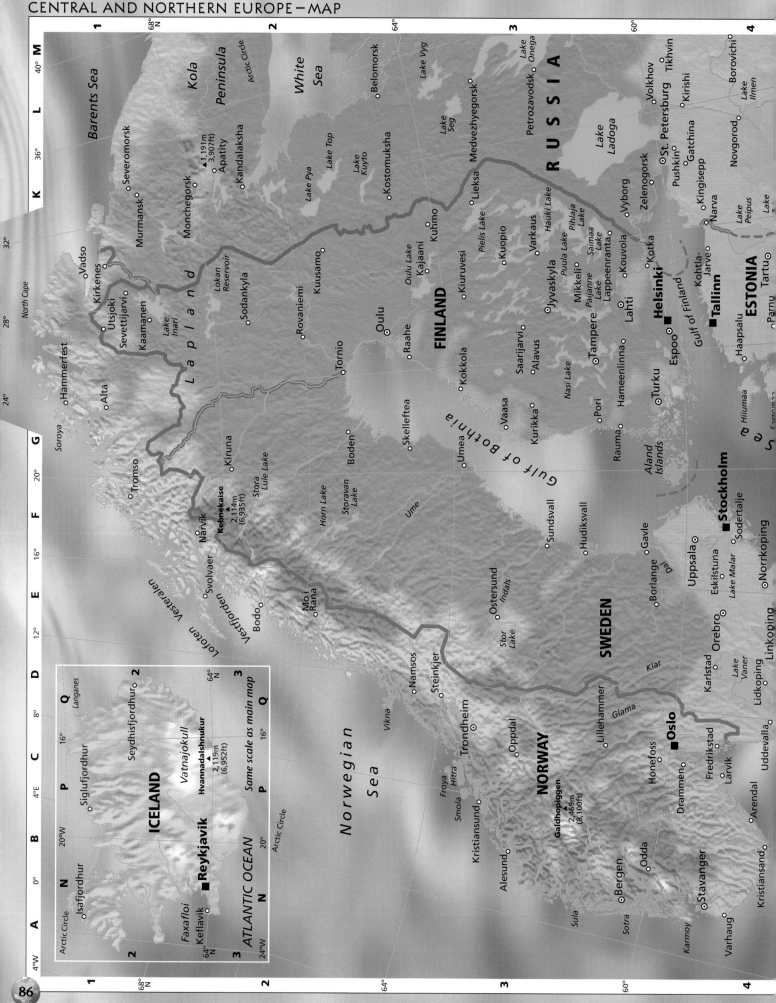

M

L

K

G

F

E

D

A

N

1   2   3   4

40° 36° 32° 28° 24° 20° 16° 12° 8° 4°E 0° 4°W

Barents Sea

North Cape

Kola Peninsula

Soroya

Severomorsk

Murmansk

Monchegorsk

Vadso

Kirkenes

Utsjoki

Sevettijarvi

Kaamanen

Lake Inari

Hammerfest

Alta

Tromso

Lapland

Lokan Reservoir

Sodankyla

Arctic Circle

▲1,191m
3,907ft

Apatity

Kandalaksha

White Sea

Belomorsk

Lake Vyg

Lake Seg

Lake Top

Lake Pya

Lake Kuyto

Kostomuksha

Medvezhyegorsk

Lake Onega

Petrozavodsk

Lieksa

Lake Ladoga

RUSSIA

Tikhvin

Volkhov

St. Petersburg

Pushkin

Kirishi

Gatchina

Borovichi

Lake Ilmen

Novgorod

Kingisepp

Narva

Lake Peipus

Lake

Tartu

ESTONIA

Parnu

Haapsalu

Kohtla-Jarve

Tallinn

Gulf of Finland

Helsinki

Espoo

Kotka

Kouvola

Vyborg

Zelenogorsk

Lappeenranta

Saimaa

Pihlaja

Hauki Lake

Varkaus

Kuopio

Pielis Lake

Kajaani

Kuhmo

Oulu Lake

Rovaniemi

Kuusamo

Tornio

Oulu

Raahe

FINLAND

Kokkola

Kiuruvesi

Saarijarvi

Alavus

Jyvaskyla

Mikkeli

Paijanne

Lahti

Hameenlinna

Tampere

Nasi Lake

Vaasa

Kurikka

Pori

Turku

Rauma

Aland Islands

Hiiumaa

Sea

Stockholm

Sodertalje

Norrtalje

Uppsala

Eskilstuna

Lake Malar

Norrkoping

Linkoping

Gavle

Borlange

Dal

SWEDEN

Orebro

Karlstad

Lake Vaner

Lidkoping

Klar

Lillehammer

Oslo

Honefoss

Drammen

Fredrikstad

Larvik

Uddevalla

Arendal

Kristiansand

Skelleftea

Boden

Kiruna

Narvik

Kebnekaise
▲2,114m
(6,935ft)

Svolvaer

Svolvaer

Bodo

Moi Rana

Namsos

Steinkjer

Trondheim

Oppdal

NORWAY

Galdhopiggen
▲2,469m
(8,100ft)

Alesund

Kristiansund

Smola

Hitra

Froya

Bergen

Odda

Stavanger

Varhaug

Karmoy

Sotra

Sula

Vikna

Norwegian Sea

Arctic Circle

Vestfjorden

Lofoten

Vesteralen

Soroya

Stora Lule Lake

Horn Lake

Storavan Lake

Ume

Ume

Gulf of Bothnia

Umea

Sundsvall

Hudiksvall

Ostersund

Stor Lake

Indals

Stor Lake

Glama

Inset map (bottom left):

D   C   P   Q

2   3

64°N   64°N

Langanes

Seydhisfjordhur

Siglufjordhur

Q

Vatnajokull

Hvannadalshnukur
▲2,119m
(6,952ft)

Same scale as main map

Q

P   P

ICELAND

Reykjavik

Keflavik

Faxafloi

Isafjordhur

Arctic Circle

N   N

ATLANTIC OCEAN

24°W   20°   16°   8°   4°E

20°W   16°   64°N

2   3

1   2

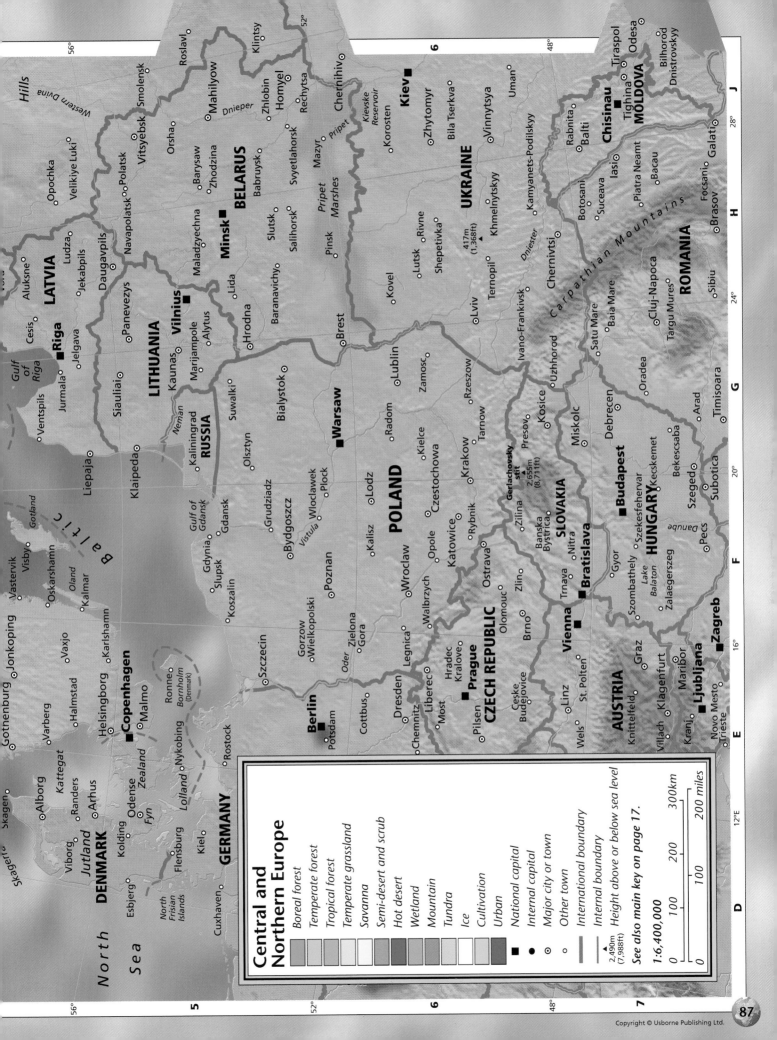

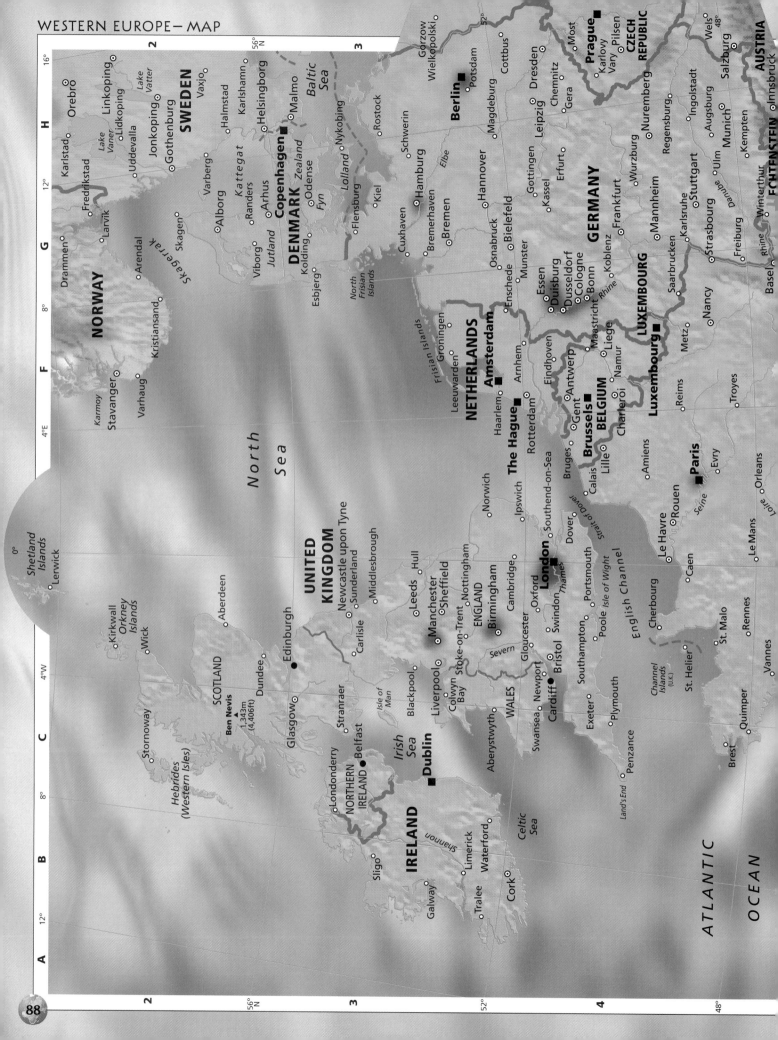

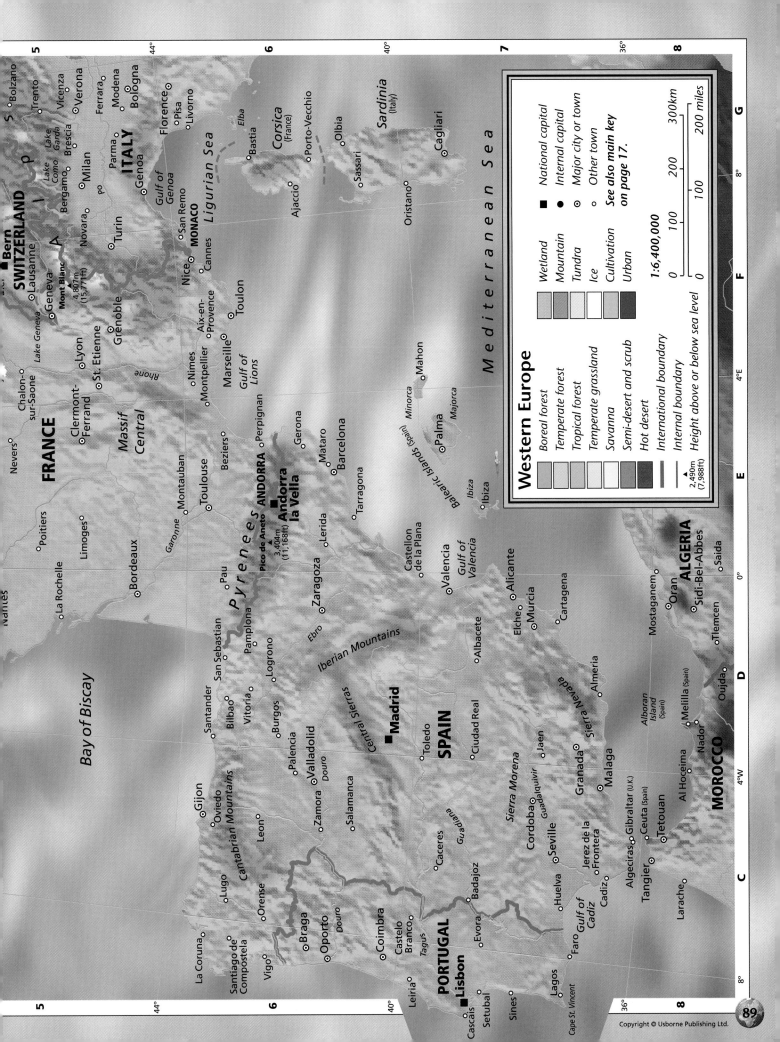

Southern Europe

- Boreal forest
- Temperate forest
- Tropical forest
- Temperate grassland
- Savanna
- Semi-desert and scrub
- Hot desert
- Wetland
- Mountain
- Tundra
- Ice
- Cultivation
- Urban

■ National capital

● Internal capital

⊙ Major city or town

○ Other town

— International boundary

— Internal boundary

▲ 2,490m (7,988ft)   Height above or below sea level

See also main key on page 17.

1:6,400,000

| 0 | 100 | 200 | 300km |
| 0 | | 100 | 200 miles |

BELGIUM

LUXEMBOURG
■ Luxembourg

GERMANY

CZECH REPUBLIC

Cherbourg
Le Havre
Rouen
Caen
Amiens
Charleroi
Namur
Koblenz
Frankfurt
Wurzburg
Erfurt
Gera
Dresden
Chemnitz
Most
Liberec
Wroclaw
Walbrzych
Oder
Opo
Hradec Kralove
Karlovy Vary
Pilsen
■ Prague
Olomouc
Brno
Zlin

Paris
Evry
Reims
Metz
Saarbrucken
Nancy
Mannheim
Karlsruhe
Nuremberg
Regensburg
Ingolstadt
Ceske Budejovice

48°N
Le Mans
Angers
Orleans
Tours
Troyes
Strasbourg
Stuttgart
Ulm
Augsburg
Munich
Linz
Wels
Vienna ■
St. Polten
Trnava
Bratislava ■

Poitiers
Nevers
Dijon
Besancon
Freiburg
Basel
Winterthur
Kempten
Innsbruck
Salzburg
AUSTRIA
Knittelfeld
Szombathely
Gyor

FRANCE

Limoges
Chalon-sur-Saone
Biel
Bern ■
Zurich
Lucerne
Vaduz ■
LIECHTENSTEIN
Grossglockner
3,798m (12,461ft)
Villach
Graz
Klagenfurt
Zalaegerszeg
Lake Balator

Clermont-Ferrand
Geneva
Lausanne
SWITZERLAND
Lake Geneva
Bolzano
Maribor

St. Etienne
Lyon
Mont Blanc
4,807m (15,771ft)
A
Lake Como
Trento
Kranj
SLOVENIA ■ Ljubljana
Novo Mesto
Zagreb ■

44°
Grenoble
Novara
Bergamo
Brescia
Vicenza
Lake Garda
Trieste
CROATIA
Karlovac
Slavonsk
Broc

Massif Central

Montauban
Turin
Milan
Po
Verona
Venice
Rijeka
Pula
Banja Luka

Garonne
Toulouse
Parma
Modena
Ferrara
Ravenna
Bologna
Rimini
Zadar
BOSNIA
AND
HERZEGOVINA
Zenica

Montpellier
Beziers
Nimes
Aix-en-Provence
MONACO
San Remo
Gulf of Genoa
Genoa
ITALY
SAN MARINO
Ancona
Split
Mostar

Andorra la Vella ■

Gulf of Lions
Marseille
Toulon
Nice
Cannes
Livorno
Pisa
Florence
Perugia
Apennines
Adriatic Sea

Ligurian Sea
Bastia
Elba
Terni
Pescara

3

Ajaccio
Corsica
(France)
VATICAN CITY
Rome ■

40°
Porto-Vecchio
Olbia
Foggia
Bari

Sassari
Naples
Pompeii
Salerno
Taranto

Oristano
Sardinia
(Italy)
Tyrrhenian
Sea

Cagliari

4
Cosenza

Mediterranean Sea
Lipari Islands
Catanzaro

Trapani
Palermo
Messina

Annaba
Menzel Bourguiba
Bizerte
Carthage
Sicily
Mount Etna
3,323m (10,902ft)
Catania

Guelma
Agrigento
Syracuse

36°
Souk Ahras
Tunis ■
Pantelleria
(Italy)
Ragusa

TUNISIA
Nabeul
MALTA
Valletta ■

5
Tebessa
Kairouan
Sousse
Pelagian Islands
(Italy)

Biskra
Kasserine
El Jem
Monastir

A   0°   B   4°E   C   8°   D   12°   E   16°

B   4°E   C   8°   D   12°   E   16°   F

Czestochowa
Kielce
Zamosc
Lutsk
Rivne
Zhytomyr
■ Kiev
Lubny
Poltava
Slovyansk

atowice
Vistula
Rzeszow
Lviv
Shepetivka
Bila Tserkva
Cherkasy
Kremenchukske Reservoir
Kramatorsk

POLAND
417m (1,368ft)▲
UKRAINE
Kremenchuk

Rybnik
Krakow
Tarnow
Ternopil
Khmelnytskyy
Vinnytsya
Dniprodzerzhynsk
Dnipropetrovsk

strava
Zilina
Gerlachovsky stit ▲ 2,655m (8,711ft)
Presov
Ivano-Frankivsk
Dniester
Kamyanets-Podilskyy
Uman
Oleksandriya
Kirovohrad
Dnieper
48° N

Banska Bystrica
Kosice
Uzhhorod
Chernivtsi
Botosani
Suceava
Balti
Rabnita
Kryvyy Rih
Nikopol
Zaporizhzhya

LOVAKIA
Miskolc
Satu Mare
Baia Mare
Iasi
MOLDOVA
■ Chisinau
Yuzhnoukrayinsk
Kakhovske Reservoir
Berdyansk
2

a
■ Budapest
Debrecen
Cluj-Napoca
Piatra Neamt
Tighina
Tiraspol
Mykolayiv
Melitopol

ekesfehervar
Oradea
Targu Mures
Bacau
Kherson
Odesa
Dzhankoy
Kerch

HUNGARY
ROMANIA
Sea of Azov

ecskemet
Bekescsaba
Focsani
Bilhorod-Dnistrovskyy
Crimea
Feodosiya

Szeged
Arad
Mount Moldoveanu 2,544m (8,346ft)▲
Sibiu
Brasov
Galati
Yevpatoriya
Simferopol

Subotica
Timisoara
Transylvanian Alps
Ramnicu Valcea
Braila
Tulcea
Sevastopol
44°

Osijek
Novi Sad
Pitesti
Ploiesti
Buzau
Mouths of the Danube

Tuzla
Belgrade
Drobeta-Turnu Severin
■ Bucharest
Constanta
Black Sea

Kragujevac
Craiova
Danube

Sarajevo
Kraljevo
Ruse
Dobrich

YUGOSLAVIA
Nis
Vratsa
Pleven
Shumen
Varna
3

Niksic
Leskovac
Balkan Mountains
BULGARIA
Sliven

rovnik
Pristina
Vranje
■ Sofia
Stara Zagora
Burgas

dgorica
Tetovo
Kumanovo
Plovdiv

Shkoder
■ Skopje
Blagoevgrad
Edirne
Zonguldak
Karabuk
Corum

MACEDONIA
Istanbul
Bosporus
Adapazari

Durres
■ Tirana
Prilep
Serres
Kavala
Tekirdag
Sea of Marmara
Bursa
Ankara ■
Kirikkale
40°

Elbasan
Bitola
Thessaloniki
Thasos
Eskisehir

ALBANIA
Korce
Canakkale
Balikesir
Kutahya
Lake Tuz

rce
Vlore
Mount Olympus ▲ 2,917m (9,570ft)
Limnos
TURKEY
Aksaray

Pindus Mountains
Larisa
Aegean Sea
Lesvos
Akhisar
Usak
Konya

Corfu
Ioannina
Volos
Manisa
Karaman

Corfu
GREECE
Euboea
Skyros
Izmir
Odemis
Isparta
Beysehir Lake

Preveza
Lamia
Chios
Aydin
Denizli
Taurus Mountains

Kefallonia
Chalkida
Ephesus
Antalya

Patra
■ Athens
Alanya

nian Sea
Peiraias
Gulf of Antalya

Pyrgos
Cyclades
Rhodes

Kalamata
Dodecanese
Rhodes
Kyrenia

Kythira
Karpathos
Nicosia ■
Larnaca

Chania
Crete
Irakleio
CYPRUS
Paphos
Limassol

Ierapetra

AFRICA

Africa is the second-biggest continent in the world, and has 53 countries. These range from the vast, dry Sudan, to small, tropical islands such as the Seychelles. More than a quarter of Africa's countries are landlocked, with no access to the sea except through other countries.

Here is a group of Masai people from East Africa, silhouetted against a sunset over the flat grasslands of Africa.

Algiers
Tunis
Rabat
Madeira (Portugal)
MOROCCO
TUNISIA
Tripoli
Canary Islands (Spain)
Laayoune
ALGERIA
LIBYA
Tropic of Cancer
WESTERN SAHARA (Morocco)
MAURITANIA
Nouakchott
MALI
NIGER
CHAD
Niger
CAPE VERDE
Praia
Dakar
SENEGAL
Banjul
THE GAMBIA
Bamako
Niamey
Ndjamena
Bissau
Ouagadougou
GUINEA-BISSAU
GUINEA
BURKINA FASO
NIGERIA
Conakry
BENIN
Abuja
Freetown
IVORY COAST
TOGO
SIERRA LEONE
GHANA
Porto-Novo
CENTRAL AFRICAN REPUBL
Monrovia
Yamoussoukro
Lome
CAMEROON
Bangui
LIBERIA
Accra
Malabo
Yaounde
EQUATORIAL GUINEA
Cong
Equator
Libreville
CONGO
SAO TOME AND PRINCIPE
GABON
Brazzaville
Kinshasa

ATLANTIC

OCEAN

Luanda

ANGOLA

NAMIBIA

Tropic of Capricorn
Windhoek

Orange

Cape Town

Facts

Total land area 30,311,690 sq km (11,703,343 sq miles)

Total population 794 million

Biggest city Lagos, Nigeria

Biggest country Sudan 2,505,810 sq km (967,493 sq miles)

Smallest country Seychelles 455 sq km (176 sq miles)

Highest mountain Kilimanjaro, Tanzania 5,895m (19,340ft)

Longest river Nile, running from to Burundi to Egypt 6,671km (4,145 miles)

Biggest lake Lake Victoria, between Tanzania, Kenya and Uganda 69,215 sq km (26,724 sq miles)

Highest waterfall Tugela Falls, on the Tugela River, South Africa 610m (2,000ft)

Biggest desert Sahara, North Africa 9,100,000 sq km (3,500,000 sq miles)

Biggest island Madagascar 587,040 sq km (226,656 sq miles)

Main mineral deposits Gold, copper, diamonds, iron ore, manganese, bauxite

Main fuel deposits Coal, uranium, natural gas

The shading on this map is there to help you see clearly the different countries that make up the continent.

Cairo

EGYPT

Tropic of Cancer

Nile

Khartoum

ERITREA
Asmara

SUDAN

DJIBOUTI Djibouti

Addis Ababa

SOMALIA

ETHIOPIA

Mogadishu

UGANDA
Kampala

KENYA

ONGO

Kigali

Nairobi

DEM.

RWANDA
BURUNDI
Bujumbura

REP.)

Dodoma

Victoria

SEYCHELLES

TANZANIA   Dar es Salaam

INDIAN

MALAWI

Moroni
COMOROS

OCEAN

AMBIA
Lusaka

Lilongwe

Zambezi

Harare
ZIMBABWE

MOZAMBIQUE

Antananarivo

MAURITIUS
Port Louis

TSWANA

MADAGASCAR

Reunion
(France)

Tropic of Capricorn

borone

Pretoria Maputo

Mbabane SWAZILAND
Lobamba

emfontein

Maseru

LESOTHO

OUTH
FRICA

This greater flamingo is from the Transvaal National Park, South Africa.

Africa is home to the world's longest river, the Nile, and its largest desert, the Sahara. In southern Africa there are two more large deserts, the Kalahari and the Namib. Africa also has enormous rainforests in central areas, near the Equator.

A convoy of camels moves across the Sahara Desert in North Africa. The strange swirls of sand are formed by strong winds.

Desert weather

Temperatures in the Sahara Desert can rise as high as 55°C (131°F) during the day, but often fall below freezing point at night. Strong winds blow across the desert and whip up mini whirlwinds called dust devils. These suck up sand and hurl it high into the air.

This satellite image clearly shows the vast Sahara Desert in North Africa. It covers an area about the size of the U.S.A.

Moroccan mountain life

The Atlas Mountains dominate the country of Morocco, north of the Sahara Desert. High in the mountains are villages which are home to groups of African people called Berbers. Berbers have lived in Morocco for thousands of years and today still follow their traditional way of life, herding sheep and goats.

This image shows the curves and folds of the Atlas Mountains in Morocco. They were formed by earthquakes and other movements of the Earth.

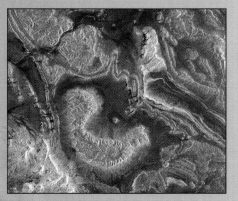

River in the desert

The River Nile winds its way through eastern Africa, from Burundi all the way to the Mediterranean Sea. It is almost the only water source in this dry, arid part of Africa, so major cities, such as Cairo in Egypt, have grown up near it. The soil near the Nile's banks is fertile enough to farm on, especially near the coast where the river splits into many streams.

Wild forests

The large, dense rainforests of central Africa are home to more than half of Africa's wild animals, including chimpanzees, gorillas and elephants. Many of these animals have never come into contact with humans.

The dense rainforest of central Africa is pink in this satellite image. Running across the middle of the picture is the large Congo River. It splits into many smaller rivers, creating a huge swampy area.

The dark blue water in the lower right of this satellite image is the Red Sea. The triangular piece of land jutting into it is part of Egypt.

This is the River Nile, running through Egypt. As the river reaches the sea, it splits into many streams that create an expanse of fertile, swampy land. This is the large green area at the top of the image.

One of Africa's most populous countries is Egypt, which has busy cities such as its capital, Cairo, as well as the remains of ancient civilizations. Africa also has many areas of natural beauty, such as the vast wildlife parks in the south and east of the continent.

Pyramids and the Sphinx

One of the ancient wonders of the world is found at Giza, in Egypt – the group of three Great Pyramids. These stone structures were built by the ancient Egyptians as tombs for their pharaohs, or kings. The biggest pyramid is about 140m (480ft) high, and probably took 20 years to build. You can see a picture of the pyramids on page 1 of this atlas.

In front of the pyramids stands the Great Sphinx, an enormous statue of a lion with a man's head. It was probably carved as a monument to a pharaoh, though no one is sure which one. Some historians believe there are secret rooms and tunnels underneath the Sphinx.

This is the Great Sphinx of Egypt. It was carved out of soft limestone which has crumbled over the years. Part of the Sphinx's nose is now missing.

Cape Town

At Africa's southern tip, in the country of South Africa, is the city of Cape Town. It is famous for its elegant buildings, sandy beaches and busy waterfront. The city is right next to Table Mountain, which gets its name from its distinctive flat top. Thick clouds often cover the mountain and are nicknamed the Table Cloth.

This is Cape Town, with Table Mountain behind.

A panther chameleon clings to a branch. It can wrap its tail around the branch too, for extra grip. Panther chameleons live only in Madagascar.

On safari

Wild animals such as lions, elephants, buffaloes and zebras live on the grasslands of eastern and southern Africa. The land is divided into many specially protected wildlife parks that tourists can visit on safari trips.

These parks are some of the last remaining places where cheetahs live. These big cats were once found all over Africa but are now endangered. Cheetahs are the world's fastest land animals, able to run at a speed of 115kph (70mph).

Wildlife island

Madagascar is a large island in the Indian Ocean, off Africa's southeastern coast. It has thick, steamy rainforests which are home to many animals not found anywhere else in the world. These include rare chameleons and over 50 species of monkey-like animals called lemurs.

Internet links

For a link to a Web site where you can discover more about Madagascar's unusual wildlife, including chameleons, go to **www.usborne-quicklinks.com**

A cheetah in Kenya, eastern Africa, hisses and spits fiercely to scare away enemies.

NORTHEAST AFRICA—MAP

GREECE · **Ath**

Annaba · Bizerte · Catania · **Sicily** (Italy)
Menzel · Carthage · Syracuse
Bourguiba · **Tunis**
Saida
Batna · Tebessa · Kairouan · Sousse · **MALTA**
Djelfa · Pantelleria (Italy) · **Valletta**
Biskra · Sfax · Monastir
Atlas Mountains · Gafsa · El Jem · Pelagian Islands (Italy)
El Oued · Tozeur · Kerkenah Islands
Touggourt · Chott · Gabes · Gulf of Gabes · **M e d i t e r r a n e a**
Ghardaia · el Jerid · Jerba
Ouargla · Tataouine · **TUNISIA** · **Tripoli** · Al Khums · Darnah
Leptis Magna · Misratah · Cyrene · Al Bayda
Gharyan · Benghazi · Tubruq
Tademait Plateau · Ghadamis · Surt · Gulf of Sidra · Ajdabiya

Great Eastern Erg

ALGERIA

Illizi · Sabha · **LIBYA** · **Libya**

Tropic of Cancer · Ahaggar Mountains · Ghat · Murzuq
Mount Tahat · 2,918m (9,573ft) · Al Jawf
Tamanrasset

Djado Plateau · Tibesti Mountains

MALI · S A H A R A

Emi Koussi · 3,415m (11,204ft)

Agadez · Faya-Largeau · Ennedi Plateau
NIGER · Bodele Depression
Tahoua

CHAD

Dosso · Maradi · Zinder · Mao · Mount Mar
Sokoto · S A H E L · Abeche · 3,088m (10,131f)
Birnin-Kebbi · Katsina
Kandi · Gusau · Kano · Lake Chad · Nyala
Zaria · Potiskum · Maiduguri · **Ndjamena** · Mongo
Kainji Reservoir · Kaduna · **NIGERIA** · Am Timan
Saki · Minna · Jos · Kumo · Maroua
Niger · Bida · **Abuja** · **CAMEROON** · Bongor · Birao

98

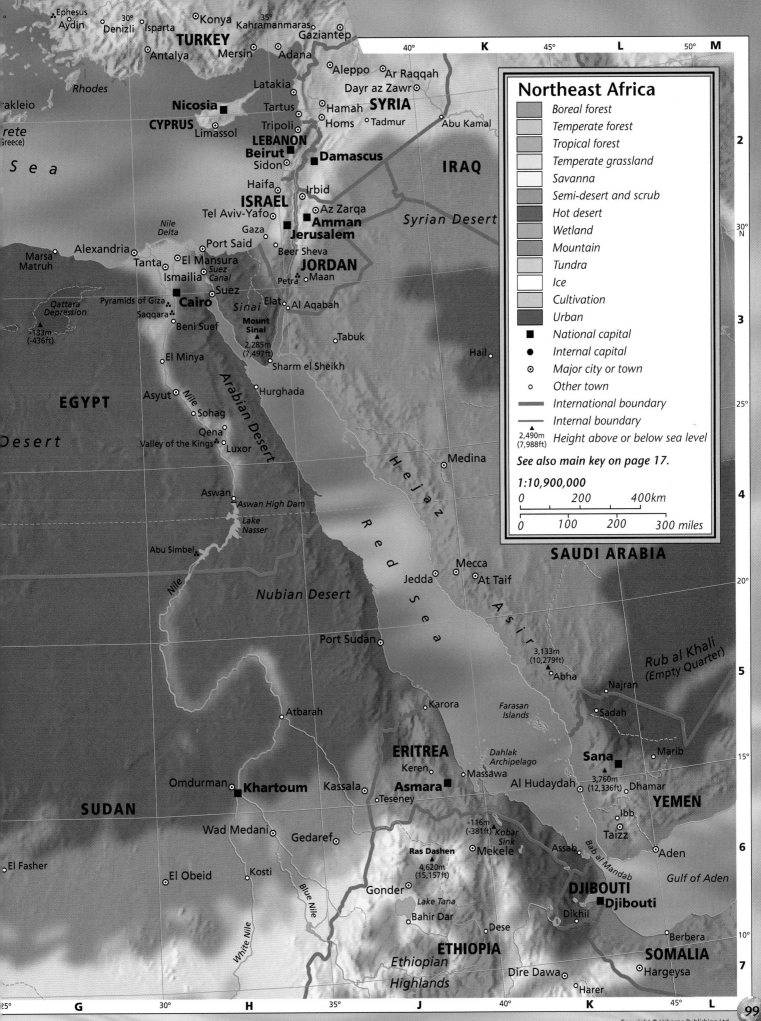

Northeast Africa

	Boreal forest
	Temperate forest
	Tropical forest
	Temperate grassland
	Savanna
	Semi-desert and scrub
	Hot desert
	Wetland
	Mountain
	Tundra
	Ice
	Cultivation
	Urban
■	National capital
●	Internal capital
⊙	Major city or town
○	Other town
	International boundary
	Internal boundary
▲ 2,490m (7,988ft)	Height above or below sea level

See also main key on page 17.

1:10,900,000

0   200   400km
0   100   200   300 miles

Map labels:

Ephesus, Aydin, Denizli, Isparta, Konya, Kahramanmaras, Gaziantep, **TURKEY**, Antalya, Mersin, Adana, Rhodes, Aleppo, Ar Raqqah, Latakia, Dayr az Zawr, Tartus, **SYRIA**, Hamah, Tadmur, Abu Kamal, **Nicosia**, Tripoli, Homs, **CYPRUS**, Limassol, **IRAQ**, **LEBANON**, **Beirut**, Sidon, **Damascus**, Haifa, Irbid, **ISRAEL**, Az Zarqa, Tel Aviv-Yafo, **Amman**, Gaza, **Jerusalem**, Port Said, Beer Sheva, **JORDAN**, Alexandria, El Mansura, Suez, Petra, Maan, Marsa Matruh, Tanta, Suez Canal, Ismailia, Suez, Qattara Depression, -133m (-436ft), Pyramids of Giza, **Cairo**, Sinai, Elat, Al Aqabah, Saqqara, Beni Suef, Mount Sinai 2,285m (7,497ft), Tabuk, El Minya, Hail, **EGYPT**, Asyut, Nile, Sohag, Hurghada, Qena, Valley of the Kings, Luxor, Arabian Desert, Desert, Aswan, Aswan High Dam, Lake Nasser, Medina, Abu Simbel, Nubian Desert, Hejaz, Red Sea, Mecca, Jedda, At Taif, **SAUDI ARABIA**, Asir, 3,133m (10,279ft), Abha, Rub al Khali (Empty Quarter), Port Sudan, Najran, Sadah, Karora, Farasan Islands, Atbarah, **ERITREA**, Dahlak Archipelago, **Sana**, Marib, Keren, Massawa, Dhamar, **Asmara**, 3,760m (12,336ft), **SUDAN**, Omdurman, **Khartoum**, Kassala, Teseney, Al Hudaydah, **YEMEN**, Ibb, Wad Medani, Gedaref, -116m (-381ft), Kobar Sink, Taizz, El Fasher, Assab, Aden, El Obeid, Kosti, Ras Dashen 4,620m (15,157ft), Mekele, Bab al Mandab, Gulf of Aden, Gonder, Berbera, Lake Tana, **DJIBOUTI**, **Djibouti**, Bahir Dar, Dikhil, **SOMALIA**, Dese, Dire Dawa, Hargeysa, **ETHIOPIA**, Ethiopian Highlands, Harer, White Nile, Blue Nile

Grid references (columns): A B C D E F G H (top); rows 1 2 3 4 5 (right side)

Longitude/latitude labels: 30°W, 20°, 10°, 5°W, 0°, 5°E, 10°, 25°, 20°, 15°, 30°, 35°, 40°N, 25°, Tropic of Cancer

Water bodies and oceans:
- ATLANTIC OCEAN
- Mediterranean Sea

Countries and regions:
- PORTUGAL
- SPAIN
- MOROCCO
- WESTERN SAHARA (Morocco)
- ALGERIA
- TUNISIA
- LIBYA
- MALI
- MAURITANIA
- SAHARA
- Azores (Portugal)
- Balearic Islands (Spain)
- Sardinia (Italy)
- Madeira (Portugal)
- Canary Islands (Spain)

Cities and towns:
Lisbon, Sines, Lagos, Seville, Cadiz, Cordoba, Granada, Malaga, Gibraltar (Spain), Ceuta (Spain), Tangier, Larache, Al Hoceima, Tetouan, Melilla (Spain), Murcia, Alicante, Almeria, Cagliari, Ibiza, Majorca, Menzel Bourguiba, Bizerte, Carthage, Tunis, Sousse, Monastir, El Jem, Sfax, Kerkenah Islands, Jerba, Gabes, Tataouine, Ghadamis, Kairouan, Annaba, Constantine, Tebessa, Skikda, Bejaia, Djemila, Setif, Batna, Biskra, El Oued, Touggourt, Ouargla, Gafsa, Tozeur, Chott el Jerid, Algiers, Blida, Mostaganem, Oran, Sidi-Bel-Abbes, Saida, Djelfa, Ghardaia, Bordj Bou Arreridj, Tlemcen, Oujda, Taza, Fes, Meknes, Kenitra, Rabat, Casablanca, El Jadida, Safi, Essaouira, Agadir, Beni Mellal, Khouribga, Marrakech, Ouarzazate, Er Rachidia, Erfoud, Bechar, Adrar, Illizi, Tamanrasset, Ad Dakhla, Nouadhibou, Nouakchott, Akjoujt, Atar, Tidjikja, Kidal, Zouerat, Es Semara, Tan-Tan, Boujdour, Laayoune, Tindouf, Funchal, Flores, Pico, Sao Miguel, Ponta Delgada, Angra do Heroismo, Terceira, Lanzarote, Fuerteventura, Gran Canaria, Tenerife, La Gomera, La Palma, El Hierro, Cape Blanc

Physical features:
- Atlas Mountains
- Morocco Mountains
- Toubkal 4,165m (13,665ft)
- Ahaggar Mountains
- Mount Tahat 2,918m (9,573ft)
- Great Eastern Erg
- Great Western Erg
- Chech Erg
- Tademait Plateau
- Tropic of Cancer

Inset box (lower left):
- Azores (Portugal)
- ATLANTIC OCEAN
- Flores, Pico, Angra do Heroismo, Terceira, Sao Miguel, Ponta Delgada
- 40°N, 30°W, 25°
- Same scale as main map
- Grid: J, K; 10

Northwest Africa

	Boreal forest	
	Temperate forest	
	Tropical forest	
	Temperate grassland	
	Savanna	
	Semi-desert and scrub	
	Hot desert	

— International boundary
— Internal boundary
▲ 2,490m (7,988ft) Height above or below sea level

	Wetland	
	Mountain	
	Tundra	
	Ice	
	Cultivation	
	Urban	

■ National capital
● Internal capital
⊙ Major city or town
○ Other town

See also main key on page 17.

1:10,900,000

0   100   200   300 miles
0   200   400km

Inset — Cape Verde / Sao Tome and Principe

ATLANTIC OCEAN

SAO TOME AND PRINCIPE
■ Sao Tome   Principe   Equator

L   25°W   ATLANTIC OCEAN   M   11
Santo Antao   Sao Nicolau   Sal
Mindelo
Boa Vista
CAPE VERDE   Sao Tiago   Maio
15°N   Fogo   ■ Praia   15°N
12
Same scale as main map

Main map labels

NIGER
Agadez
Maradi
Tahoua
Katsina
Sokoto
Gusau
Zaria
Birnin-Kebbi
Kaduna
Minna
Bida
Abuja ■
Gao
Tillaberi
Niamey ■
Dosso
Kainji Reservoir
Niger
Ilorin
NIGERIA
Ogbomoso
Enugu
Onitsha
Owo
Benin City
Warri
Port Harcourt
Niger Delta

S A H E L
BURKINA FASO
Ouagadougou ■
Fada-Ngourma
Dori
Ouahigouya
Tenkodogo
Bawku
White Volta
BENIN
Kandi
Natitingou
Djougou
Parakou
Saki
Ibadan
Abeokuta
Lagos
Porto-Novo ■
Cotonou
Lome ■
Bight of Benin
Gulf of Guinea

TOGO
Abomey
Sokode
Damongo
Tamale
Wa
Wenchi
GHANA
Lake Volta
Koforidua
Accra ■
Cape Coast
Tarkwa
Sekondi-Takoradi
Cape Three Points

Tombouctou (Timbuktu)
Goundam
Mopti
San
Segou
Niono
Koudougou
Bobo Dioulasso
Banfora
Sikasso
Bougouni
Koutiala
Kita
Bamako ■
Niger
Black Volta
Tougan

Nema
Nioro du Sahel
Ayoun el Atrous
Kiffa
Kaedi
Selibabi
Kita

IVORY COAST
Odienne
Korhogo
Katiola
Bouna
Bondoukou
Bouake
Yamoussoukro ■
Man
Daloa
Gagnoa
Divo
Adzope
Abidjan
San Pedro
Cape Palmas
Harper
Nzerekore
1,752m (5,748ft)

GUINEA
Siguiri
Kankan
Kindia
Labe
Boke
Conakry ■
Gueckedou
Kedougou
Zorzor

SIERRA LEONE
Makeni
Sefadu
Bo
Kenema
Freetown ■
Tubmanburg
Monrovia ■
LIBERIA

SENEGAL
St. Louis
Rosso
Louga
Thies
Dakar ■
Kaolack
Tambacounda
Kolda
Senegal
Kayes
Dara

THE GAMBIA
Banjul ■
Bignona
Ziguinchor

GUINEA-BISSAU
Bissau ■
Bissagos Archipelago

CAPE VERDE

ATLANTIC OCEAN

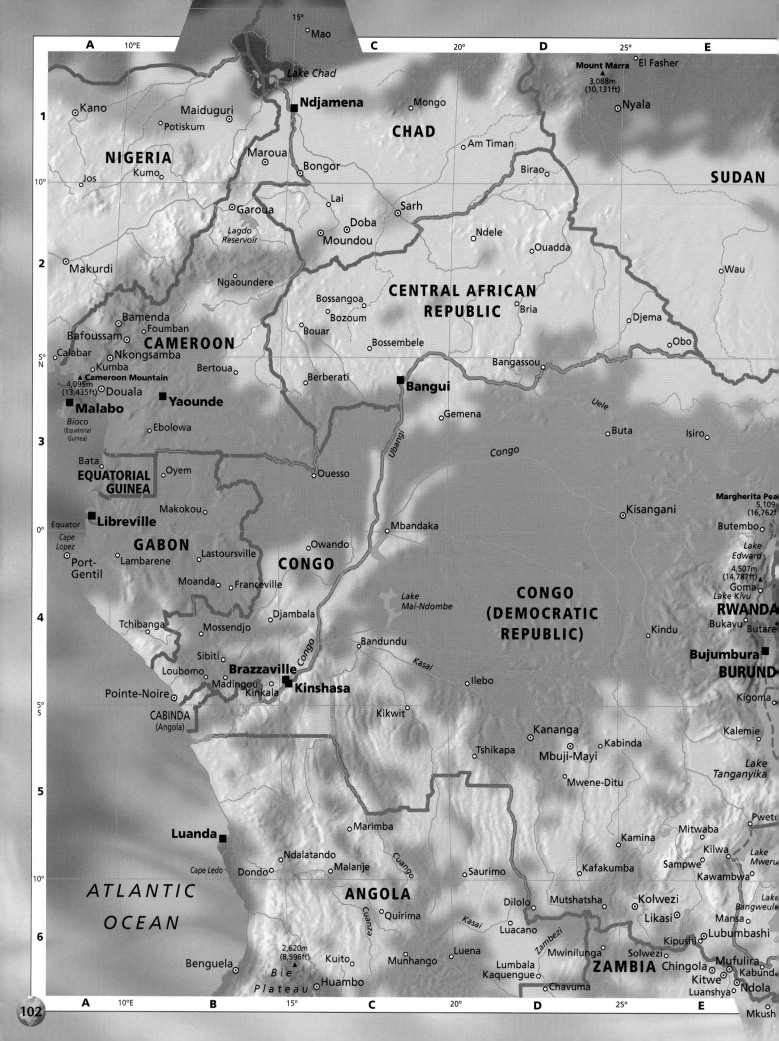

ATLANTIC OCEAN

NIGERIA
Kano
Maiduguri
Potiskum
Jos
Kumo
Makurdi

CAMEROON
Bamenda
Foumban
Bafoussam
Calabar
Nkongsamba
Kumba
▲ Cameroon Mountain
4,095m
(13,435ft) Douala
Malabo
*Bioco
(Equatorial
Guinea)*
Bertoua
Ebolowa
Maroua
Garoua
*Lagdo
Reservoir*
Yaounde

CHAD
Mao
Lake Chad
Ndjamena
Bongor
Lai
Doba
Moundou
Mongo
Am Timan
Sarh
Ndele

Mount Marra ▲
3,088m
(10,131ft)
El Fasher
Nyala

SUDAN
Wau

**CENTRAL AFRICAN
REPUBLIC**
Bossangoa
Bozoum
Bouar
Bossembele
Berberati
Bangui
Gemena
Bria
Djema
Obo
Bangassou
Uele
Buta
Isiro

**EQUATORIAL
GUINEA**
Bata
Oyem
Ngaoundere

GABON
Makokou
Lambarene
Lastoursville
Moanda
Franceville
Tchibanga
Mossendjo

LIBREVILLE
Equator
*Cape
Lopez*
Port-
Gentil

CONGO
Owando
Djambala
Sibiti
Loubomo
Madingou
Kinkala
Brazzaville
Ouesso
Ubangi
Mbandaka
Congo
Kisangani

Margherita Pea
5,109
(16,762f
Butembo
*Lake
Edward*
4,507m
(14,787ft) ▲
Goma
Lake Kivu

RWANDA
Bukavu
Butare
Kindu

Bujumbura
BURUND
Kigoma

*Lake
Tanganyika*

**CONGO
(DEMOCRATIC
REPUBLIC)**
*Lake
Mai-Ndombe*
Bandundu
Kasai
Ilebo
Kikwit
Kinshasa
Congo
Kananga
Tshikapa
Mbuji-Mayi
Kabinda
Mwene-Ditu
Kalemie

CABINDA
(Angola)
Pointe-Noire

Luanda
Cape Ledo
Dondo
Ndalatando
Malanje
Marimba
Saurimo
Cuango
Cuanza
Quirima
Kamina
Mitwaba
Kilwa
Sampwe
Kawambwa
*Lake
Mweru*
Mansa

ANGOLA
Benguela
Kuito
Munhango
2,620m
(8,596ft) ▲
*Bie
Plateau*
Huambo
Kasai
Dilolo
Luacano
Luena
Zambezi
Mwinilunga
Lumbala
Kaquengue
Chavuma
Mutshatsha
Kafakumba
Kolwezi
Likasi
Kipushi
Solwezi

ZAMBIA
Chingola
Kitwe
Luanshya
Mufulira
Kabund
Ndola
Lubumbashi

*Lake
Bangweul*

Mkush

Pwet
Kamina

102

A   10°E   B   15°   C   20°   D   25°   E

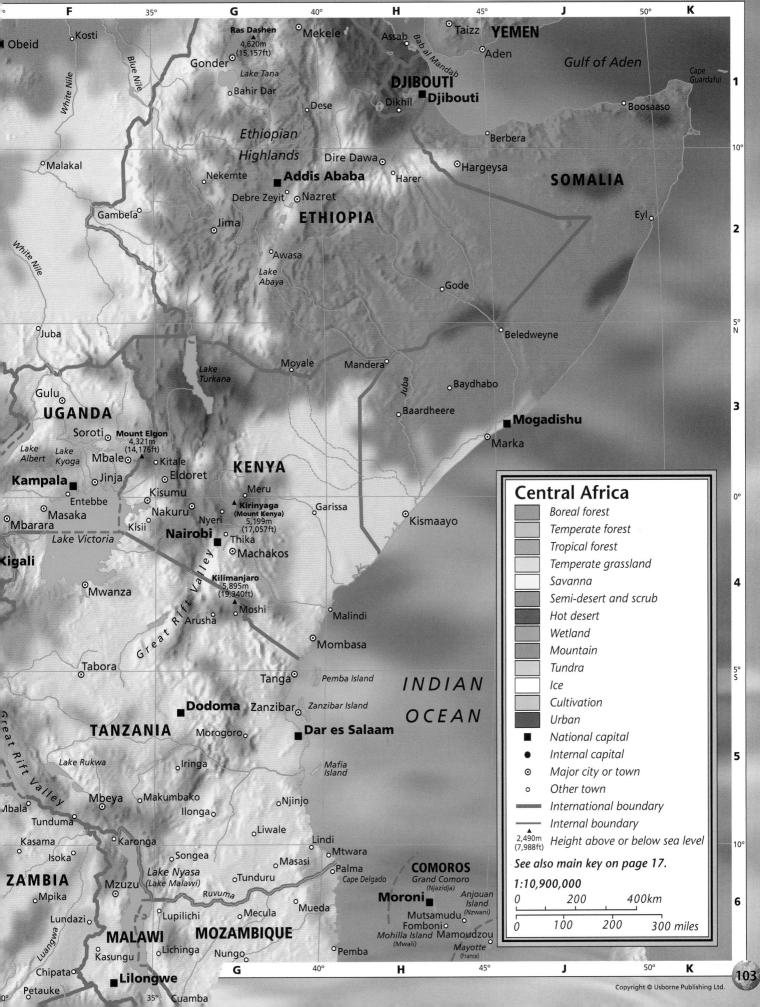

Central Africa

- Boreal forest
- Temperate forest
- Tropical forest
- Temperate grassland
- Savanna
- Semi-desert and scrub
- Hot desert
- Wetland
- Mountain
- Tundra
- Ice
- Cultivation
- Urban
- ■ National capital
- ● Internal capital
- ⊙ Major city or town
- ○ Other town
- ▬▬ International boundary
- ▬ Internal boundary
- ▲ 2,490m (7,988ft) Height above or below sea level

See also main key on page 17.

1:10,900,000

0   200   400km

0   100   200   300 miles

103

ATLANTIC OCEAN

ANGOLA

NAMIBIA

BOTSWANA

ZAMBIA

CONGO (DEMOCRATIC REPUBLIC)

ZIMBABWE

SOUTH AFRICA

LESOTHO

SWAZILAND

Luanda
Ndalatando
Dondo
Marimba
Malanje
Saurimo
Kafakumba
Dilolo
Mutshatsha
Kolwezi
Likasi
Kamina
Mitwaba
Kilwa
Sampwe
Pweto
Kawambwa
Mbala
Kasam
Lake Mweru
Lake Bangweulu
Mansa
Mpika
Kasenga
Lubumbashi
Kipushi
Mufulira
Kabunda
Solwezi
Chingola
Kitwe
Ndola
Luanshya
Mkushi
Mwinilunga
Chavuma
Zambezi
Quirima
Cuanza
Luacano
Lumbala Kaquengueo
Luena
Kuito
Munhango
Cangombe
Lumbala Nguimbo
Lukulu
Mongu
Kataba
Ngoma
Lusaka
Kafue
Rufunsa
Zumbo
Kabwe
Petauke
Mumbue
Menongue
Caiundo
Mavinga
Luiana
Cuangar
Rundu
Andara
Luana
Sesheke
Livingstone or Victoria Falls
Zimba
Binga
Kariba
Chinhoyi
Bindura
Harare
Kadoma
Mutoko
Mour Darw
Cabora Bassa Reservoir
Lake Kariba
Benguela
Lucira
Namibe
Xangongo
Ondangwa
Opuwo
Okaukuejo
Kamanjab
Otjiwarongo
Sukses
Karibib
Okahandja
Windhoek
Gobabis
Leonardville
Rehoboth
Kalkrand
Mariental
Gochas
Tses
Keetmanshoop
Seeheim
Grunau
Luderitz
Alexander Bay
Mamuno
Tshwane
Serowe
Mahalapye
Kang
Molepolole
Mochudi
Gaborone
Kanye
Werda
Tshane
Mmabatho
Terra Firma
Kalahari Desert
Tshabong
Hotazel
Upington
Kenhardt
Douglas
Kimberley
Prieska
Carnarvon
De Aar
Beaufort West
Bitterfontein
Paarl
Worcester
Oudtshoorn
Stellenbosch
Cape Town
Uitenhage
Port Elizabeth
Grahamstown
East London
Bisho
Cradock
Graaff-Reinet
Umtata
Kokstad
Durban
Pietermaritzburg
Richards Bay
Ladysmith
Harrismith
Bethlehem
Kroonstad
Welkom
Maseru
Mafeteng
Bloemfontein
Standerton
Orkneyo
Springs
Johannesburg
Benoni
Krugersdorp
Pretoria
Warmbad
Pietersburg
Graskop
Nelspruit
Mbabane
Lobamba
Messina
Pafu
Limpo
Bulawayo
Gweru
Masvinge
Zvishavane
Chiredzi
Plumtree
Francistown
Orapa
Selebi-Phikwe
Rakops
Maun
Nokaneng
Tsau
Lake Ngami
Makgadikgadi Pans (Makarikari)
Hwange
Kamativi
Tsumeb
Otavi
Etosha Pan
Namib Desert
Kaukau Veld
Okavango
Okavango Swamp
Caprivi Strip
Zambezi
Huambo
Matala
Lubango
Cuito
Bie Plateau
Kuanza
Kasai
Kaquengueo
Mwinilunga
Lumbala
Swakopmund
Walvis Bay

2,620m (8,596ft)

2,770m (9,088ft)

Cape Ledo
Cape St. Martha
Albino Point
Foz do Cunene
Cape Columbine
Cape of Good Hope
Cape Agulhas
Cape St. Francis

Tropic of Capricorn

Great Karoo
Drakensberg
Orange
Molopo
Groot
Cunene
Cuango

15°E
20°
25°
30°
10°E
15°
25°
30°
10°S
15°
20°
25°
30°

104

A   B   C   D   E   F
1   2   3   4   5   6

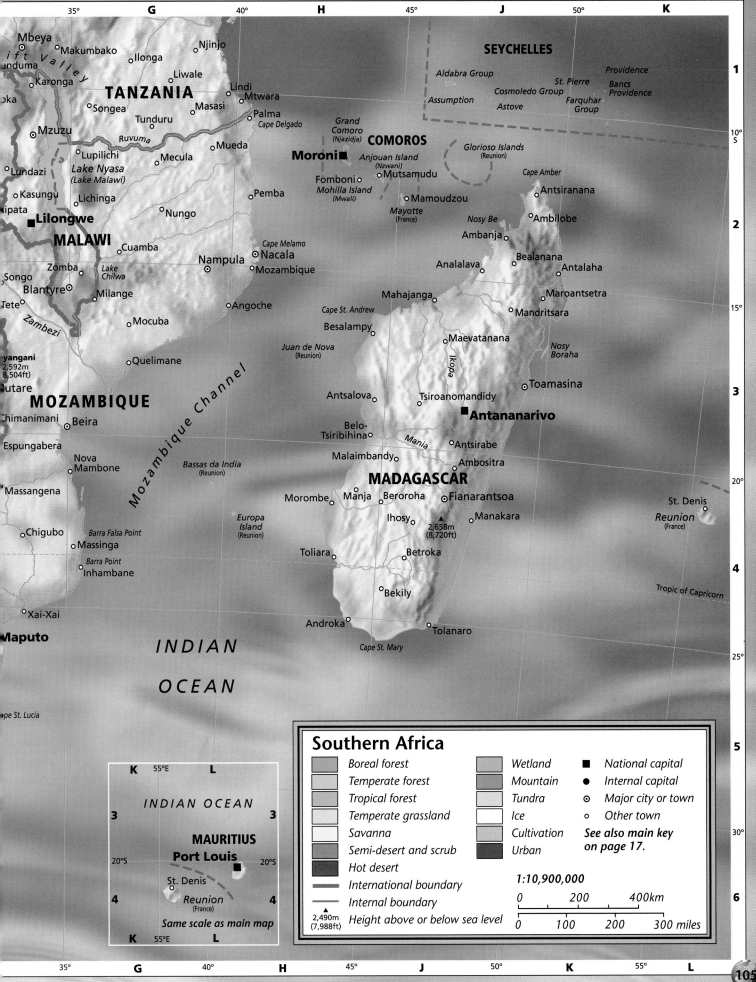

Southern Africa

	Boreal forest		Wetland	■ National capital
	Temperate forest		Mountain	● Internal capital
	Tropical forest		Tundra	⊙ Major city or town
	Temperate grassland		Ice	○ Other town
	Savanna		Cultivation	*See also main key*
	Semi-desert and scrub		Urban	*on page 17.*
	Hot desert			

─── International boundary

─── Internal boundary

▲ 2,490m (7,988ft) Height above or below sea level

1:10,900,000

0   200   400km

0   100   200   300 miles

Map labels (main map):

Mbeya, Makumbako, Njinjo, Ilonga, Liwale, Karonga, **TANZANIA**, Lindi, Songea, Masasi, Mtwara, Tunduru, Palma, Cape Delgado, Mueda, Mzuzu, Ruvuma, Mecula, Lupilichi, Mamoudzou, Lundazi, Lake Nyasa (Lake Malawi), Lichinga, Nungo, Kasungu, ipata, **Lilongwe**, **MALAWI**, Cuamba, Nampula, Nacala, Zomba, Lake Chilwa, Mozambique, Songo, Blantyre, Milange, Cape Melamo, Tete, Mocuba, Angoche, Zambezi, yangani 2,592m 8,504ft, Quelimane, utare, **MOZAMBIQUE**, Chimanimani, Beira, Espungabera, Nova Mambone, Bassas da India (Reunion), Massangena, Chigubo, Barra Falsa Point, Massinga, Barra Point, Inhambane, Xai-Xai, Maputo

SEYCHELLES, Aldabra Group, St. Pierre, Providence, Cosmoledo Group, Bancs Providence, Assumption, Astove, Farquhar Group

Grand Comoro (Njazidja), **COMOROS**, Glorioso Islands (Reunion), **Moroni**, Anjouan Island (Nzwani), Fomboni, Mutsamudu, Cape Amber, Mohilla Island (Mwali), Antsiranana, Mayotte (France), Nosy Be, Ambilobe, Ambanja, Cape St. Andrew, Analalava, Bealanana, Antalaha, Mahajanga, Maroantsetra, Besalampy, Mandritsara, Juan de Nova (Reunion), Maevatanana, Nosy Boraha, Ikopa, Toamasina, Antsalova, Tsiroanomandidy, **Antananarivo**, Belo-Tsiribihina, Mania, Antsirabe, Malaimbandy, Ambositra, **MADAGASCAR**, Morombe, Manja, Beroroha, Fianarantsoa, St. Denis, Reunion (France), Ihosy, Manakara, 2,658m (8,720ft), Toliara, Betroka, Bekily, Tropic of Capricorn, Androka, Tolanaro, Cape St. Mary

INDIAN OCEAN

pe St. Lucia

Inset:

INDIAN OCEAN

MAURITIUS

Port Louis

St. Denis

Reunion (France)

Same scale as main map

55°E, 20°S, K, L

THE ARCTIC AND ANTARCTICA

The Arctic and Antarctica are the world's coldest places. The Arctic is the area around the North Pole, including the Arctic Ocean and the most northerly parts of Europe, North America and Asia. Antarctica is a huge continent at the South Pole.

Frozen island

Within the Arctic is Greenland, the world's largest island. Most Greenlanders live along the rocky coast, as the main body of land is covered in thick ice for most of the year.

The large white area in this satellite image is ice, covering the Arctic Ocean and Greenland. At the top left of the image is the edge of Russia and at the top right is part of Europe.

This is the entrance to Sweden's Arctic ice hotel. The hotel is open in winter, then melts in the spring when the weather gets milder. The next winter, it is built all over again.

Internet links

For a link to a Web site where you can discover all kinds of information about animals that live in the Arctic, such as walruses, snowy owls, polar bears and arctic foxes, go to
www.usborne-quicklinks.com

A hotel of ice

Every winter, a hotel made entirely of ice is built in the far north of Sweden. Each piece of furniture is sculpted from ice, and even the beds are made of ice blocks. Guests sleep in special thermal sleeping bags with animal skins piled on top for extra warmth.

Icy continent

A huge, jagged sheet of ice permanently covers almost all of Antarctica, and spreads out over nearby seas as well. Scientists think that the area in the far west of the continent may be made up of many islands, but it is hard to tell because they are so far beneath the ice.

Mountains run down the middle of Antarctica, and in the west there are volcanoes. Amazingly, one volcano heats the sea near it so much that it is warm enough to swim in.

The darkest shading on this satellite image of Antarctica indicates ice that is over 3km (2 miles) deep.

These penguins are on the coast of Antarctica. They live in the ocean but come onto land to breed.

Life in Antarctica

The temperature in Antarctica can fall as low as -80°C (-112°F) in winter. It is too cold for people to live there, though scientists visit to study the area. No plants grow in the ice, and the only land animals are tiny mites. But many animals live in the seas around Antarctica, including penguins, seals, whales and fish.

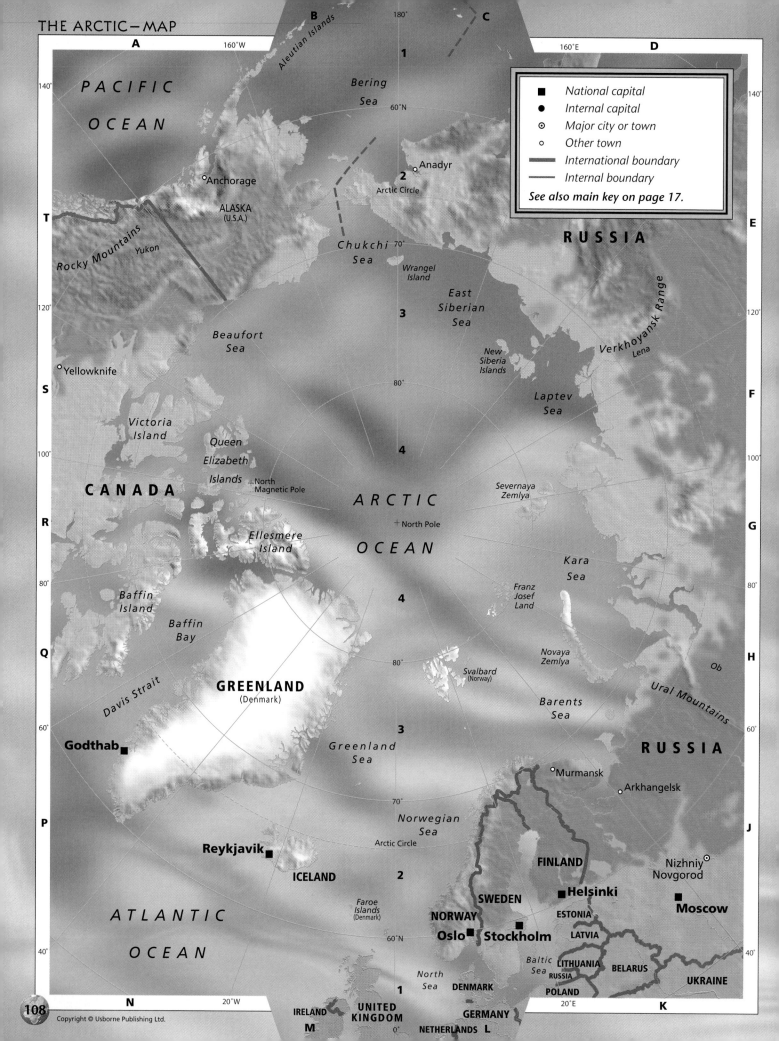

THE ARCTIC—MAP

Key

■	National capital
●	Internal capital
⊙	Major city or town
○	Other town
━━	International boundary
───	Internal boundary

See also main key on page 17.

A   160°W   B   180°   C   160°E   D

PACIFIC OCEAN

Aleutian Islands

Bering Sea

1

60°N

°Anchorage

2   °Anadyr

Arctic Circle

ALASKA (U.S.A.)

RUSSIA   E

Rocky Mountains   Yukon

Chukchi Sea   70°

Wrangel Island

East Siberian Sea

3

Verkhoyansk Range   Lena

Beaufort Sea

New Siberia Islands

Laptev Sea

120°

°Yellowknife

80°

4

F

S

Victoria Island

Queen Elizabeth Islands

CANADA

North Magnetic Pole

Severnaya Zemlya

100°

ARCTIC

+North Pole

OCEAN

R   Ellesmere Island

Kara Sea

G

80°

Baffin Island

Baffin Bay

Franz Josef Land

4

80°

Q   Davis Strait

GREENLAND (Denmark)

Svalbard (Norway)

Novaya Zemlya

Ob

Ural Mountains

H

60°

Godthab ■

3

Barents Sea

RUSSIA

60°

P   Greenland Sea

°Murmansk

°Arkhangelsk

J

40°

70°

Norwegian Sea

Arctic Circle

Reykjavik ■

2

FINLAND

Nizhniy° Novgorod

ICELAND

SWEDEN   Helsinki ■

ATLANTIC

Faroe Islands (Denmark)

ESTONIA

Moscow ■

NORWAY

LATVIA

OCEAN

Oslo ■ Stockholm ■

LITHUANIA

Baltic Sea   RUSSIA   BELARUS

60°N

1

North Sea   DENMARK

POLAND   UKRAINE

N   20°W   IRELAND   UNITED KINGDOM   M   0°   GERMANY   NETHERLANDS   L   20°E   K

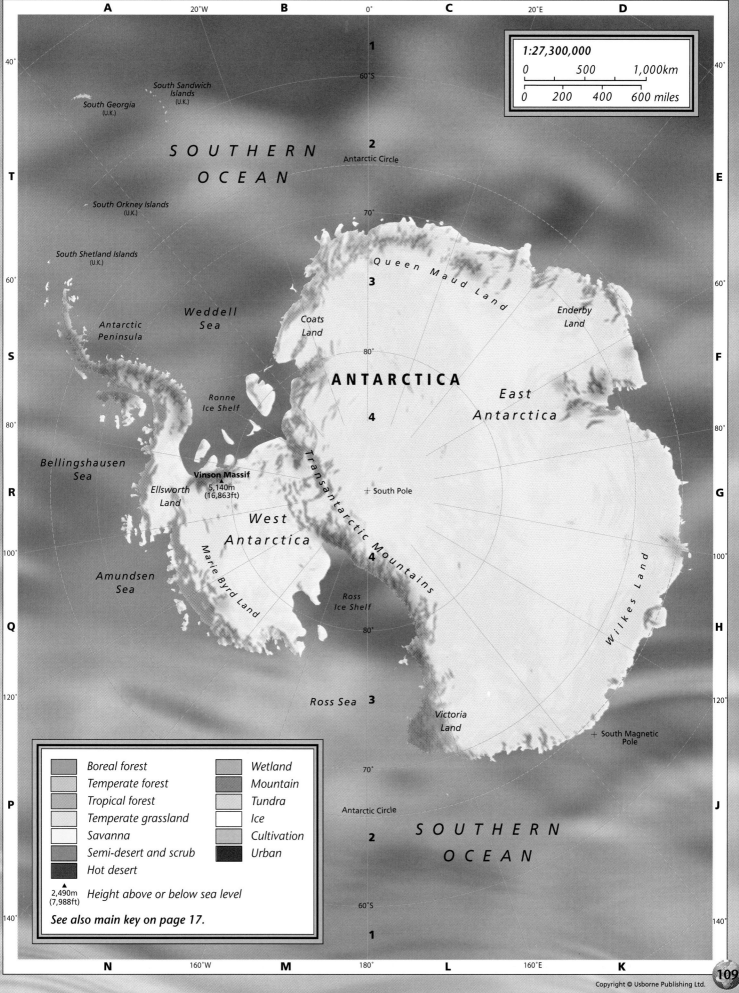

1

1:27,300,000

0	500	1,000km

0	200	400	600 miles

40°

60°S

T

2

Antarctic Circle

70°

S O U T H E R N

O C E A N

South Georgia
(U.K.)

South Sandwich
Islands
(U.K.)

60°

South Orkney Islands
(U.K.)

S

80°

South Shetland Islands
(U.K.)

3

Q u e e n   M a u d   L a n d

Weddell
Sea

Coats
Land

Enderby
Land

Antarctic
Peninsula

ANTARCTICA

East
Antarctica

Ronne
Ice Shelf

4

Bellingshausen
Sea

R

Vinson Massif
▲
5,140m
(16,863ft)

Ellsworth
Land

+ South Pole

G

West
Antarctica

Marie Byrd Land

Amundsen
Sea

Transantarctic Mountains

4

W i l k e s   L a n d

Q

100°

Ross
Ice Shelf

80°

H

Ross Sea

3

120°

Victoria
Land

+ South Magnetic
Pole

P

70°

Antarctic Circle

J

S O U T H E R N

O C E A N

2

60°S

1

▮ Boreal forest		▮ Wetland	
▮ Temperate forest		▮ Mountain	
▮ Tropical forest		▮ Tundra	
▮ Temperate grassland		▮ Ice	
▮ Savanna		▮ Cultivation	
▮ Semi-desert and scrub		▮ Urban	
▮ Hot desert			

▲
2,490m
(7,988ft)   Height above or below sea level

See also main key on page 17.

GEOGRAPHY QUIZ

Test your knowledge of the world's countries, cities, sights and animals with these quiz questions. The answers are on page 129.

The enormous, elaborate church above was designed by a famous Spanish architect named Antonio Gaudí.

Mystery places

Which famous sights are shown in the photographs on this page? Each has clues to help you.

The marble building on the left is one of the Seven Wonders of the World. It was built by an Indian emperor.

This famous steel bridge crosses the bay of a large North American city. It opened in 1937 and for many years was the longest suspension bridge in the world.

This city skyline is dominated by the tallest freestanding structure in the world. Visitors can go up the tower to a glass-bottomed viewing platform and a revolving restaurant. Can you name the tower and the city?

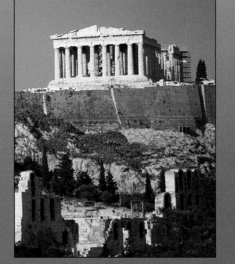

The ruins above are the remains of some of Europe's most important ancient temples and other public buildings.

Quick quiz

1. Which country's flag consists of a red circle on a white background?

2. When it is noon in Britain, what time is it in Mexico?

3. In which country is the Great Victoria Desert?

4. Which continent is the third-largest in the world?

5. In which country is Brno?

6. What is the world's deepest lake?

7. Name the smallest country in Europe.

8. Which country lies between Nicaragua and Panama?

9. In which country would you pay using naira and kobo as currency?

10. What is Turkey's capital city?

Internet links

For a link to a Web site where you can test and improve your knowledge of the countries and cities of the world, go to **www.usborne-quicklinks.com**

Survival challenge

Could you survive in the world's toughest terrains? Take this test to find out.

1. Which of the following would not be very useful on a trip to Antarctica?
a) A warm hat and gloves
b) An umbrella
c) Sunglasses and sunscreen

2. You are in the Sahara Desert and are short of drinking water. What should you do?
a) Stay active, so you produce sweat to cool yourself down.
b) Put on extra clothes and rest as much as possible.
c) Talk and sing songs to keep yourself alert.

3. When on safari in Africa, which of these spiders should you avoid?
a) Six-eyed crab spiders
b) Button spiders
c) Violin spiders

4. You are walking in the Rocky Mountains and meet a grizzly bear. What should you do?
a) Lie on the ground and play dead.
b) Turn and run away as fast as possible.
c) Back away slowly and calmly.

This grizzly bear is in the Rocky Mountains in Utah, U.S.A. Grizzly bears like to keep well away from humans, but will occasionally attack if they feel threatened.

GAZETTEER OF STATES

Afghanistan

Albania

Algeria

Andorra

Angola

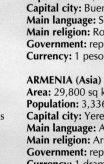
Antigua and Barbuda

• **Argentina**

Armenia

Australia

Austria

Azerbaijan

Bahamas, The

Bahrain

Bangladesh

This gazetteer lists the world's 193 independent states, along with key facts about each one. In the lists of languages, the language that is most widely spoken is given first, even if it is not the official language. In the lists of religions, the one followed by the most people is also placed first. Every state has a national flag, which is usually used to represent the country abroad. A few states also have a state flag which they prefer to use instead. The state flags appear here with a dot beside them.

AFGHANISTAN (Asia)
Area: 647,500 sq km (249,935 sq miles)
Population: 25,838,797
Capital city: Kabul
Main languages: Dari, Pashto
Main religion: Muslim
Government: transitional
Currency: 1 afghani = 100 puls

ALBANIA (Europe)
Area: 28,750 sq km (11,100 sq miles)
Population: 3,510,484
Capital city: Tirana
Main language: Albanian
Main religions: Muslim, Albanian Orthodox
Government: emerging democracy
Currency: 1 lek = 100 qintars

ALGERIA (Africa)
Area: 2,381,740 sq km (919,589 sq miles)
Population: 31,193,917
Capital city: Algiers
Main languages: Arabic, French, Berber dialects
Main religion: Sunni Muslim
Government: republic
Currency: 1 Algerian dinar = 100 centimes

ANDORRA (Europe)
Area: 468 sq km (181 sq miles)
Population: 67,627
Capital city: Andorra la Vella
Main languages: Catalan, Spanish
Main religion: Roman Catholic
Government: parliamentary democracy
Currency: 1 euro = 100 cents

ANGOLA (Africa)
Area: 1,246,700 sq km (481,351 sq miles)
Population: 10,366,031
Capital city: Luanda
Main languages: Kilongo, Kimbundu, other Bantu languages, Portuguese
Main religions: indigenous, Roman Catholic, Protestant
Government: transitional
Currency: 1 kwanza = 100 lwei

ANTIGUA AND BARBUDA (North America)
Area: 442 sq km (171 sq miles)
Population: 66,970
Capital city: Saint John's
Main languages: Caribbean Creole, English
Main religion: Protestant
Government: constitutional monarchy
Currency: 1 East Caribbean dollar = 100 cents

ARGENTINA (South America)
Area: 2,780,400 sq km (1,073,512 sq miles)
Population: 36,955,182
Capital city: Buenos Aires
Main language: Spanish
Main religion: Roman Catholic
Government: republic
Currency: 1 peso = 100 centavos

ARMENIA (Asia)
Area: 29,800 sq km (11,506 sq miles)
Population: 3,336,100
Capital city: Yerevan
Main language: Armenian
Main religion: Armenian Orthodox
Government: republic
Currency: 1 dram = 100 luma

AUSTRALIA (Australasia/Oceania)
Area: 7,686,850 sq km (2,967,124 sq miles)
Population: 19,357,594
Capital city: Canberra
Main language: English
Main religion: Christian
Government: federal democratic monarchy
Currency: 1 Australian dollar = 100 cents

AUSTRIA (Europe)
Area: 83,858 sq km (32,378 sq miles)
Population: 8,150,835
Capital city: Vienna
Main language: German
Main religion: Roman Catholic
Government: federal republic
Currency: 1 euro = 100 cents

Barbados

Belarus

Belgium

Belize

Benin

Bhutan

• **Bolivia**

AZERBAIJAN (Asia)
Area: 86,600 sq km (33,436 sq miles)
Population: 7,771,092
Capital city: Baku
Main language: Azeri
Main religion: Muslim
Government: republic
Currency: 1 manat = 100 gopiks

BAHAMAS, THE (North America)
Area: 13,940 sq km (5,382 sq miles)
Population: 297,852
Capital city: Nassau
Main languages: Bahamian Creole, English
Main religion: Christian
Government: parliamentary democracy
Currency: 1 Bahamian dollar = 100 cents

BAHRAIN (Asia)
Area: 678 sq km (261 sq miles)
Population: 645,361
Capital city: Manama
Main languages: Arabic, English
Main religion: Muslim
Government: traditional monarchy
Currency: 1 Bahraini dinar = 1,000 fils

BANGLADESH (Asia)
Area: 144,000 sq km (55,598 sq miles)
Population: 131,269,860
Capital city: Dhaka
Main languages: Bengali, English
Main religions: Muslim, Hindu
Government: republic
Currency: 1 taka = 100 poisha

BARBADOS (North America)
Area: 430 sq km (166 sq miles)
Population: 275,330
Capital city: Bridgetown
Main languages: Bajan, English
Main religion: Christian
Government: parliamentary democracy
Currency: 1 Barbadian dollar = 100 cents

BELARUS (Europe)
Area: 207,600 sq km (80,154 sq miles)
Population: 10,350,194
Capital city: Minsk
Main language: Belarusian
Main religion: Eastern Orthodox
Government: republic
Currency: 1 Belarusian ruble = 100 kopecks

BELGIUM (Europe)
Area: 30,510 sq km (11,780 sq miles)
Population: 10,258,762
Capital city: Brussels
Main languages: Dutch, French
Main religions: Roman Catholic, Protestant
Government: constitutional monarchy
Currency: 1 euro = 100 cents

BELIZE (North America)
Area: 22,960 sq km (8,865 sq miles)
Population: 256,062
Capital city: Belmopan
Main languages: Spanish, Belize Creole,
English, Garifuna, Maya

Main religions: Roman Catholic, Protestant
Government: parliamentary democracy
Currency: 1 Belizean dollar = 100 cents

BENIN (Africa)
Area: 112,620 sq km (43,483 sq miles)
Population: 6,590,782
Capital city: Porto-Novo
Main languages: Fon, French, Yoruba
Main religions: indigenous, Christian, Muslim
Government: republic
Currency: 1 CFA* franc = 100 centimes

BHUTAN (Asia)
Area: 47,000 sq km (18,146 sq miles)
Population: 2,049,412
Capital city: Thimphu
Main languages: Dzongkha, Nepali
Main religions: Muslim, Hindu
Government: monarchy
Currency: 1 ngultrum = 100 chetrum

BOLIVIA (South America)
Area: 1,098,580 sq km (424,162 sq miles)
Population: 8,300,463
Capital cities: La Paz, Sucre
Main languages: Spanish, Quechua, Aymara
Main religion: Roman Catholic
Government: republic
Currency: 1 boliviano = 100 centavos

BOSNIA AND HERZEGOVINA (Europe)
Area: 51,129 sq km (19,741 sq miles)
Population: 3,922,205
Capital city: Sarajevo
Main languages: Bosnian, Serbian, Croatian
Main religions: Muslim, Orthodox, Roman
Catholic
Government: emerging federal democracy
Currency: 1 marka = 100 pfenninga

BOTSWANA (Africa)
Area: 600,372 sq km (231,743 sq miles)
Population: 1,586,119
Capital city: Gaborone
Main languages: Setswana, Kalanga,
English
Main religions: indigenous, Christian
Government: parliamentary republic
Currency: 1 pula = 100 thebe

BRAZIL (South America)
Area: 8,547,400 sq km (3,300,151 sq miles)
Population: 174,468,575
Capital city: Brasilia
Main language: Portuguese
Main religion: Roman Catholic
Government: federal republic
Currency: 1 real = 100 centavos

BRUNEI (Asia)
Area: 5,770 sq km (2,228 sq miles)
Population: 343,653
Capital city: Bandar Seri Begawan
Main languages: Malay, English, Chinese
Main religions: Muslim, Buddhist
Government: constitutional sultanate (a type
of monarchy)
Currency: 1 Bruneian dollar = 100 cents

**Bosnia and
Herzegovina**

Botswana

Brazil

Brunei

Bulgaria

Burkina Faso

Burma (Myanmar)

113

GAZETTEER OF STATES CONTINUED:

Burundi

Cambodia

Cameroon

Canada

Cape Verde

Central African Republic

Chad

BULGARIA (Europe)
Area: 110,910 sq km (42,822 sq miles)
Population: 7,707,495
Capital city: Sofia
Main language: Bulgarian
Main religions: Bulgarian Orthodox, Muslim
Government: republic
Currency: 1 lev = 100 stotinki

BURKINA FASO (Africa)
Area: 274,200 sq km (105,869 sq miles)
Population: 12,272,289
Capital city: Ouagadougou
Main languages: Moore, Jula, French
Main religions: Muslim, indigenous
Government: republic
Currency: 1 CFA* franc = 100 centimes

BURMA (MYANMAR) (Asia)
Area: 678,500 sq km (261,969 sq miles)
Population: 50,438,300
Capital city: Rangoon
Main language: Burmese
Main religion: Buddhist
Government: military dictatorship
Currency: 1 kyat = 100 pyas

BURUNDI (Africa)
Area: 27,830 sq km (10,745 sq miles)
Population: 6,223,897
Capital city: Bujumbura
Main languages: Kirundi, French, Swahili
Main religions: Christian, indigenous
Government: republic
Currency: 1 Burundi franc = 100 centimes

CAMBODIA (Asia)
Area: 181,040 sq km (69,900 sq miles)
Population: 12,491,501
Capital city: Phnom Penh
Main language: Khmer
Main religion: Buddhist
Government: constitutional monarchy
Currency: 1 new riel = 100 sen

CAMEROON (Africa)
Area: 475,440 sq km (183,567 sq miles)
Population: 15,803,220
Capital city: Yaounde
Main languages: Cameroon Pidgin English, Ewondo, Fula, French, English
Main religions: indigenous, Christian, Muslim
Government: republic
Currency: 1 CFA* franc = 100 centimes

CANADA (North America)
Area: 9,970,610 sq km (3,849,653 sq miles)
Population: 31,592,805
Capital city: Ottawa
Main languages: English, French
Main religions: Roman Catholic, Protestant
Government: federal democracy
Currency: 1 Canadian dollar = 100 cents

CAPE VERDE (Africa)
Area: 4,033 sq km (1,557 sq miles)
Population: 405,163
Capital city: Praia
Main languages: Crioulo*, Portuguese

Main religions: Roman Catholic, Protestant
Government: republic
Currency: 1 Cape Verdean escudo = 100 centavos

CENTRAL AFRICAN REPUBLIC (Africa)
Area: 622,436 sq km (240,322 sq miles)
Population: 3,576,884
Capital city: Bangui
Main languages: Sangho, French
Main religions: indigenous, Christian, Muslim
Government: republic
Currency: 1 CFA* franc = 100 centimes

CHAD (Africa)
Area: 1,284,000 sq km (495,752 sq miles)
Population: 8,707,078
Capital city: Ndjamena
Main languages: Arabic, Sara, French
Main religions: Muslim, Christian, indigenous
Government: republic
Currency: 1 CFA* franc = 100 centimes

CHILE (South America)
Area: 756,626 sq km (292,133 sq miles)
Population: 15,328,467
Capital city: Santiago
Main language: Spanish
Main religions: Roman Catholic, Protestant
Government: republic
Currency: 1 Chilean peso = 100 centavos

CHINA (Asia)
Area: 9,596,960 sq km (3,705,386 sq miles)
Population: 1,273,111,290
Capital city: Beijing
Main languages: Mandarin Chinese, Yue, Wu
Main religions: Taoist, Buddhist
Government: Communist state
Currency: 1 yuan = 10 jiao

COLOMBIA (South America)
Area: 1,138,910 sq km (439,733 sq miles)
Population: 40,349,388
Capital city: Bogota
Main language: Spanish
Main religion: Roman Catholic
Government: republic
Currency: 1 Colombian peso = 100 centavos

COMOROS (Africa)
Area: 1,862 sq km (719 sq miles)
Population: 596,202
Capital city: Moroni
Main languages: Comorian*, French, Arabic
Main religion: Sunni Muslim
Government: republic
Currency: 1 Comoran franc = 100 centimes

CONGO (Africa)
Area: 342,000 sq km (132,046 sq miles)
Population: 2,894,336
Capital city: Brazzaville
Main languages: Munukutuba, Lingala, French
Main religions: Christian, animist
Government: republic
Currency: 1 CFA* franc = 100 centimes

Chile

China

Colombia

Comoros

Congo

Congo (Democratic Republic)

Costa Rica

*CFA = Communaute Financiere Africaine; Comorian = a blend of Swahili and Arabic; Crioulo = a blend of Portuguese and West African

Croatia

Cuba

Cyprus

Czech Republic

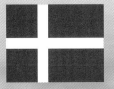

Denmark

Djibouti

Dominica

CONGO (DEMOCRATIC REPUBLIC) (Africa)
Area: 2,345,410 sq km (905,563 sq miles)
Population: 53,624,718
Capital city: Kinshasa
Main languages: Lingala, Swahili, Kikongo, Tshiluba, French
Main religions: Roman Catholic, Protestant, Kimbanguist, Muslim
Government: transitional
Currency: 1 Congolese franc = 100 centimes

COSTA RICA (North America)
Area: 51,100 sq km (19,730 sq miles)
Population: 3,773,057
Capital city: San Jose
Main language: Spanish
Main religions: Roman Catholic, Evangelical
Government: democratic republic
Currency: 1 Costa Rican colon = 100 centimos

CROATIA (Europe)
Area: 56,538 sq km (21,829 sq miles)
Population: 4,334,142
Capital city: Zagreb
Main language: Croatian
Main religions: Roman Catholic, Orthodox
Government: parliamentary democracy
Currency: 1 kuna = 100 lipas

CUBA (North America)
Area: 110,860 sq km (42,803 sq miles)
Population: 11,184,023
Capital city: Havana
Main language: Spanish
Main religion: Roman Catholic
Government: Communist state
Currency: 1 Cuban peso = 100 centavos

CYPRUS (Europe)
Area: 9,250 sq km (3,571 sq miles)
Population: 762,887
Capital city: Nicosia
Main languages: Greek, Turkish
Main religions: Greek Orthodox, Muslim
Government: republic with a self-proclaimed independent Turkish area
Currency: Greek Cypriot area: 1 Cypriot pound = 100 cents; Turkish Cypriot area: 1 Turkish lira = 100 kurus

CZECH REPUBLIC (Europe)
Area: 78,866 sq km (30,450 sq miles)
Population: 10,264,212
Capital city: Prague
Main language: Czech
Main religion: Roman Catholic
Government: parliamentary democracy
Currency: 1 koruna = 100 haleru

DENMARK (Europe)
Area: 43,094 sq km (16,639 sq miles)
Population: 5,352,815
Capital city: Copenhagen
Main language: Danish
Main religion: Evangelical Lutheran
Government: constitutional monarchy
Currency: 1 Danish krone = 100 oere

DJIBOUTI (Africa)
Area: 23,200 sq km (8,957 sq miles)
Population: 460,700
Capital city: Djibouti
Main languages: Afar, Somali, Arabic, French
Main religion: Muslim
Government: republic
Currency: 1 Djiboutian franc = 100 centimes

DOMINICA (North America)
Area: 751 sq km (290 sq miles)
Population: 70,786
Capital city: Roseau
Main languages: English, French patois
Main religions: Roman Catholic, Protestant
Government: democratic republic
Currency: 1 East Caribbean dollar = 100 cents

DOMINICAN REPUBLIC (North America)
Area: 48,511 sq km (18,731 sq miles)
Population: 8,581,477
Capital city: Santo Domingo
Main language: Spanish
Main religion: Roman Catholic
Government: democratic republic
Currency: 1 Dominican peso = 100 centavos

EAST TIMOR (Asia)
Area: 24,000 sq km (9,266 sq miles)
Population: 737,811
Capital city: Dili
Main languages: Tetun (Tetum), Bahasa Indonesia, Portuguese
Main religions: Roman Catholic, animist
Government: republic
Currency: 1 U.S. dollar = 100 cents

ECUADOR (South America)
Area: 283,560 sq km (109,483 sq miles)
Population: 13,183,978
Capital city: Quito
Main languages: Spanish, Quechua
Main religion: Roman Catholic
Government: republic
Currency: 1 sucre = 100 centavos

EGYPT (Africa)
Area: 1,001,450 sq km (386,660 sq miles)
Population: 69,536,644
Capital city: Cairo
Main language: Arabic
Main religion: Sunni Muslim
Government: republic
Currency: 1 Egyptian pound = 100 piasters

EL SALVADOR (North America)
Area: 21,040 sq km (8,124 sq miles)
Population: 6,237,662
Capital city: San Salvador
Main language: Spanish
Main religion: Roman Catholic
Government: republic
Currency: 1 Salvadoran colon = 100 centavos

EQUATORIAL GUINEA (Africa)
Area: 28,050 sq km (10,830 sq miles)
Population: 486,060
Capital city: Malabo
Main languages: Fang, Bubi, other Bantu

• **Dominican Republic**

East Timor

• **Ecuador**

Egypt

• **El Salvador**

Equatorial Guinea

Eritrea

GAZETTEER OF STATES CONTINUED:

Estonia

Ethiopia

Federated States of Micronesia

Fiji

Finland

France

Gabon

languages, Spanish, French, Pidgin English
Main religion: Christian
Government: republic
Currency: 1 CFA* franc = 100 centimes

ERITREA (Africa)
Area: 117,600 sq km (45,405 sq miles)
Population: 4,298,269
Capital city: Asmara
Main languages: Tigrinya, Afar, Arabic
Main religions: Muslim, Coptic Christian, Roman Catholic, Protestant
Government: transitional
Currency: 1 nafka = 100 cents

ESTONIA (Europe)
Area: 45,226 sq km (17,462 sq miles)
Population: 1,423,316
Capital city: Tallinn
Main languages: Estonian, Russian
Main religions: Evangelical Lutheran, Russian and Estonian Orthodox, other Christian
Government: parliamentary democracy
Currency: 1 Estonian kroon = 100 senti

ETHIOPIA (Africa)
Area: 1,127,127 sq km (435,184 sq miles)
Population: 65,891,874
Capital city: Addis Ababa
Main languages: Amharic, Tigrinya, Arabic
Main religions: Muslim, Ethiopian Orthodox, animist
Government: federal republic
Currency: 1 birr = 100 cents

FEDERATED STATES OF MICRONESIA (Australasia/Oceania)
Area: 702 sq km (271 sq miles)
Population: 134,597
Capital city: Palikir
Main languages: Chuuk, Ponapean, English
Main religions: Roman Catholic, Protestant
Government: democracy
Currency: 1 U.S. dollar = 100 cents

FIJI (Australasia/Oceania)
Area: 18,270 sq km (7,054 sq miles)
Population: 844,330
Capital city: Suva
Main languages: Fijian, Hindustani, English
Main religions: Christian, Hindu
Government: republic
Currency: 1 Fijian dollar = 100 cents

FINLAND (Europe)
Area: 337,030 sq km (130,127 sq miles)
Population: 5,175,783
Capital city: Helsinki
Main language: Finnish
Main religion: Evangelical Lutheran
Government: republic
Currency: 1 euro = 100 cents

FRANCE (Europe)
Area: 547,030 sq km (211,208 sq miles)
Population: 59,551,227
Capital city: Paris
Main language: French

Main religion: Roman Catholic
Government: republic
Currency: 1 euro = 100 cents

GABON (Africa)
Area: 267,670 sq km (103,347 sq miles)
Population: 1,221,175
Capital city: Libreville
Main languages: Fang, Myene, French
Main religions: Christian, animist
Government: republic
Currency: 1 CFA* franc = 100 centimes

GAMBIA, THE (Africa)
Area: 11,300 sq km (4,363 sq miles)
Population: 1,411,205
Capital city: Banjul
Main languages: Mandinka, Fula, Wolof, English
Main religion: Muslim
Government: democratic republic
Currency: 1 dalasi = 100 butut

GEORGIA (Asia)
Area: 69,700 sq km (26,911 sq miles)
Population: 4,989,285
Capital city: Tbilisi
Main languages: Georgian, Russian
Main religions: Georgian Orthodox, Muslim, Russian Orthodox
Government: republic
Currency: 1 lari = 100 tetri

GERMANY (Europe)
Area: 357,021 sq km (137,846 sq miles)
Population: 83,029,536
Capital city: Berlin
Main language: German
Main religions: Protestant, Roman Catholic
Government: federal republic
Currency: 1 euro = 100 cents

GHANA (Africa)
Area: 238,540 sq km (92,100 sq miles)
Population: 19,894,014
Capital city: Accra
Main languages: Twi, Fante, Ga, Hausa, Dagbani, Ewe, Nzemi, English
Main religions: indigenous, Muslim, Christian
Government: democratic republic
Currency: 1 new cedi = 100 pesewas

GREECE (Europe)
Area: 131,940 sq km (50,942 sq miles)
Population: 10,623,835
Capital city: Athens
Main language: Greek
Main religion: Greek Orthodox
Government: parliamentary republic
Currency: 1 euro = 100 cents

GRENADA (North America)
Area: 340 sq km (131 sq miles)
Population: 89,227
Capital city: Saint George's
Main languages: English, French patois
Main religions: Roman Catholic, Protestant
Government: constitutional monarchy
Currency: 1 East Caribbean dollar = 100 cents

Gambia, The

Georgia

Germany

Ghana

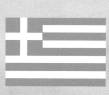

Greece

Grenada

Guatemala

*CFA = Communaute Financiere Africaine

Guinea

Guinea-Bissau

Guyana

• Haiti

Honduras

Hungary

Iceland

GUATEMALA (North America)
Area: 108,890 sq km (42,042 sq miles)
Population: 12,974,361
Capital city: Guatemala City
Main languages: Spanish, Amerindian languages including Quiche, Kekchi, Cakchiquel, Mam
Main religions: Roman Catholic, Protestant, indigenous Mayan beliefs
Government: democratic republic
Currency: 1 quetzal = 100 centavos

GUINEA (Africa)
Area: 245,860 sq km (94,927 sq miles)
Population: 7,613,870
Capital city: Conakry
Main languages: Fuuta Jalon, Mallinke, Susu, French
Main religion: Muslim
Government: republic
Currency: 1 Guinean franc = 100 centimes

GUINEA-BISSAU (Africa)
Area: 36,120 sq km (13,946 sq miles)
Population: 1,315,822
Capital city: Bissau
Main languages: Crioulo*, Balante, Pulaar, Mandjak, Mandinka, Portuguese
Main religions: indigenous, Muslim
Government: republic
Currency: 1 CFA* franc = 100 centimes

GUYANA (South America)
Area: 214,970 sq km (83,000 sq miles)
Population: 697,181
Capital city: Georgetown
Main languages: Guyanese Creole, English, Amerindian languages, Caribbean Hindi
Main religions: Christian, Hindu
Government: republic
Currency: 1 Guyanese dollar = 100 cents

HAITI (North America)
Area: 27,750 sq km (10,714 sq miles)
Population: 6,964,549
Capital city: Port-au-Prince
Main languages: Haitian Creole, French
Main religions: Roman Catholic, Protestant, Voodoo
Government: republic
Currency: 1 gourde = 100 centimes

HONDURAS (North America)
Area: 112,090 sq km (43,278 sq miles)
Population: 6,406,052
Capital city: Tegucigalpa
Main language: Spanish
Main religion: Roman Catholic
Government: republic
Currency: 1 lempira = 100 centavos

HUNGARY (Europe)
Area: 93,030 sq km (35,919 sq miles)
Population: 10,106,017
Capital city: Budapest
Main language: Hungarian
Main religions: Roman Catholic, Calvinist
Government: parliamentary democracy
Currency: 1 forint = 100 filler

ICELAND (Europe)
Area: 103,000 sq km (39,768 sq miles)
Population: 277,906
Capital city: Reykjavik
Main language: Icelandic
Main religion: Evangelical Lutheran
Government: republic
Currency: 1 Icelandic krona = 100 aurar

INDIA (Asia)
Area: 3,287,590 sq km (1,269,339 sq miles)
Population: 1,029,991,145
Capital city: New Delhi
Main languages: Hindi, English, Bengali, Urdu, over 1,600 other languages and dialects
Main religions: Hindu, Muslim
Government: federal republic
Currency: 1 Indian rupee = 100 paise

INDONESIA (Asia)
Area: 1,919,440 sq km (741,096 sq miles)
Population: 228,437,870
Capital city: Jakarta
Main languages: Bahasa Indonesia, English, Dutch, Javanese
Main religion: Muslim
Government: republic
Currency: 1 Indonesian rupiah = 100 sen

IRAN (Asia)
Area: 1,648,000 sq km (636,293 sq miles)
Population: 66,128,965
Capital city: Tehran
Main languages: Farsi and other Persian dialects, Azeri
Main religions: Shi'a Muslim, Sunni Muslim
Government: Islamic republic
Currency: 10 Iranian rials = 1 toman

IRAQ (Asia)
Area: 437,072 sq km (168,754 sq miles)
Population: 23,331,985
Capital city: Baghdad
Main languages: Arabic, Kurdish
Main religion: Muslim
Government: republic under a military regime
Currency: 1 Iraqi dinar = 1,000 fils

IRELAND (Europe)
Area: 70,280 sq km (27,135 sq miles)
Population: 3,840,838
Capital city: Dublin
Main languages: English, Irish (Gaelic)
Main religion: Roman Catholic
Government: republic
Currency: 1 euro = 100 cents

ISRAEL (Asia)
Area: 20,770 sq km (8,019 sq miles)
Population: 5,938,093
Capital city: Jerusalem
Main languages: Hebrew, Arabic
Main religions: Jewish, Muslim
Government: parliamentary democracy
Currency: 1 Israeli shekel = 100 agorot

ITALY (Europe)
Area: 301,230 sq km (116,305 sq miles)

India

Indonesia

Iran

Iraq

Ireland

Israel

Italy

*CFA = Communaute Financiere Africaine;
Crioulo = a blend of Portuguese and West African

GAZETTEER OF STATES CONTINUED:

Ivory Coast

Population: 57,679,825
Capital city: Rome
Main language: Italian
Main religion: Roman Catholic
Government: republic
Currency: 1 euro = 100 cents

Jamaica

IVORY COAST (Africa)
Area: 322,460 sq km (124,502 sq miles)
Population: 16,393,221
Capital city: Yamoussoukro
Main languages: Baoule, Dioula, French
Main religions: Christian, Muslim, animist
Government: republic
Currency: 1 CFA* = 100 centimes

Japan

JAMAICA (North America)
Area: 10,990 sq km (4,243 sq miles)
Population: 2,665,636
Capital city: Kingston
Main languages: Southwestern Caribbean Creole, English
Main religion: Protestant
Government: parliamentary democracy
Currency: 1 Jamaican dollar = 100 cents

Jordan

JAPAN (Asia)
Area: 377,835 sq km (145,882 sq miles)
Population: 126,771,662
Capital city: Tokyo
Main language: Japanese
Main religions: Shinto, Buddhist
Government: constitutional monarchy
Currency: 1 yen = 100 sen

Kazakhstan

JORDAN (Asia)
Area: 92,190 sq km (35,585 sq miles)
Population: 5,153,378
Capital city: Amman
Main languages: Arabic, English
Main religion: Sunni Muslim
Government: constitutional monarchy
Currency: 1 Jordanian dinar = 1,000 fils

KAZAKHSTAN (Asia)
Area: 2,717,300 sq km (1,049,150 sq miles)
Population: 16,731,303
Capital city: Astana
Main languages: Kazakh, Russian
Main religions: Muslim, Russian Orthodox
Government: republic
Currency: 1 Kazakhstani tenge = 100 tiyn

Kenya

KENYA (Africa)
Area: 582,650 sq km (224,961 sq miles)
Population: 30,765,916
Capital city: Nairobi
Main languages: Swahili, English, Bantu languages
Main religions: Christian, indigenous
Government: republic
Currency: 1 Kenyan shilling = 100 cents

Kiribati

KIRIBATI (Australasia/Oceania)
Area: 717 sq km (277 sq miles)
Population: 94,149
Capital city: Bairiki (on Tarawa island)
Main languages: Gilbertese, English
Main religions: Roman Catholic, Protestant

Government: republic
Currency: 1 Australian dollar = 100 cents

KUWAIT (Asia)
Area: 17,820 sq km (6,880 sq miles)
Population: 2,041,961
Capital city: Kuwait City
Main languages: Arabic, English
Main religion: Muslim
Government: monarchy
Currency: 1 Kuwaiti dinar = 1,000 fils

Kuwait

KYRGYZSTAN (Asia)
Area: 198,500 sq km (76,641 sq miles)
Population: 4,753,003
Capital city: Bishkek
Main languages: Kyrgyz, Russian
Main religions: Muslim, Russian Orthodox
Government: republic
Currency: 1 Kyrgyzstani som = 100 tyiyn

Kyrgyzstan

LAOS (Asia)
Area: 236,800 sq km (91,428 sq miles)
Population: 5,638,967
Capital city: Vientiane
Main languages: Lao, French, English
Main religions: Buddhist, animist
Government: Communist state
Currency: 1 new kip = 100 at

Laos

LATVIA (Europe)
Area: 64,589 sq km (24,938 sq miles)
Population: 2,385,231
Capital city: Riga
Main languages: Latvian, Russian
Main religions: Lutheran, Roman Catholic, Russian Orthodox
Government: parliamentary democracy
Currency: 1 Latvian lat = 100 santims

Latvia

LEBANON (Asia)
Area: 10,400 sq km (4,015 sq miles)
Population: 3,627,774
Capital city: Beirut
Main languages: Arabic, French, English
Main religions: Muslim, Christian
Government: republic
Currency: 1 Lebanese pound = 100 piasters

Lebanon

LESOTHO (Africa)
Area: 30,350 sq km (11,718 sq miles)
Population: 2,177,062
Capital cities: Maseru, Lobamba
Main languages: Sesotho, English, Zulu, Xhosa
Main religions: Christian, indigenous
Government: constitutional monarchy
Currency: 1 loti = 100 lisente

Lesotho

LIBERIA (Africa)
Area: 111,370 sq km (43,000 sq miles)
Population: 3,225,837
Capital city: Monrovia
Main languages: Kpelle, English, Bassa
Main religions: indigenous, Christian, Muslim
Government: republic
Currency: 1 Liberian dollar = 100 cents

LIBYA (Africa)
Area: 1,759,540 sq km (679,358 sq miles)

Liberia

*CFA = Communaute Financiere Africaine

Libya

Population: 5,240,599
Capital city: Tripoli
Main languages: Arabic, Italian, English
Main religion: Sunni Muslim
Government: military rule
Currency: 1 Libyan dinar = 1,000 dirhams

Liechtenstein

LIECHTENSTEIN (Europe)
Area: 160 sq km (62 sq miles)
Population: 32,528
Capital city: Vaduz
Main languages: German, Alemannic
Main religion: Roman Catholic
Government: constitutional monarchy
Currency: 1 Swiss franc = 100 centimes

Lithuania

LITHUANIA (Europe)
Area: 65,200 sq km (25,174 sq miles)
Population: 3,610,535
Capital city: Vilnius
Main languages: Lithuanian, Polish, Russian
Main religions: Roman Catholic, Lutheran, Russian Orthodox
Government: democracy
Currency: 1 Lithuanian litas = 100 centas

Luxembourg

LUXEMBOURG (Europe)
Area: 2,586 sq km (998 sq miles)
Population: 442,972
Capital city: Luxembourg
Main languages: Luxemburgish, German, French
Main religion: Roman Catholic
Government: constitutional monarchy
Currency: 1 euro = 100 cents

Macedonia

MACEDONIA (Europe)
Area: 25,333 sq km (9,781 sq miles)
Population: 2,046,209
Capital city: Skopje
Main languages: Macedonian, Albanian
Main religions: Macedonian Orthodox, Muslim
Government: emerging democracy
Currency: 1 Macedonian denar = 100 deni

Madagascar

MADAGASCAR (Africa)
Area: 587,040 sq km (226,656 sq miles)
Population: 15,982,563
Capital city: Antananarivo
Main languages: Malagasy, French
Main religions: indigenous beliefs, Christian
Government: republic
Currency: 1 Malagasy franc = 100 centimes

Malawi

MALAWI (Africa)
Area: 118,480 sq km (45,745 sq miles)
Population: 10,548,250
Capital city: Lilongwe
Main languages: Chichewa, English
Main religions: Protestant, Roman Catholic, Muslim
Government: parliamentary democracy
Currency: 1 Malawian kwacha = 100 tambala

MALAYSIA (Asia)
Area: 329,750 sq km (127,316 sq miles)
Population: 22,229,040
Capital city: Kuala Lumpur

Main languages: Bahasa Melayu, English, Chinese dialects, Tamil
Main religions: Muslim, Buddhist, Daoist
Government: constitutional monarchy
Currency: 1 ringgit = 100 sen

MALDIVES (Asia)
Area: 300 sq km (116 sq miles)
Population: 310,764
Capital city: Male
Main languages: Maldivian, English
Main religion: Sunni Muslim
Government: republic
Currency: 1 rufiyaa = 100 laari

MALI (Africa)
Area: 1,240,000 sq km (478,764 sq miles)
Population: 11,008,518
Capital city: Bamako
Main languages: Bambara, Fulani, Songhai, French
Main religion: Muslim
Government: republic
Currency: 1 CFA* franc = 100 centimes

MALTA (Europe)
Area: 316 sq km (122 sq miles)
Population: 394,583
Capital city: Valletta
Main languages: Maltese, English
Main religion: Roman Catholic
Government: democratic republic
Currency: 1 Maltese lira = 100 cents

MARSHALL ISLANDS (Australasia/Oceania)
Area: 181 sq km (70 sq miles)
Population: 70,822
Capital city: Majuro
Main languages: Marshallese, English
Main religion: Protestant
Government: republic
Currency: 1 U.S. dollar = 100 cents

MAURITANIA (Africa)
Area: 1,030,700 sq km (397,953 sq miles)
Population: 2,747,312
Capital city: Nouakchott
Main languages: Arabic, Wolof, French
Main religion: Muslim
Government: republic
Currency: 1 ouguiya = 5 khoums

MAURITIUS (Africa)
Area: 1,860 sq km (718 sq miles)
Population: 1,189,825
Capital city: Port Louis
Main languages: Mauritius Creole French, French, Hindi, Bhojpuri, Urdu, Tamil, English
Main religions: Hindu, Christian, English
Government: parliamentary democracy
Currency: 1 Mauritian rupee = 100 cents

MEXICO (North America)
Area: 1,972,550 sq km (761,602 sq miles)
Population: 101,879,171
Capital city: Mexico City
Main languages: Spanish, Mayan, Nahuatl

Malaysia

Maldives

Mali

Malta

Marshall Islands

Mauritania

Mauritius

*CFA = Communaute Financiere Africaine

GAZETTEER OF STATES CONTINUED:

Mexico

Main religion: Roman Catholic
Government: federal republic
Currency: 1 New Mexican peso = 100 centavos

Moldova

MOLDOVA (Europe)
Area: 33,843 sq km (13,067 sq miles)
Population: 4,431,570
Capital city: Chisinau
Main languages: Moldovan, Russian, Gagauz
Main religion: Eastern Orthodox
Government: republic
Currency: 1 Moldovan leu = 100 bani

Monaco

MONACO (Europe)
Area: 1.95 sq km (0.75 sq miles)
Population: 31,842
Capital city: Monaco
Main languages: French, Monegasque, Italian
Main religion: Roman Catholic
Government: constitutional monarchy
Currency: 1 euro = 100 cents

Mongolia

MONGOLIA (Asia)
Area: 1,565,000 sq km (604,247 sq miles)
Population: 2,654,999
Capital city: Ulan Bator
Main language: Khalkha Mongol
Main religion: Tibetan Buddist Lamaist
Government: republic
Currency: 1 tugrik = 100 mongos

Morocco

MOROCCO (Africa)
Area: 446,550 sq km (172,413 sq miles)
Population: 30,645,305
Capital city: Rabat
Main languages: Arabic, Berber, French
Main religion: Muslim
Government: constitutional monarchy
Currency: 1 Moroccan dirham = 100 centimes

Mozambique

MOZAMBIQUE (Africa)
Area: 801,590 sq km (309,494 sq miles)
Population: 19,371,057
Capital city: Maputo
Main languages: Makua, Tsonga, Portuguese
Main religions: indigenous, Christian, Muslim
Government: republic
Currency: 1 metical = 100 centavos

NAMIBIA (Africa)
Area: 825,418 sq km (318,694 sq miles)
Population: 1,797,677
Capital city: Windhoek
Main languages: Afrikaans, German, English
Main religions: Christian, indigenous
Government: republic
Currency: 1 Namibian dollar = 100 cents

Namibia

NAURU (Australasia/Oceania)
Area: 21 sq km (8 sq miles)
Population: 12,088
Capital: Yaren
Main languages: Nauruan, English
Main religion: Christian
Government: republic
Currency: 1 Australian dollar = 100 cents

NEPAL (Asia)
Area: 147,181 sq km (56,827 sq miles)
Population: 25,284,463
Capital city: Kathmandu
Main languages: Nepali, Maithili
Main religions: Hindu, Buddhist
Government: constitutional monarchy
Currency: 1 Nepalese rupee = 100 paisa

NETHERLANDS (Europe)
Area: 41,532 sq km (16,036 sq miles)
Population: 15,981,472
Capital cities: Amsterdam, The Hague
Main language: Dutch
Main religion: Christian
Government: constitutional monarchy
Currency: 1 euro = 100 cents

NEW ZEALAND (Australasia/Oceania)
Area: 268,680 sq km (103,737 sq miles)
Population: 3,864,129
Capital city: Wellington
Main languages: English, Maori
Main religion: Christian
Government: parliamentary democracy
Currency: 1 New Zealand dollar = 100 cents

NICARAGUA (North America)
Area: 129,494 sq km (49,998 sq miles)
Population: 4,918,393
Capital city: Managua
Main language: Spanish
Main religion: Roman Catholic
Government: republic
Currency: 1 gold cordoba = 100 centavos

NIGER (Africa)
Area: 1,267,000 sq km (489,189 sq miles)
Population: 10,355,156
Capital city: Niamey
Main languages: Hausa, Djerma, French
Main religion: Muslim
Government: republic
Currency: 1 CFA* franc = 100 centimes

NIGERIA (Africa)
Area: 923,768 sq km (356,667 sq miles)
Population: 126,635,626
Capital city: Abuja
Main languages: Hausa, Yoruba, Igbo, English
Main religions: Muslim, Christian, indigenous
Government: republic
Currency: 1 naira = 100 kobo

NORTH KOREA (Asia)
Area: 120,540 sq km (46,540 sq miles)
Population: 21,968,228
Capital city: Pyongyang
Main language: Korean
Main religions: Buddhist, Confucianist
Government: authoritarian socialist
Currency: 1 North Korean won = 100 chon

NORWAY (Europe)
Area: 324,220 sq km (125,181 sq miles)
Population: 4,503,440
Capital city: Oslo
Main language: Norwegian

Nauru

Nepal

Netherlands

New Zealand

Nicaragua

Niger

Nigeria

*CFA = Communaute Financiere Africaine

North Korea

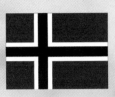

Norway

Oman

Pakistan

Palau

Panama

**Papua
New Guinea**

Main religion: Evangelical Lutheran
Government: constitutional monarchy
Currency: 1 Norwegian krone = 100 oere

OMAN (Asia)
Area: 212,460 sq km (82,031 sq miles)
Population: 2,622,198
Capital city: Muscat
Main languages: Arabic, English, Baluchi
Main religion: Muslim
Government: monarchy
Currency: 1 Omani rial = 1,000 baiza

PAKISTAN (Asia)
Area: 803,940 sq km (310,401 sq miles)
Population: 144,616,639
Capital city: Islamabad
Main languages: Punjabi, Sindhi, Urdu,
English
Main religion: Muslim
Government: federal republic
Currency: 1 Pakistani rupee = 100 paisa

PALAU (Australasia/Oceania)
Area: 459 sq km (177 sq miles)
Population: 19,092
Capital city: Koror
Main languages: Palauan, English
Main religions: Christian, Modekngei
Government: democratic republic
Currency: 1 U.S. dollar = 100 cents

PANAMA (North America)
Area: 78,200 sq km (30,193 sq miles)
Population: 2,845,647
Capital city: Panama City
Main languages: Spanish, English
Main religions: Roman Catholic, Protestant
Government: democracy
Currency: 1 balboa = 100 centesimos

**PAPUA NEW GUINEA
(Australasia/Oceania)**
Area: 462,840 sq km (178,703 sq miles)
Population: 5,049,055
Capital city: Port Moresby
Main languages: Tok Pisin, Hiri Motu,
English
Main religions: Christian, indigenous
Government: parliamentary democracy
Currency: 1 kina = 100 toea

PARAGUAY (South America)
Area: 406,750 sq km (157,046 sq miles)
Population: 5,734,139
Capital city: Asuncion
Main languages: Guarani, Spanish
Main religion: Roman Catholic
Government: republic
Currency: 1 guarani = 100 centimos

PERU (South America)
Area: 1,285,220 sq km (496,223 sq miles)
Population: 27,483,864
Capital city: Lima
Main languages: Spanish, Quechua, Aymara
Main religion: Roman Catholic
Government: republic
Currency: 1 nuevo sol = 100 centimos

PHILIPPINES (Asia)
Area: 300,000 sq km (115,830 sq miles)
Population: 82,841,518
Capital city: Manila
Main languages: Tagalog, English, Ilocano
Main religion: Roman Catholic
Government: republic
Currency: 1 Philippine peso = 100 centavos

POLAND (Europe)
Area: 312,685 sq km (120,727 sq miles)
Population: 38,633,912
Capital city: Warsaw
Main language: Polish
Main religion: Roman Catholic
Government: democratic republic
Currency: 1 zloty = 100 groszy

PORTUGAL (Europe)
Area: 92,391 sq km (35,672 sq miles)
Population: 10,066,253
Capital city: Lisbon
Main language: Portuguese
Main religion: Roman Catholic
Government: democratic republic
Currency: 1 euro = 100 cents

QATAR (Asia)
Area: 11,437 sq km (4,416 sq miles)
Population: 769,152
Capital city: Doha
Main languages: Arabic, English
Main religion: Muslim
Government: monarchy
Currency: 1 Qatari riyal = 100 dirhams

ROMANIA (Europe)
Area: 237,500 sq km (91,699 sq miles)
Population: 22,364,022
Capital city: Bucharest
Main languages: Romanian, Hungarian, German
Main religion: Romanian Orthodox
Government: republic
Currency: 1 leu = 100 bani

RUSSIA (Europe and Asia)
Area: 17,075,200 sq km (6,592,735 sq miles)
Population: 145,470,197
Capital city: Moscow
Main language: Russian
Main religions: Russian Orthodox, Muslim
Government: federal government
Currency: 1 ruble = 100 kopeks

RWANDA (Africa)
Area: 26,338 sq km (10,169 sq miles)
Population: 7,312,756
Capital city: Kigali
Main languages: Kinyarwanda, French,
English, Swahili
Main religions: Roman Catholic, Protestant,
Adventist
Government: transitional
Currency: 1 Rwandan franc = 100 centimes

**SAINT KITTS AND NEVIS
(North America)**
Area: 269 sq km (104 sq miles)
Population: 38,756

Paraguay

• **Peru**

Philippines

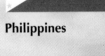

Poland

Portugal

Qatar

Romania

GAZETTEER OF STATES CONTINUED:

Russia

Capital city: Basseterre
Main language: English
Main religions: Protestant, Roman Catholic
Government: constitutional monarchy
Currency: 1 East Caribbean dollar = 100 cents

SAINT LUCIA (North America)
Area: 620 sq km (239 sq miles)
Population: 158,178
Capital city: Castries
Main languages: French patois, English
Main religion: Roman Catholic
Government: parliamentary democracy
Currency: 1 East Caribbean dollar = 100 cents

Rwanda

SAINT VINCENT AND THE GRENADINES (North America)
Area: 389 sq km (150 sq miles)
Population: 115,942
Capital city: Kingstown
Main languages: English, French patois
Main religions: Protestant, Roman Catholic
Government: parliamentary democracy
Currency: 1 East Caribbean dollar = 100 cents

Saint Kitts and Nevis

SAMOA (Australasia/Oceania)
Area: 2,860 sq km (1,104 sq miles)
Population: 179,058
Capital city: Apia
Main languages: Samoan, English
Main religion: Christian
Government: constitutional monarchy
Currency: 1 tala = 100 sene

SAN MARINO (Europe)
Area: 61 sq km (24 sq miles)
Population: 27,336
Capital city: San Marino
Main language: Italian
Main religion: Roman Catholic
Government: republic
Currency: 1 euro = 100 cents

Saint Lucia

SAO TOME AND PRINCIPE (Africa)
Area: 1,001 sq km (386 sq miles)
Population: 165,034
Capital city: Sao Tome
Main languages: Crioulo* dialects, Portuguese
Main religion: Christian
Government: republic
Currency: 1 dobra = 100 centimos

Saint Vincent and the Grenadines

SAUDI ARABIA (Asia)
Area: 2,149,690 sq km (829,995 sq miles)
Population: 22,757,092
Capital city: Riyadh
Main language: Arabic
Main religion: Muslim
Government: monarchy
Currency: 1 Saudi riyal = 100 halalah

Samoa

SENEGAL (Africa)
Area: 196,190 sq km (75,749 sq miles)
Population: 10,284,929
Capital city: Dakar
Main languages: Wolof, French, Pulaar
Main religion: Muslim
Government: democratic republic
Currency: 1 CFA* franc = 100 centimes

• San Marino

SEYCHELLES (Africa)
Area: 455 sq km (176 sq miles)
Population: 79,715
Capital city: Victoria
Main language: Seselwa
Main religion: Roman Catholic
Government: republic
Currency: 1 Seychelles rupee = 100 cents

SIERRA LEONE (Africa)
Area: 71,740 sq km (27,699 sq miles)
Population: 5,426,618
Capital city: Freetown
Main languages: Mende, Temne, Krio, English
Main religions: Muslim, indigenous, Christian
Government: republic
Currency: 1 leone = 100 cents

SINGAPORE (Asia)
Area: 648 sq km (250 sq miles)
Population: 4,300,419
Capital city: Singapore
Main languages: Chinese, Malay, English, Tamil
Main religions: Buddhist, Muslim
Government: parliamentary republic
Currency: 1 Singapore dollar = 100 cents

SLOVAKIA (Europe)
Area: 48,845 sq km (18,859 sq miles)
Population: 5,414,937
Capital city: Bratislava
Main languages: Slovak, Hungarian
Main religion: Roman Catholic
Government: parliamentary democracy
Currency: 1 koruna = 100 halierov

SLOVENIA (Europe)
Area: 20,253 sq km (7,820 sq miles)
Population: 1,930,132
Capital city: Ljubljana
Main language: Slovenian
Main religion: Roman Catholic
Government: democratic republic
Currency: 1 tolar = 100 stotins

SOLOMON ISLANDS (Australasia/Oceania)
Area: 28,450 sq km (10,985 sq miles)
Population: 480,442
Capital city: Honiara
Main languages: Solomon pidgin, Kwara'ae, To'abaita, English
Main religion: Christian
Government: parliamentary democracy
Currency: 1 Solomon Islands dollar = 100 cents

SOMALIA (Africa)
Area: 637,657 sq km (246,199 sq miles)
Population: 7,488,773
Capital city: Mogadishu
Main languages: Somali, Arabic, Oromo
Main religion: Sunni Muslim
Government: transitional
Currency: 1 Somali shilling = 100 cents

SOUTH AFRICA (Africa)
Area: 1,219,912 sq km (471,008 sq miles)
Population: 43,586,097
Capital cities: Pretoria, Cape Town, Bloemfontein
Main languages: Zulu, Xhosa, Afrikaans, Pedi,

Sao Tome and Principe

Saudi Arabia

Senegal

Seychelles

Sierra Leone

Singapore

Slovakia

*CFA = Communaute Financiere Africaine; Crioulo = a blend of Portuguese and West African

• Slovenia

Solomon Islands

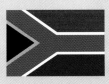

Somalia

South Africa

South Korea

• Spain

Sri Lanka

English, Tswana, Sotho, Tsonga, Swati, Venda, Ndebele
Main religions: Christian, indigenous
Government: republic
Currency: 1 rand = 100 cents

SOUTH KOREA (Asia)
Area: 98,480 sq km (38,023 sq miles)
Population: 47,904,370
Capital city: Seoul
Main language: Korean
Main religions: Christian, Buddhist
Government: republic
Currency: 1 South Korean won = 100 chun

SPAIN (Europe)
Area: 504,750 sq km (194,884 sq miles)
Population: 40,037,995
Capital city: Madrid
Main languages: Castilian Spanish, Catalan
Main religion: Roman Catholic
Government: constitutional monarchy
Currency: 1 euro = 100 cents

SRI LANKA (Asia)
Area: 65,610 sq km (25,332 sq miles)
Population: 19,408,635
Capital cities: Colombo, Sri Jayewardenepura Kotte
Main languages: Sinhala, Tamil, English
Main religions: Buddhist, Hindu
Government: republic
Currency: 1 Sri Lankan rupee = 100 cents

SUDAN (Africa)
Area: 2,505,810 sq km (967,493 sq miles)
Population: 36,080,373
Capital city: Khartoum
Main languages: Arabic, English
Main religions: Sunni Muslim, indigenous
Government: Islamic republic
Currency: 1 Sudanese dinar = 100 piastres

SURINAM (South America)
Area: 163,270 sq km (63,039 sq miles)
Population: 433,998
Capital city: Paramaribo
Main languages: Sranang Tongo, Dutch, English
Main religions: Christian, Hindu, Muslim
Government: republic
Currency: 1 Surinamese guilder, gulden or florin = 100 cents

SWAZILAND (Africa)
Area: 17,363 sq km (6,704 sq miles)
Population: 1,104,343
Capital cities: Mbabane, Lobamba
Main languages: Swati, English
Main religions: Protestant, indigenous, Muslim
Government: monarchy
Currency: 1 lilangeni = 100 cents

SWEDEN (Europe)
Area: 449,964 sq km (173,731 sq miles)
Population: 8,875,053
Capital city: Stockholm
Main language: Swedish

Main religion: Lutheran
Government: constitutional monarchy
Currency: 1 Swedish krona = 100 oere

SWITZERLAND (Europe)
Area: 41,290 sq km (15,942 sq miles)
Population: 7,283,274
Capital city: Bern
Main languages: German, French, Italian
Main religions: Roman Catholic, Protestant
Government: federal republic
Currency: 1 Swiss franc, franken or frano = 100 centimes, rappen or centesimi

SYRIA (Asia)
Area: 185,180 sq km (71,498 sq miles)
Population: 16,728,808
Capital city: Damascus
Main languages: Arabic, Kurdish
Main religions: Muslim, Christian
Government: republic under military regime
Currency: 1 Syrian pound = 100 piastres

TAIWAN (Asia)
Area: 35,980 sq km (13,892 sq miles)
Population: 22,370,461
Capital city: Taipei
Main languages: Taiwanese, Mandarin Chinese, Hakka Chinese
Main religions: Buddhist, Confucian, Daoist
Government: democracy
Currency: 1 New Taiwan dollar = 100 cents

TAJIKISTAN (Asia)
Area: 143,100 sq km (55,251 sq miles)
Population: 6,578,681
Capital city: Dushanbe
Main languages: Tajik, Russian
Main religion: Sunni Muslim
Government: republic
Currency: 1 somoni = 100 dirams

TANZANIA (Africa)
Area: 945,087 sq km (364,898 sq miles)
Population: 36,232,074
Capital cities: Dar es Salaam, Dodoma
Main languages: Swahili, English, Sukuma
Main religions: Christian, Muslim, indigenous
Government: republic
Currency: 1 Tanzanian shilling = 100 cents

THAILAND (Asia)
Area: 514,000 sq km (198,455 sq miles)
Population: 61,797,751
Capital city: Bangkok
Main languages: Thai, English, Chaochow
Main religion: Buddhist
Government: constitutional monarchy
Currency: 1 baht = 100 satang

TOGO (Africa)
Area: 56,785 sq km (21,925 sq miles)
Population: 5,153,088
Capital city: Lome
Main languages: Mina, Ewe, Kabye, French
Main religions: indigenous, Christian, Muslim
Government: republic
Currency: 1 CFA* franc = 100 centimes

Sudan

Surinam

Swaziland

Sweden

Switzerland

Syria

Taiwan

123

GAZETTEER OF STATES CONTINUED:

Tajikistan

Tanzania

Thailand

Togo

Tonga

Trinidad and Tobago

TONGA (Australasia/Oceania)
Area: 748 sq km (289 sq miles)
Population: 104,227
Capital city: Nukualofa
Main languages: Tongan, English
Main religion: Christian
Government: constitutional monarchy
Currency: 1 pa'anga = 100 seniti

TRINIDAD AND TOBAGO (North America)
Area: 5,128 sq km (1,980 sq miles)
Population: 1,169,682
Capital city: Port-of-Spain
Main languages: English, French, Spanish, Hindi
Main religions: Christian, Hindu
Government: republic
Currency: 1 Trinidad and Tobago dollar = 100 cents

TUNISIA (Africa)
Area: 163,610 sq km (63,170 sq miles)
Population: 9,705,102
Capital city: Tunis
Main languages: Arabic, French
Main religion: Muslim
Government: republic
Currency: 1 Tunisian dinar = 1,000 millimes

TURKEY (Europe and Asia)
Area: 780,580 sq km (301,382 sq miles)
Population: 66,493,970
Capital city: Ankara
Main language: Turkish
Main religion: Muslim
Government: democratic republic
Currency: 1 Turkish lira = 100 kurus

TURKMENISTAN (Asia)
Area: 488,100 sq km (188,455 sq miles)
Population: 4,603,244
Capital city: Ashgabat (Ashkhabad)
Main languages: Turkmen, Russian
Main religion: Muslim
Government: republic
Currency: 1 Turkmen manat = 100 tenesi

TUVALU (Australasia/Oceania)
Area: 26 sq km (10 sq miles)
Population: 10,991
Capital city: Funafuti
Main languages: Tuvaluan, English
Main religion: Congregationalist
Government: constitutional monarchy
Currency: 1 Tuvaluan dollar or 1 Australian dollar = 100 cents

UGANDA (Africa)
Area: 236,040 sq km (91,135 sq miles)
Population: 23,985,712
Capital city: Kampala
Main languages: Luganda, English, Swahili
Main religions: Christian, Muslim, indigenous
Government: republic
Currency: 1 Ugandan shilling = 100 cents

UKRAINE (Europe)
Area: 603,700 sq km (233,089 sq miles)
Population: 49,153,027
Capital city: Kiev

Main languages: Ukrainian, Russian
Main religion: Ukrainain Orthodox
Government: republic
Currency: 1 hryvnia = 100 kopiykas

UNITED ARAB EMIRATES (Asia)
Area: 82,880 sq km (32,000 sq miles)
Population: 2,407,460
Capital city: Abu Dhabi
Main languages: Arabic, English
Main religion: Muslim
Government: federation
Currency: 1 Emirati dirham = 100 fils

UNITED KINGDOM (Europe)
Area: 244,820 sq km (94,525 sq miles)
Population: 59,647,790
Capital city: London
Main language: English
Main religions: Anglican, Roman Catholic
Government: constitutional monarchy
Currency: 1 British pound = 100 pence

UNITED STATES OF AMERICA (North America)
Area: 9,629,091 sq km (3,717,792 sq miles)
Population: 278,058,881
Capital city: Washington D.C.
Main language: English
Main religions: Protestant, Roman Catholic
Government: federal republic
Currency: 1 U.S. dollar = 100 cents

URUGUAY (South America)
Area: 176,220 sq km (68,039 sq miles)
Population: 3,360,105
Capital city: Montevideo
Main language: Spanish
Main religion: Roman Catholic
Government: republic
Currency: 1 Uruguayan peso = 100 centesimos

UZBEKISTAN (Asia)
Area: 447,400 sq km (172,741 sq miles)
Population: 25,155,064
Capital city: Tashkent
Main languages: Uzbek, Russian
Main religions: Muslim, Eastern Orthodox
Government: republic
Currency: 1 Uzbekistani sum = 100 tyyn

VANUATU (Australasia/Oceania)
Area: 12,189 sq km (4,706 sq miles)
Population: 192,910
Capital city: Port-Vila
Main languages: Bislama, French, English
Main religion: Christian
Government: republic
Currency: 1 vatu = 100 centimes

VATICAN CITY (Europe)
Area: 0.44 sq km (0.17 sq miles)
Population: 880
Capital city: Vatican City
Main languages: Italian, Latin
Main religion: Roman Catholic
Government: led by the Pope
Currency: 1 euro = 100 cents

Tunisia

Turkey

Turkmenistan

Tuvalu

Uganda

Ukraine

United Arab Emirates

United Kingdom

United States of America

Uruguay

Uzbekistan

Vanuatu

VENEZUELA (South America)
Area: 912,050 sq km (352,143 sq miles)
Population: 23,916,810
Capital city: Caracas
Main language: Spanish
Main religion: Roman Catholic
Government: federal republic
Currency: 1 bolivar = 100 centimos

VIETNAM (Asia)
Area: 329,560 sq km (127,243 sq miles)
Population: 79,939,014
Capital city: Hanoi
Main languages: Vietnamese, French, English, Khmer, Chinese
Main religion: Buddhist
Government: Communist state
Currency: 1 new dong = 100 xu

YEMEN (Asia)
Area: 527,970 sq km (203,849 sq miles)
Population: 18,078,035
Capital city: Sana
Main language: Arabic
Main religion: Muslim
Government: republic
Currency: 1 Yemeni rial = 100 fils

YUGOSLAVIA (Europe)
Area: 102,350 sq km (39,517 sq miles)
Population: 10,677,290
Capital city: Belgrade
Main language: Serbian
Main religions: Orthodox, Muslim
Government: republic
Currency: 1 Yugoslavian new dinar = 100 paras

ZAMBIA (Africa)
Area: 752,614 sq km (290,584 sq miles)
Population: 9,770,199
Capital city: Lusaka
Main languages: Bemba, Tonga, Nyanja, English
Main religions: Christian, Muslim, Hindu
Government: republic
Currency: 1 Zambian kwacha = 100 ngwee

ZIMBABWE (Africa)
Area: 390,580 sq km (150,803 sq miles)
Population: 11,365,366
Capital city: Harare
Main languages: Shona, Ndebele, English
Main religions: Christian, indigenous
Government: republic
Currency: 1 Zimbabwean dollar = 100 cents

The United Nations

The United Nations (U.N.) is an organization which aims to bring countries together to work for peace and development. Of the world's 193 states, 189 belong to the U.N. Those that don't belong are Taiwan, Switzerland, East Timor and the Vatican City.

Kofi Annan, the Secretary-General of the U.N., with U.N. ambassador Pele

Internet links

For a link to a Web site where you can test your flag knowledge by playing a game where you have to match countries and their flags, go to **www.usborne-quicklinks.com**

Vatican City

Venezuela

Vietnam

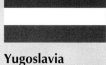

Yemen

Yugoslavia

Zambia

Zimbabwe

TIME ZONES

When it's midday in Rio de Janeiro, it's midnight in Tokyo. This is because the Earth is divided into different time zones. Within each zone, people usually set their clocks to the same time. If you fly between two zones, you change your watch to the time in the new zone.

Summer time

Some countries adjust their clocks in summer. For example, in the U.K. all clocks go forward one hour. This is known as Daylight Saving Time or Summer Time. It is a way of getting more out of the days by having an extra hour of daylight in the evening. It reduces energy use as people don't use as much electricity for lights.

Dividing up time

There are 25 main time zones. They are separated by one-hour intervals and there is a new time zone every 15 degrees of longitude. There are 12 one-hour zones both ahead of and behind Greenwich Mean Time, or GMT, which is the time at the Prime Meridian Line.

Governments can change their countries' time zones. So, for convenience, whole countries usually keep the same local time instead of sticking to the zones exactly. For example, China could be divided into several time zones, but instead the whole country keeps the same time. A few areas, such as India, use non-standard half hour deviations.

Changing dates

On the opposite side of the world from the Prime Meridian Line is the International Date Line, which runs mostly through the Pacific Ocean and bends to avoid the land. Places to the west of it are 24 hours ahead of places to the east. This means that if you travel east across it you lose a day and if you travel west across it you gain a day.

This map shows the time zones. The times at the top of the map tell you the time in the different zones when it is noon at the Prime Meridian Line. There are two midnight zones, one for each day on either side of the International Date Line. The numbers in circles tell you how many hours ahead of or behind Greenwich Mean Time an area is.

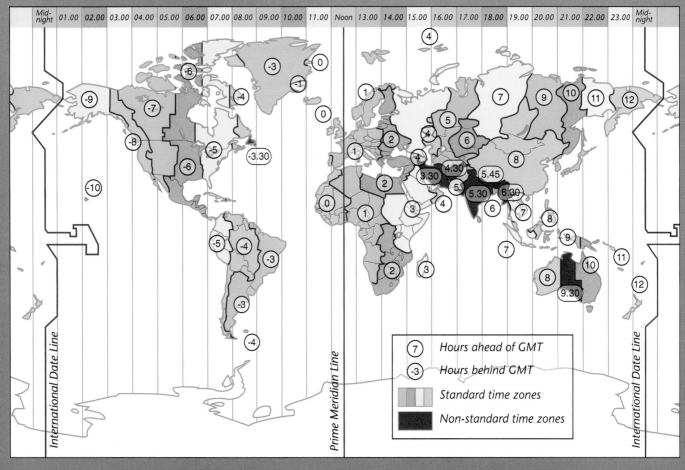

GENERAL INDEX

Places featured in the maps in this atlas are listed in a separate index on pages 130–143.

Answers to geography quiz (pages 110–111)

Mystery places

Top left: La Sagrada Familia church in Barcelona, Spain
Top right: The Taj Mahal near Agra, India
Middle left: The Golden Gate Bridge in San Francisco, U.S.A.
Middle right: The Acropolis in Athens, Greece
Bottom: The CN Tower in Toronto, Canada

Quick quiz

1. Japan
2. 6 a.m.
3. Australia
4. North America
5. Czech Republic
6. Lake Baikal, Russia
7. Vatican City
8. Costa Rica
9. Nigeria
10. Ankara

Survival challenge

1. b. An umbrella would not be useful as it doesn't rain in Antarctica. It's also the world's windiest continent, so an umbrella wouldn't last long! You would need sunglasses and sunscreen, however, as the reflection of the sun off snow is dazzling and can cause sunburn.

2. b. Extra clothes would help to conserve your sweat, which cools down your skin, and resting in the shade (if there is any) would help your body stay as cool as possible. Being active, talking or singing would cause your body to lose moisture and your mouth to dry out – which would make you even thirstier.

3. All of them. Six-eyed crab spiders are one of the most venomous types of spiders in the world. Their bites are so severe that they can cause death. Button spiders have a bite which is very painful, though not lethal, while a bite from a violin spider causes painful swelling.

4. c. A bear will only attack if it thinks you are a threat to it. If you moved away slowly, not making any sudden movements, it would probably leave you alone. You should only lie down (preferably curled into a ball) and play dead if the bear actually takes a swipe at you.

MAP INDEX

This is an index of the places and features named on the maps. Each entry consists of the following parts: the name (given in bold type), the country or region within which it is located (given in italics), the page on which the name can be found (given in bold type), and the grid reference (also given in bold type). For some names, there is also a description explaining what kind of place it is – for example a country, internal administrative area (state or province), national capital or internal capital. To find a place on a map, first find the map indicated by the page reference. Then use the grid reference to find the square containing the name or town symbol. See page 11 for help with using the grid.

Himalayas, *Asia*, 70 E4
Hindu Kush, *Asia*, 70 B3
Hinton, *Canada*, 30 H3
Hiroshima, *Japan*, 69 M4
Hispaniola, *North America*, 35 K4
Hitra, *Norway*, 86 D3
Hobart, *Australia, internal capital*, 54 J8
Ho Chi Minh City, *Vietnam*, 66 E5
Hohhot, *China*, 68 H2
Hokkaido, *Japan*, 69 P2
Holguin, *Cuba*, 35 J3
Homs, *Syria*, 72 C5
Homyel, *Belarus*, 87 J5
Honduras, *North America, country*, 35 G4
Honduras, Gulf of, *North America*, 35 G4
Honefoss, *Norway*, 86 D3
Hong Kong, *China*, 69 H6
Honiara, *Solomon Islands, national capital*, 52 D5
Honolulu, *U.S.A., internal capital*, 33 P7
Honshu, *Japan*, 69 N3
Horlivka, *Ukraine*, 84 D4
Hormuz, Strait of, *Asia*, 73 G6
Horn, Cape, *Chile*, 45 D11
Horn Lake, *U.S.A.*, 33 K2
Hotan, *China*, 70 D3
Hotazel, *South Africa*, 104 D5
Houston, *U.S.A.*, 33 G5
Hradec Kralove, *Czech Republic*, 90 E1
Hrodna, *Belarus*, 87 H5
Huacrachuco, *Peru*, 42 C5
Huaihua, *China*, 68 H5
Huambo, *Angola*, 104 C2
Huancayo, *Peru*, 42 C6
Huang He, *China*, 69 H3
Huanuco, *Peru*, 42 C5
Huascaran, Mount, *Peru*, 42 C5
Hubli, *India*, 71 D7
Hudiksvall, *Sweden*, 86 F3
Hudson Bay, *Canada*, 31 L3
Hudson Strait, *Canada*, 31 M2
Hue, *Vietnam*, 66 E4
Huelva, *Spain*, 89 C7
Hull, *United Kingdom*, 88 D3
Hulun Lake, *China*, 69 J1
Hungary, *Europe, country*, 87 F7
Huntsville, *Canada*, 31 M4
Huntsville, *U.S.A.*, 33 J4
Hurghada, *Egypt*, 99 H3
Huron, Lake, *U.S.A.*, 33 J3
Hvannadalshnukur, *Iceland*, 86 P2
Hwange, *Zimbabwe*, 104 E3
Hyderabad, *India*, 71 D7
Hyderabad, *Pakistan*, 70 B5
Hyesan, *North Korea*, 69 L2

i

Iasi, *Romania*, 91 H2
Ibadan, *Nigeria*, 101 F7
Ibague, *Colombia*, 42 C3
Ibarra, *Ecuador*, 42 C3
Ibb, *Yemen*, 73 D9
Iberian Mountains, *Spain*, 89 D6
Ibiza, *Spain*, 89 E7
Ica, *Peru*, 42 C6
Iceland, *Europe, country*, 86 P2
Idaho, *U.S.A., internal admin. area*, 32 C2
Idaho Falls, *U.S.A.*, 32 D2
Ierapetra, *Greece*, 91 H5
Iguacu Falls, *South America*, 44 H5
Ihosy, *Madagascar*, 105 J4
Ikopa, *Madagascar*, 105 J3
Ilagan, *Philippines*, 67 H4
Ilebo, *Democratic Republic of Congo*, 102 D4
Ilheus, *Brazil*, 44 L2
Iliamna Lake, *U.S.A.*, 30 D2
Iligan, *Philippines*, 67 H6
Illapel, *Chile*, 44 D6
Illimani, Mount, *Bolivia*, 44 E3
Illinois, *U.S.A., internal admin. area*, 33 J2
Illizi, *Algeria*, 100 G3
Ilmen, Lake, *Russia*, 86 J4
Iloilo, *Philippines*, 67 H5
Ilonga, *Tanzania*, 103 G5
Ilorin, *Nigeria*, 101 F7

Imperatriz, *Brazil*, 43 J5
Imphal, *India*, 71 G6
Inari, Lake, *Finland*, 86 H1
Inchon, *South Korea*, 69 L3
Indals, *Sweden*, 86 E3
Inderbor, *Kazakhstan*, 85 G4
India, *Asia, country*, 71 D6
Indiana, *U.S.A., internal admin. area*, 33 J2
Indianapolis, *U.S.A., internal capital*, 33 J3
Indian Ocean, 21
Indonesia, *Asia, country*, 64 C5
Indore, *India*, 71 D6
Indus, *Asia*, 70 B5
Inner Mongolia, *China*, 69 H2
Innsbruck, *Austria*, 90 D2
Inhambane, *Mozambique*, 105 G4
Ingolstadt, *Germany*, 88 G4
Inukjuak, *Canada*, 31 M3
Inuvik, *Canada*, 30 F2
Invercargill, *New Zealand*, 55 N9
Inyangani, *Zimbabwe*, 105 F3
Ioannina, *Greece*, 91 G4
Ionian Sea, *Europe*, 91 F4
Iowa, *U.S.A., internal admin. area*, 33 H2
Ipiales, *Colombia*, 42 C3
Ipoh, *Malaysia*, 64 B3
Ipswich, *United Kingdom*, 88 E3
Iqaluit, *Canada, internal capital*, 31 N2
Iquique, *Chile*, 44 D4
Iquitos, *Peru*, 42 D4
Irakleio, *Greece*, 91 H5
Iran, *Asia, country*, 72 F5
Iranshahr, *Iran*, 73 H6
Iraq, *Asia, country*, 72 D5
Irbid, *Jordan*, 72 C5
Ireland, *Europe, country*, 88 B3
Iringa, *Tanzania*, 103 G5
Irish Sea, *Europe*, 88 C3
Irkutsk, *Russia*, 75 F3
Irrawaddy, *Burma*, 66 C4
Irrawaddy, Mouths of the, *Burma*, 66 B4
Irtysh, *Asia*, 74 D3
Isabela, *Ecuador*, 42 N10
Isafjordhur, *Iceland*, 86 N2
Isiro, *Democratic Republic of Congo*, 102 E3
Islamabad, *Pakistan, national capital*, 70 C4
Isle of Man, *Europe*, 88 C3
Isle of Wight, *United Kingdom*, 88 D4
Ismailia, *Egypt*, 99 H2
Ismailia, *Egypt*, 99 H2
Isoka, *Zambia*, 105 F2
Isparta, *Turkey*, 91 J4
Israel, *Asia, country*, 73 B5
Issyk, Lake, *Kyrgyzstan*, 70 D2
Istanbul, *Turkey*, 91 J3
Itaituba, *Brazil*, 43 G4
Itajai, *Brazil*, 44 J5
Italy, *Europe, country*, 90 D2
Itapetininga, *Brazil*, 44 J4
Ivano-Frankivsk, *Ukraine*, 87 H6
Ivanovo, *Russia*, 84 E2
Ivdel, *Russia*, 85 J1
Ivory Coast, *Africa, country*, 101 D7
Ivujivik, *Canada*, 31 M2
Izhevsk, *Russia*, 85 G2
Izmir, *Turkey*, 91 H4

j

Jabalpur, *India*, 71 D6
Jackson, *Mississippi, U.S.A., internal capital*, 33 H4
Jackson, *Tennessee, U.S.A.*, 33 J3
Jacksonville, *U.S.A.*, 33 K4
Jaen, *Spain*, 89 D7
Jaffna, *Sri Lanka*, 71 E9
Jaipur, *India*, 70 D5
Jakarta, *Indonesia, national capital*, 64 C5
Jalalabad, *Afghanistan*, 70 C4
Jalal-Abad, *Kyrgyzstan*, 70 C2
Jamaica, *North America, country*, 35 J4
Jambi, *Indonesia*, 64 B4
James Bay, *Canada*, 31 L3
Jamestown, *U.S.A.*, 33 L2

Jammu, *India*, 70 C4
Jammu and Kashmir, *Asia*, 70 D4
Jamnagar, *India*, 71 C6
Jamshedpur, *India*, 71 F6
Japan, *Asia, country*, 69 N3
Japan, Sea of, *Asia*, 69 M2
Japura, *Brazil*, 42 E4
Jatai, *Brazil*, 44 H3
Java, *Indonesia*, 64 C5
Java Sea, *Indonesia*, 64 C5
Jayapura, *Indonesia*, 65 K4
Jedda, *Saudi Arabia*, 73 C7
Jefferson City, *U.S.A., internal capital*, 33 H3
Jekabpils, *Latvia*, 87 H4
Jelgava, *Latvia*, 87 G4
Jember, *Indonesia*, 64 D5
Jerba, *Tunisia*, 98 D2
Jerez de la Frontera, *Spain*, 89 C7
Jerusalem, *Israel, national capital*, 73 C5
Jhansi, *India*, 70 D5
Jiamusi, *China*, 69 M1
Jilin, *China*, 69 L2
Jima, *Ethiopia*, 103 G2
Jinhua, *China*, 69 J5
Jining, *China*, 69 J3
Jinja, *Uganda*, 103 F3
Jinzhou, *China*, 69 K2
Jixi, *China*, 69 M1
Jizzax, *Uzbekistan*, 70 B2
Joao Pessoa, *Brazil*, 43 M5
Jodhpur, *India*, 70 C5
Johannesburg, *South Africa*, 104 E5
Johnston Atoll, *Oceania*, 52 G3
Johor Bahru, *Malaysia*, 64 B3
Jolo, *Philippines*, 67 H6
Jonesboro, *U.S.A.*, 33 H3
Jonkoping, *Sweden*, 87 E4
Jordan, *Asia, country*, 73 C5
Jorhat, *India*, 70 G5
Jos, *Nigeria*, 102 A2
Juan de Nova, *Africa*, 105 H3
Juazeiro, *Brazil*, 43 K5
Juazeiro do Norte, *Brazil*, 43 L5
Juba, *Africa*, 103 N10
Juba, *Sudan*, 103 F3
Juchitan, *Mexico*, 34 E4
Juiz de Fora, *Brazil*, 44 K4
Juliaca, *Peru*, 42 D7
Juneau, *U.S.A., internal capital*, 30 F3
Jurmala, *Latvia*, 87 G4
Jurua, *Brazil*, 42 E5
Jutland, *Europe*, 87 D4
Jyvaskyla, *Finland*, 86 H3

k

K2, *Asia*, 70 D3
Kaamanen, *Finland*, 86 H1
Kabinda, *Democratic Republic of Congo*, 102 D5
Kabul, *Afghanistan, national capital*, 70 B4
Kabunda, *Democratic Republic of Congo*, 102 E6
Kabwe, *Zambia*, 104 E2
Kadoma, *Zimbabwe*, 104 E3
Kaduna, *Nigeria*, 101 G6
Kaedi, *Mauritania*, 101 C5
Kafakumba, *Democratic Republic of Congo*, 102 D5
Kafue, *Zambia*, 104 E3
Kagoshima, *Japan*, 69 M4
Kahramanmaras, *Turkey*, 72 C4
Kahului, *U.S.A.*, 33 P7
Kainji Reservoir, *Nigeria*, 101 F6
Kairouan, *Tunisia*, 98 D1
Kajaani, *Finland*, 86 H2
Kakhovske Reservoir, *Ukraine*, 84 C4
Kalahari Desert, *Africa*, 104 D4
Kalamata, *Greece*, 91 G4
Kalemie, *Democratic Republic of Congo*, 102 E5
Kalgoorlie, *Australia*, 54 D6
Kaliningrad, *Russia*, 87 G5
Kalisz, *Poland*, 87 F6
Kalkrand, *Namibia*, 104 C4

Kalmar, *Sweden*, 87 F4
Kaluga, *Russia*, 84 D3
Kamanjab, *Namibia*, 104 B3
Kama Reservoir, *Russia*, 85 H2
Kamativi, *Zimbabwe*, 104 E3
Kamchatka Peninsula, *Russia*, 75 H3
Kamenka, *Russia*, 84 E3
Kamina, *Democratic Republic of Congo*, 102 E5
Kamloops, *Canada*, 30 G3
Kampala, *Uganda, national capital*, 103 F3
Kampong Cham, *Cambodia*, 66 E5
Kampong Chhnang, *Cambodia*, 66 D5
Kampong Saom, *Cambodia*, 66 D5
Kamyanets-Podilskyy, *Ukraine*, 87 H6
Kamyshin, *Russia*, 84 F3
Kananga, *Democratic Republic of Congo*, 102 D5
Kanazawa, *Japan*, 69 N3
Kandahar, *Afghanistan*, 70 B4
Kandalaksha, *Russia*, 86 K2
Kandi, *Benin*, 101 F6
Kandy, *Sri Lanka*, 71 E9
Kang, *Botswana*, 104 D4
Kangaroo Island, *Australia*, 54 G7
Kanggye, *North Korea*, 69 L2
Kankan, *Guinea*, 101 D6
Kano, *Nigeria*, 98 C6
Kanpur, *India*, 70 E5
Kansas, *U.S.A., internal admin. area*, 32 G3
Kansas City, *U.S.A.*, 33 H3
Kanye, *Botswana*, 104 E4
Kaohsiung, *Taiwan*, 69 K6
Kaolack, *Senegal*, 101 B6
Kara-Balta, *Kyrgyzstan*, 70 C2
Karabuk, *Turkey*, 91 K3
Karachi, *Pakistan*, 71 B6
Karaj, *Iran*, 72 F4
Karakol, *Kyrgyzstan*, 70 D2
Karakorum Range, *Asia*, 70 D3
Kara Kum Desert, *Turkmenistan*, 72 G3
Karaman, *Turkey*, 91 K4
Karamay, *China*, 70 E1
Kara Sea, *Russia*, 74 D2
Kariba, *Zimbabwe*, 104 E3
Kariba, Lake, *Africa*, 104 E3
Karibib, *Namibia*, 104 C4
Karimata Strait, *Indonesia*, 64 C4
Karlovac, *Croatia*, 90 E2
Karlovy Vary, *Czech Republic*, 90 E1
Karlshamn, *Sweden*, 87 E4
Karlsruhe, *Germany*, 88 G4
Karlstad, *Sweden*, 87 E4
Karmoy, *Norway*, 86 C4
Karonga, *Malawi*, 105 F1
Karora, *Eritrea*, 99 J5
Karpathos, *Greece*, 91 H5
Karratha, *Australia*, 54 C4
Kasai, *Africa*, 102 C4
Kasama, *Zambia*, 104 F2
Kashi, *China*, 70 D3
Kassala, *Sudan*, 99 J5
Kassel, *Germany*, 88 G4
Kasungu, *Malawi*, 105 F2
Kataba, *Zambia*, 104 E3
Kathmandu, *Nepal, national capital*, 70 F5
Katiola, *Ivory Coast*, 101 D7
Katowice, *Poland*, 87 F6
Katsina, *Nigeria*, 101 G6
Kattegat, *Europe*, 87 D4
Kauai, *U.S.A.*, 33 P7
Kaukau Veld, *Africa*, 104 C4
Kaunas, *Lithuania*, 87 G5
Kavala, *Greece*, 91 H3
Kawambwa, *Zambia*, 104 E1
Kayes, *Mali*, 101 C6
Kayseri, *Turkey*, 72 C4
Kazakhstan, *Asia, country*, 74 C3
Kazan, *Russia*, 85 F2
Kaztalovka, *Kazakhstan*, 85 F4
Kebnekaise, *Sweden*, 86 F2
Kecskemet, *Hungary*, 87 F7
Kedougou, *Senegal*, 101 C6
Keetmanshoop, *Namibia*, 104 C5

Kefallonia, *Greece*, 91 F4
Keflavik, *Iceland*, 86 N2
Kelowna, *Canada*, 30 H4
Kempten, *Germany*, 88 G5
Kendari, *Indonesia*, 65 F4
Kenema, *Sierra Leone*, 101 C7
Kenhardt, *South Africa*, 104 D5
Kenitra, *Morocco*, 100 D2
Kenora, *Canada*, 31 K4
Kentucky, *U.S.A., internal admin. area*, 33 J3
Kentucky Lake, *U.S.A.*, 33 J3
Kenya, *Africa, country*, 103 G3
Kenya, Mount, *Kenya*, 103 G4
Kerch, *Ukraine*, 91 L2
Kerema, *Papua New Guinea*, 65 L5
Keren, *Eritrea*, 99 J5
Kerkenah Islands, *Tunisia*, 98 D2
Kermadec Islands, *New Zealand*, 55 Q6
Kerman, *Iran*, 73 G5
Kermanshah, *Iran*, 72 E5
Key West, *U.S.A.*, 33 K6
Khabarovsk, *Russia*, 75 G3
Khanka, Lake, *Asia*, 69 M2
Kharkiv, *Ukraine*, 84 D3
Khartoum, *Sudan, national capital*, 99 H5
Kherson, *Ukraine*, 84 C4
Khmelnytskyy, *Ukraine*, 87 H6
Khon Kaen, *Thailand*, 66 D4
Khorugh, *Tajikistan*, 70 C3
Khouribga, *Morocco*, 100 D2
Khujand, *Tajikistan*, 70 B2
Khulna, *Bangladesh*, 71 F6
Kidal, *Mali*, 100 F5
Kiel, *Germany*, 88 G3
Kielce, *Poland*, 87 G6
Kiev, *Ukraine, national capital*, 87 J6
Kievske Reservoir, *Ukraine*, 84 C3
Kiffa, *Mauritania*, 101 C5
Kigali, *Rwanda, national capital*, 103 F4
Kigoma, *Tanzania*, 102 E4
Kikwit, *Democratic Republic of Congo*, 102 C5
Kilimanjaro, *Africa*, 103 G4
Kilwa, *Democratic Republic of Congo*, 102 E5
Kimberley, *South Africa*, 104 D5
Kimberley Plateau, *Australia*, 54 E3
Kimchaek, *North Korea*, 69 L2
Kindia, *Guinea*, 101 C6
Kindu, *Democratic Republic of Congo*, 102 E4
Kineshma, *Russia*, 84 E2
King George Island, *Atlantic Ocean*, 45 G12
Kingisepp, *Russia*, 86 J4
King Island, *Australia*, 54 H7
Kings Peak, *U.S.A.*, 32 D2
Kingston, *Canada*, 31 M4
Kingston, *Jamaica, national capital*, 35 J4
Kingstown, *St. Vincent and the Grenadines, national capital*, 34 M5
King William Island, *Canada*, 31 K2
Kinkala, *Congo*, 102 B4
Kinshasa, *Democratic Republic of Congo, national capital*, 102 C4
Kipushi, *Democratic Republic of Congo*, 102 E6
Kiribati, *Oceania, country*, 52 F5
Kirikkale, *Turkey*, 91 K4
Kirinyaga, *Kenya*, 103 G4
Kirishi, *Russia*, 86 K4
Kirkenes, *Norway*, 86 J1
Kirkland Lake, *Canada*, 31 L4
Kirkuk, *Iraq*, 72 D4
Kirkwall, *United Kingdom*, 88 D2
Kirov, *Russia*, 85 F2
Kirovohrad, *Ukraine*, 84 C4
Kiruna, *Sweden*, 86 G2
Kisangani, *Democratic Republic of Congo*, 102 E4
Kisii, *Kenya*, 103 F4
Kismaayo, *Somalia*, 103 H4
Kisumu, *Kenya*, 103 F4
Kita, *Mali*, 101 D6

Kitakyushu, *Japan*, 69 M4
Kitale, *Kenya*, 103 G3
Kitwe, *Zambia*, 104 E2
Kiuruvesi, *Finland*, 86 H3
Kivu, Lake, *Africa*, 102 E4
Klagenfurt, *Austria*, 90 E2
Klaipeda, *Lithuania*, 87 G5
Klar, *Europe*, 86 E3
Klintsy, *Russia*, 87 K5
Knittelfeld, *Austria*, 90 E2
Knoxville, *U.S.A.*, 33 K3
Kobar Sink, *Ethiopia*, 99 K6
Koblenz, *Germany*, 88 F4
Kochi, *India*, 71 D9
Kodiak Island, *U.S.A.*, 30 D3
Koforidua, *Ghana*, 101 E7
Kohtla-Jarve, *Estonia*, 86 H4
Kokkola, *Finland*, 86 G3
Kokshetau, *Kazakhstan*, 72 J1
Kola Peninsula, *Russia*, 86 L2
Kolda, *Senegal*, 101 C6
Kolding, *Denmark*, 87 D5
Kolhapur, *India*, 71 C7
Kolkata, *India*, 71 F6
Kolomna, *Russia*, 84 D2
Kolwezi, *Democratic Republic of Congo*, 102 E6
Kolyma Range, *Russia*, 75 H2
Komsomolets, *Kazakhstan*, 85 J3
Komsomolsk, *Russia*, 75 G3
Konduz, *Afghanistan*, 70 B3
Kongur Shan, *China*, 70 D3
Konosha, *Russia*, 84 E1
Konya, *Turkey*, 91 K4
Korce, *Albania*, 91 G3
Korea Bay, *Asia*, 69 K3
Korea Strait, *Asia*, 69 L4
Korhogo, *Ivory Coast*, 101 D7
Korla, *China*, 70 F2
Koror, *Palau, national capital*, 52 A4
Korosten, *Ukraine*, 87 J6
Kosciuszko, Mount, *Australia*, 55 J7
Kosice, *Slovakia*, 87 G6
Kosti, *Sudan*, 99 H6
Kostomuksha, *Russia*, 86 J2
Kostroma, *Russia*, 84 E2
Koszalin, *Poland*, 87 F5
Kota, *India*, 70 D5
Kota Bharu, *Malaysia*, 64 B2
Kota Kinabalu, *Malaysia*, 64 E2
Kotka, *Finland*, 86 H3
Kotlas, *Russia*, 85 F1
Koudougou, *Burkina Faso*, 101 E6
Koutiala, *Mali*, 101 D6
Kouvola, *Finland*, 86 H3
Kovel, *Ukraine*, 87 H6
Kozhikode, *India*, 71 D8
Kragujevac, *Yugoslavia*, 91 G2
Krakatoa, *Indonesia*, 64 C5
Krakow, *Poland*, 87 G6
Kraljevo, *Yugoslavia*, 91 G3
Kramatorsk, *Ukraine*, 84 D4
Kranj, *Slovenia*, 90 E2
Krasnodar, *Russia*, 72 C2
Krasnoyarsk, *Russia*, 74 E3
Kremenchuk, *Ukraine*, 84 C4
Kremenchukske Reservoir, *Ukraine*, 84 C4
Krishna, *India*, 71 D7
Kristiansand, *Norway*, 86 C4
Kristiansund, *Norway*, 86 C3
Krong Kaoh Kong, *Cambodia*, 66 D5
Kroonstad, *South Africa*, 104 E5
Krugersdorp, *South Africa*, 104 E5
Kryvyy Rih, *Ukraine*, 84 C4
Kuala Lumpur, *Malaysia, national capital*, 64 B3
Kuala Terengganu, *Malaysia*, 64 B2
Kuantan, *Malaysia*, 64 B3
Kuching, *Malaysia*, 64 D3
Kuhmo, *Finland*, 86 J2
Kuito, *Angola*, 104 C2
Kulob, *Tajikistan*, 70 B3
Kumamoto, *Japan*, 69 M4
Kumanovo, *Macedonia*, 91 G3
Kumasi, *Ghana*, 101 E7

Kumba, *Cameroon*, 102 A3
Kumo, *Nigeria*, 98 D6
Kunlun Mountains, *China*, 70 E3
Kunming, *China*, 68 F5
Kuopio, *Finland*, 86 H2
Kupang, *Indonesia*, 65 F6
Kuressaare, *Estonia*, 87 G4
Kurgan, *Russia*, 85 K2
Kurikka, *Finland*, 86 G3
Kuril Islands, *Russia*, 75 H3
Kursk, *Russia*, 84 D3
Kushiro, *Japan*, 69 P2
Kutahya, *Turkey*, 91 J4
Kutaisi, *Georgia*, 72 D3
Kutch, Rann of, *India*, 71 B6
Kuujjuaq, *Canada*, 31 N3
Kuusamo, *Finland*, 86 J2
Kuwait, *Asia, country*, 73 E6
Kuwait City, *Kuwait, national capital*, 73 E6
Kuybyshev Reservoir, *Russia*, 85 F3
Kuyto, Lake, *Russia*, 86 K2
Kuytun, *China*, 70 F2
Kwangju, *South Korea*, 69 L3
Kyoga, Lake, *Uganda*, 103 F3
Kyoto, *Japan*, 69 N3
Kyrenia, *Cyprus*, 91 K5
Kyrgyzstan, *Asia, country*, 70 C2
Kythira, *Greece*, 91 G4
Kyushu, *Japan*, 69 M4
Kyzyl, *Russia*, 74 E3

L

Laayoune, *Western Sahara, national capital*, 100 C3
Labe, *Guinea*, 101 C6
Labrador City, *Canada*, 31 N3
Labrador Sea, *North America*, 31 P2
La Chorrera, *Colombia*, 42 D4
La Coruna, *Spain*, 89 B6
Ladoga, Lake, *Russia*, 86 J3
Ladysmith, *South Africa*, 104 E5
Lae, *Papua New Guinea*, 65 L5
Lagdo Reservoir, *Cameroon*, 102 B2
La Gomera, *Canary Islands*, 100 B3
Lagos, *Nigeria*, 101 F7
Lagos, *Portugal*, 89 B7
La Grande Reservoir, *Canada*, 31 M3
Lagunillas, *Venezuela*, 42 D1
Lahat, *Indonesia*, 64 B4
Lahore, *Pakistan*, 70 C4
Lahti, *Finland*, 86 H3
Lai, *Chad*, 102 C2
La Libertad, *Ecuador*, 42 B4
Lambarene, *Gabon*, 102 B4
Lamia, *Greece*, 91 G4
Lancaster Sound, *Canada*, 31 L1
Land's End, *United Kingdom*, 88 C4
Langanes, *Iceland*, 86 Q2
Langsa, *Indonesia*, 64 A3
Lansing, *U.S.A., internal capital*, 33 K2
Lanzarote, *Canary Islands*, 100 C3
Lanzhou, *China*, 68 F3
Laoag, *Philippines*, 67 H4
Lao Cai, *Vietnam*, 66 D3
La Oroya, *Peru*, 42 C6
Laos, *Asia, country*, 66 D4
La Palma, *Canary Islands*, 100 B3
La Palma, *Panama*, 35 J6
La Paz, *Bolivia, national capital*, 44 E3
La Paz, *Mexico*, 34 B3
La Perouse Strait, *Asia*, 69 P1
Lapland, *Europe*, 86 H1
La Plata, *Argentina*, 44 G6
Lappeenranta, *Finland*, 86 J3
Laptev Sea, *Russia*, 75 G2
Larache, *Morocco*, 100 D1
Laredo, *U.S.A.*, 32 G5
La Rioja, *Argentina*, 44 E5
Larisa, *Greece*, 91 G4
Larkana, *Pakistan*, 70 B5
Larnaca, *Cyprus*, 91 K5
La Rochelle, *France*, 89 D5
La Romana, *Dominican Republic*, 35 L4
Larvik, *Norway*, 86 D4
Lashio, *Burma*, 66 C3

Lastoursville, *Gabon*, 102 B4
Las Vegas, *U.S.A.*, 32 C3
Latakia, *Syria*, 72 C4
Latvia, *Europe, country*, 87 H4
Launceston, *Australia*, 54 J8
Lausanne, *Switzerland*, 90 C2
Lautoka, *Fiji*, 55 Q3
Lebanon, *Asia, country*, 72 C5
Lecce, *Italy*, 91 F3
Ledo, Cape, *Angola*, 104 B1
Leeds, *United Kingdom*, 88 D3
Leeuwarden, *Netherlands*, 88 F3
Leeuwin, Cape, *Australia*, 54 B6
Leeward Islands, *North America*, 34 M4
Legaspi, *Philippines*, 67 H5
Legnica, *Poland*, 87 F6
Le Havre, *France*, 88 E4
Leipzig, *Germany*, 88 H4
Leiria, *Portugal*, 89 B7
Le Mans, *France*, 88 E4
Lena, *Russia*, 75 G2
Leon, *Mexico*, 34 D3
Leon, *Nicaragua*, 35 G5
Leon, *Spain*, 89 C6
Leonardville, *Namibia*, 104 C4
Lerida, *Spain*, 89 E6
Lerwick, *United Kingdom*, 88 D1
Les Cayes, *Haiti*, 35 K4
Leshan, *China*, 68 F5
Leskovac, *Yugoslavia*, 91 G3
Lesotho, *Africa, country*, 104 E5
Lesser Antilles, *North America*, 34 M5
Lesser Sunda Islands, *Indonesia*, 64 E5
Lesvos, *Greece*, 91 H4
Lethbridge, *Canada*, 30 H4
Leticia, *Brazil*, 42 E4
Lewiston, *U.S.A.*, 32 C1
Lexington, *U.S.A.*, 33 K3
Lhasa, *China*, 70 G5
Lhokseumawe, *Indonesia*, 64 A2
Lianyungang, *China*, 69 J4
Liaoyuan, *China*, 69 L2
Liberec, *Czech Republic*, 90 E1
Liberia, *Africa, country*, 101 D7
Liberia, *Costa Rica*, 35 G5
Libreville, *Gabon, national capital*, 102 A3
Libya, *Africa, country*, 98 E3
Libyan Desert, *Africa*, 98 F3
Lichinga, *Mozambique*, 105 G2
Lida, *Belarus*, 87 H5
Lidkoping, *Sweden*, 86 E4
Liechtenstein, *Europe, country*, 90 D2
Liege, *Belgium*, 88 F4
Lieksa, *Finland*, 86 J3
Liepaja, *Latvia*, 87 G4
Ligurian Sea, *Europe*, 90 C3
Likasi, *Democratic Republic of Congo*, 102 E6
Lille, *France*, 88 E4
Lillehammer, *Norway*, 86 D3
Lilongwe, *Malawi, national capital*, 105 F2
Lima, *Peru, national capital*, 42 C6
Limassol, *Cyprus*, 91 K5
Limerick, *Ireland*, 88 B3
Limnos, *Greece*, 84 C3
Limoges, *France*, 89 E5
Limon, *Costa Rica*, 35 H5
Limpopo, *Africa*, 104 F4
Linares, *Chile*, 45 D7
Linchuan, *China*, 69 J5
Lincoln, *U.S.A., internal capital*, 33 G2
Lindi, *Tanzania*, 103 G6
Line Islands, *Kiribati*, 53 H4
Linhares, *Brazil*, 44 K3
Linkoping, *Sweden*, 86 E4
Linz, *Austria*, 90 E1
Lions, Gulf of, *Europe*, 89 F6
Lipari Islands, *Italy*, 90 E4
Lipetsk, *Russia*, 84 D3
Lisbon, *Portugal, national capital*, 89 B7
Lithuania, *Europe, country*, 87 G5
Little Andaman, *India*, 71 G8
Little Rock, *U.S.A., internal capital*, 33 H4
Liuzhou, *China*, 68 G6

Liverpool, *United Kingdom,* 88 D3
Livingstone, *Zambia,* 104 E3
Livorno, *Italy,* 90 D3
Liwale, *Tanzania,* 103 G5
Ljubljana, *Slovenia, national capital,* 90 E2
Llanos, *South America,* 42 D2
Lloydminster, *Canada,* 30 J3
Lobamba, *Lesotho, national capital,* 104 F5
Lodz, *Poland,* 87 F6
Lofoten, *Norway,* 86 E1
Logan, Mount, *Canada,* 30 F2
Logrono, *Spain,* 89 D6
Loire, *France,* 88 E5
Loja, *Ecuador,* 42 C4
Lokan Reservoir, *Finland,* 86 H2
Lolland, *Denmark,* 87 D5
Lombok, *Indonesia,* 64 E5
Lome, *Togo, national capital,* 101 F7
London, *Canada,* 31 L4
London, *United Kingdom, national capital,* 88 D4
Londonderry, *United Kingdom,* 88 C3
Londrina, *Brazil,* 44 H4
Long Island, *The Bahamas,* 33 L6
Long Xuyen, *Vietnam,* 66 E5
Lopez, Cape, *Gabon,* 102 A4
Lop Nur, *China,* 70 G2
Lord Howe Island, *Australia,* 55 L6
Los Angeles, *Chile,* 45 D7
Los Angeles, *U.S.A.,* 32 C4
Los Mochis, *Mexico,* 34 C2
Louangphrabang, *Laos,* 66 D4
Loubomo, *Congo,* 102 B4
Louga, *Senegal,* 101 B5
Louisiana, *U.S.A., internal admin. area,* 33 H4
Lower California, *Mexico,* 34 B2
Loyalty Islands, *New Caledonia,* 55 N4
Luacano, *Angola,* 104 D2
Luanda, *Angola, national capital,* 104 B1
Luangwa, *Africa,* 104 F2
Luanshya, *Zambia,* 104 E2
Lubango, *Angola,* 104 B2
Lubbock, *U.S.A.,* 32 F4
Lublin, *Poland,* 87 G6
Lubny, *Ukraine,* 84 C3
Lubumbashi, *Democratic Republic of Congo,* 102 E6
Lucena, *Philippines,* 67 H5
Lucerne, *Switzerland,* 90 D2
Lucira, *Angola,* 104 B2
Lucknow, *India,* 70 E5
Luderitz, *Namibia,* 104 C5
Ludhiana, *India,* 70 D4
Ludza, *Latvia,* 87 H4
Luena, *Angola,* 104 C2
Luganville, *Vanuatu,* 55 N3
Lugo, *Spain,* 89 C6
Luhansk, *Ukraine,* 84 D4
Luiana, *Angola,* 104 D3
Lukulu, *Zambia,* 104 D2
Lumbala Kaquengue, *Angola,* 104 D2
Lumbala Nguimbo, *Angola,* 104 D2
Lundazi, *Zambia,* 105 F2
Lupilichi, *Mozambique,* 105 G2
Lusaka, *Zambia, national capital,* 104 E3
Lutsk, *Ukraine,* 87 H6
Luxembourg, *Europe, country,* 88 F4
Luxembourg, *Luxembourg, national capital,* 88 F4
Luxor, *Egypt,* 99 H3
Luzhou, *China,* 68 G5
Luzon, *Philippines,* 67 H4
Luzon Strait, *Philippines,* 67 H4
Lviv, *Ukraine,* 87 H6
Lyon, *France,* 89 F5
Lysychansk, *Ukraine,* 84 D4

m

Maan, *Jordan,* 73 C5
Maastricht, *Netherlands,* 88 F4
Macae, *Brazil,* 44 K4
Macapa, *Brazil,* 43 H3
Macau, *China,* 69 H6

Macedonia, *Europe, country,* 91 G3
Maceio, *Brazil,* 43 L5
Machakos, *Kenya,* 103 G4
Machala, *Ecuador,* 42 C4
Machu Picchu, *Peru,* 42 D6
Mackay, *Australia,* 55 J4
Mackenzie, *Canada,* 30 G2
Mackenzie Bay, *Canada,* 30 F2
Mackenzie Mountains, *Canada,* 30 F2
Macon, *U.S.A.,* 33 K4
Madagascar, *Africa, country,* 105 J4
Madang, *Papua New Guinea,* 65 L5
Madeira, *Atlantic Ocean,* 100 B2
Madeira, *Brazil,* 42 F5
Madingou, *Congo,* 102 B4
Madison, *U.S.A., internal capital,* 33 J2
Madras, *India,* 71 E8
Madrid, *Spain, national capital,* 89 D6
Madurai, *India,* 71 D9
Maevatanana, *Madagascar,* 105 J3
Mafeteng, *Lesotho,* 104 E5
Mafia Island, *Tanzania,* 103 H5
Magadan, *Russia,* 75 H3
Magangue, *Colombia,* 42 D2
Magdalena, *Bolivia,* 44 F2
Magdeburg, *Germany,* 88 G3
Magellan, Strait of, *South America,* 45 E10
Magnitogorsk, *Russia,* 85 H3
Mahajanga, *Madagascar,* 105 J3
Mahalapye, *Botswana,* 104 E4
Mahilyow, *Belarus,* 87 J5
Mahon, *Spain,* 89 F7
Maiduguri, *Nigeria,* 98 D6
Mai-Ndombe, Lake, *Democratic Republic of Congo,* 102 C4
Maine, *U.S.A., internal admin. area,* 33 N1
Maine, Gulf of, *U.S.A.,* 33 N2
Maio, *Cape Verde,* 101 M11
Majorca, *Spain,* 89 E7
Majuro, *Marshall Islands, national capital,* 52 E4
Makarikari, *Botswana,* 104 D4
Makassar Strait, *Indonesia,* 65 E4
Makeni, *Sierra Leone,* 101 C7
Makgadikgadi Pans, *Botswana,* 104 D4
Makhachkala, *Russia,* 72 E3
Makkovik, *Canada,* 31 P3
Makokou, *Gabon,* 102 B3
Makumbako, *Tanzania,* 103 F5
Makurdi, *Nigeria,* 102 A2
Mala, *Peru,* 42 C6
Malabo, *Equatorial Guinea, national capital,* 102 A3
Maladzyechna, *Belarus,* 87 H5
Malaga, *Spain,* 89 C7
Malaimbandy, *Madagascar,* 105 J4
Malakal, *Sudan,* 103 F2
Malakula, *Vanuatu,* 55 N3
Malang, *Indonesia,* 64 D5
Malanje, *Angola,* 104 C1
Malar, Lake, *Sweden,* 86 F4
Malatya, *Turkey,* 72 C4
Malawi, *Africa, country,* 105 F2
Malawi, Lake, *Africa,* 103 F6
Malaysia, *Asia, country,* 64 B2
Maldives, *Asia, country,* 71 C9
Male, *Maldives, national capital,* 71 C10
Malegaon, *India,* 71 C6
Malindi, *Kenya,* 103 H4
Malmo, *Sweden,* 87 E5
Malpelo Island, *Colombia,* 42 B3
Malta, *Europe, country,* 90 E4
Mamoudzou, *Mayotte,* 105 J2
Mamuno, *Botswana,* 104 D4
Man, *Ivory Coast,* 101 D7
Manado, *Indonesia,* 65 F3
Managua, *Nicaragua, national capital,* 35 G5
Manakara, *Madagascar,* 105 J4
Manama, *Bahrain, national capital,* 73 F6
Manaus, *Brazil,* 43 G4
Manchester, *United Kingdom,* 88 D3
Manchuria, *China,* 69 K2
Mandalay, *Burma,* 66 C3

Mandera, *Kenya,* 103 H3
Mandritsara, *Madagascar,* 105 J3
Mandurah, *Australia,* 54 C6
Mangalore, *India,* 71 C8
Mania, *Madagascar,* 105 J3
Manicouagan Reservoir, *Canada,* 31 N3
Manila, *Philippines, national capital,* 67 H5
Manisa, *Turkey,* 91 H4
Man, Isle of, *Europe,* 88 C3
Manitoba, *Canada, internal admin. area,* 31 K3
Manitoba, Lake, *Canada,* 31 K3
Manizales, *Colombia,* 42 C2
Manja, *Madagascar,* 105 H4
Mannar, *Sri Lanka,* 71 E9
Mannar, Gulf of, *Asia,* 71 D9
Mannheim, *Germany,* 88 G4
Mansa, *Zambia,* 104 E2
Manta, *Ecuador,* 42 B4
Manzhouli, *China,* 75 F3
Mao, *Chad,* 98 E6
Maoke Range, *Indonesia,* 65 J4
Maputo, *Mozambique, national capital,* 105 F5
Maraba, *Brazil,* 43 J5
Maracaibo, *Venezuela,* 42 D1
Maracaibo, Lake, *Venezuela,* 42 D2
Maracay, *Venezuela,* 42 E1
Maradi, *Niger,* 98 C6
Maranon, *Peru,* 42 C4
Marathon, *Canada,* 31 L4
Mar del Plata, *Argentina,* 45 G7
Margarita Island, *Venezuela,* 42 F1
Margherita Peak, *Africa,* 102 E3
Marib, *Yemen,* 73 E8
Mariental, *Namibia,* 104 C4
Marie Byrd Land, *Antarctica,* 109 Q3
Marijampole, *Lithuania,* 87 G5
Marilia, *Brazil,* 44 H4
Marimba, *Angola,* 104 C1
Mariupol, *Ukraine,* 84 D4
Marka, *Somalia,* 103 H3
Marmara, Sea of, *Turkey,* 91 J3
Maroantsetra, *Madagascar,* 105 J3
Maroua, *Cameroon,* 102 B1
Marquesas Islands, *French Polynesia,* 53 K5
Marrakech, *Morocco,* 100 D2
Marra, Mount, *Sudan,* 98 F6
Marsa Matruh, *Egypt,* 99 G2
Marseille, *France,* 89 F6
Marshall Islands, *Oceania, country,* 52 D3
Martapura, *Indonesia,* 64 D4
Martinique, *North America,* 34 M5
Mary, *Turkmenistan,* 72 H4
Maryland, *U.S.A., internal admin. area,* 33 L3
Masaka, *Uganda,* 103 F4
Masasi, *Tanzania,* 103 G6
Masbate, *Philippines,* 67 H5
Maseru, *Lesotho, national capital,* 104 E5
Mashhad, *Iran,* 72 G4
Masirah Island, *Oman,* 73 G7
Massachusetts, *U.S.A., internal admin. area,* 33 M2
Massangena, *Mozambique,* 105 F4
Massawa, *Eritrea,* 99 J5
Massif Central, *France,* 89 E5
Massinga, *Mozambique,* 105 G4
Masvingo, *Zimbabwe,* 104 F4
Matagalpa, *Nicaragua,* 35 G5
Matala, *Angola,* 104 B2
Matamoros, *Mexico,* 34 E2
Matanzas, *Cuba,* 35 H3
Mataram, *Indonesia,* 64 E5
Mataro, *Spain,* 89 E6
Matehuala, *Mexico,* 34 D3
Mato Grosso, Plateau of, *Brazil,* 43 G6
Matsuyama, *Japan,* 69 M4
Maturin, *Venezuela,* 42 F2
Maui, *U.S.A.,* 33 P7
Maun, *Botswana,* 104 D3
Mauritania, *Africa, country,* 100 C5
Mauritius, *Indian Ocean, country,* 105 L3

Mavinga, *Angola,* 104 D3
Mayotte, *Africa,* 105 J2
Mazar-e Sharif, *Afghanistan,* 70 B3
Mazatlan, *Mexico,* 34 C3
Mazyr, *Belarus,* 87 J5
Mbabane, *Swaziland, national capital,* 104 F5
Mbala, *Zambia,* 104 F1
Mbale, *Uganda,* 103 F3
Mbandaka, *Democratic Republic of Congo,* 102 C3
Mbarara, *Uganda,* 103 F4
Mbeya, *Tanzania,* 103 F5
Mbuji-Mayi, *Democratic Republic of Congo,* 102 D5
McClintock Channel, *Canada,* 30 J1
McClure Strait, *Canada,* 30 G1
McKinley, Mount, *U.S.A.,* 30 D2
Mead, Lake, *U.S.A.,* 32 D3
Mecca, *Saudi Arabia,* 73 C7
Mecula, *Mozambique,* 105 G2
Medan, *Indonesia,* 64 A3
Medellin, *Colombia,* 42 C2
Medford, *U.S.A.,* 32 B2
Medina, *Saudi Arabia,* 73 C7
Mediterranean Sea, *Africa/Europe,* 21
Medvezhyegorsk, *Russia,* 86 K3
Meerut, *India,* 70 D5
Meiktila, *Burma,* 66 C3
Meizhou, *China,* 69 J6
Mekele, *Ethiopia,* 103 G1
Meknes, *Morocco,* 100 D2
Mekong, *Asia,* 66 E5
Melaka, *Malaysia,* 64 B3
Melamo, Cape, *Mozambique,* 105 H2
Melanesia, *Oceania,* 52 D5
Melbourne, *Australia, internal capital,* 54 H7
Melilla, *Africa,* 89 D7
Melitopol, *Ukraine,* 84 D4
Melo, *Uruguay,* 44 H6
Melville Island, *Australia,* 54 F2
Melville Island, *Canada,* 30 H1
Melville Peninsula, *Canada,* 31 L2
Memphis, *U.S.A.,* 33 J3
Mendoza, *Argentina,* 44 E6
Menongue, *Angola,* 104 C2
Mentawai Islands, *Indonesia,* 64 A4
Menzel Bourguiba, *Tunisia,* 98 C1
Mergui, *Burma,* 66 C5
Mergui Archipelago, *Burma,* 66 C5
Merida, *Mexico,* 34 G3
Meridian, *U.S.A.,* 33 J4
Merlo, *Argentina,* 44 E6
Mersin, *Turkey,* 72 B4
Meru, *Kenya,* 103 G3
Messina, *Italy,* 90 E4
Messina, *South Africa,* 104 F4
Metz, *France,* 88 F4
Mexicali, *Mexico,* 34 A1
Mexico, *North America, country,* 34 D3
Mexico City, *Mexico, national capital,* 34 E4
Mexico, Gulf of, *North America,* 34 F3
Mexico, Plateau of, *Mexico,* 34 D2
Miami, *U.S.A.,* 33 K5
Michigan, *U.S.A., internal admin. area,* 33 J2
Michigan, Lake, *U.S.A.,* 33 J2
Michurinsk, *Russia,* 84 E3
Micronesia, *Oceania,* 52 C4
Micronesia, Federated States of, *Oceania, country,* 52 C4
Middlesbrough, *United Kingdom,* 88 D3
Midway Islands, *Pacific Ocean,* 52 F2
Mikkeli, *Finland,* 86 H3
Milan, *Italy,* 90 D2
Milange, *Mozambique,* 105 G3
Mildura, *Australia,* 54 H6
Minas, *Uruguay,* 44 G6
Mindanao, *Philippines,* 67 H6
Mindelo, *Cape Verde,* 101 M11
Mindoro, *Philippines,* 67 H5
Mingacevir, *Azerbaijan,* 72 E3
Minna, *Nigeria,* 101 G7

Minneapolis, *U.S.A.*, 33 H2
Minnesota, *U.S.A.*, *internal admin. area*, 33 G1
Minorca, *Spain*, 89 E6
Minot, *U.S.A.*, 32 F1
Minsk, *Belarus*, *national capital*, 87 H5
Miri, *Malaysia*, 64 D3
Mirim Lake, *Brazil*, 44 H6
Miskolc, *Hungary*, 87 G6
Misool, *Indonesia*, 65 H4
Misratah, *Libya*, 98 E2
Mississippi, *U.S.A.*, 33 H4
Mississippi, *U.S.A.*, *internal admin. area*, 33 H4
Mississippi Delta, *U.S.A.*, 33 J5
Missoula, *U.S.A.*, 32 D1
Missouri, *U.S.A.*, 32 G2
Missouri, *U.S.A.*, *internal admin. area*, 33 H3
Mistassini, Lake, *Canada*, 31 M3
Mitwaba, *Democratic Republic of Congo*, 102 E5
Mkushi, *Zambia*, 104 E2
Mmabatho, *South Africa*, 104 E5
Moanda, *Gabon*, 102 B4
Mobile, *U.S.A.*, 33 J4
Mochudi, *Botswana*, 104 E4
Mocuba, *Mozambique*, 105 G3
Modena, *Italy*, 90 D2
Mogadishu, *Somalia*, *national capital*, 103 J3
Mogao Caves, *China*, 68 E2
Mohilla Island, *Comoros*, 105 H2
Mo i Rana, *Norway*, 86 E2
Mojave Desert, *U.S.A.*, 32 C4
Moldova, *Europe*, *country*, 91 J2
Moldoveanu, Mount, *Romania*, 84 C4
Molepolole, *Botswana*, 104 E4
Mollendo, *Peru*, 42 D7
Molokai, *U.S.A.*, 33 P7
Molopo, *Africa*, 104 D5
Molucca Sea, *Indonesia*, 65 F4
Mombasa, *Kenya*, 103 G4
Monaco, *Europe*, *country*, 89 F6
Monastir, *Tunisia*, 98 D1
Monchegorsk, *Russia*, 86 K2
Monclova, *Mexico*, 34 D2
Moncton, *Canada*, 31 N4
Mongo, *Chad*, 98 E6
Mongolia, *Asia*, *country*, 68 F1
Mongu, *Zambia*, 104 D3
Monrovia, *Liberia*, *national capital*, 101 C7
Montalvo, *Ecuador*, 42 C4
Montana, *U.S.A.*, *internal admin. area*, 32 E1
Montauban, *France*, 89 E5
Montego Bay, *Jamaica*, 35 J4
Monterrey, *Mexico*, 34 D2
Montes Claros, *Brazil*, 44 K3
Montevideo, *Uruguay*, *national capital*, 44 G6
Montgomery, *U.S.A.*, *internal capital*, 33 J4
Montpelier, *U.S.A.*, *internal capital*, 33 M2
Montpellier, *France*, 89 E6
Montreal, *Canada*, 31 M4
Montserrat, *North America*, 34 M4
Monywa, *Burma*, 66 C3
Moose Jaw, *Canada*, 30 J3
Mopti, *Mali*, 101 E6
Moree, *Australia*, 55 J5
Morelia, *Mexico*, 34 D4
Morocco, *Africa*, *country*, 100 D2
Morogoro, *Tanzania*, 103 G5
Morombe, *Madagascar*, 105 H4
Moroni, *Comoros*, *national capital*, 105 H2
Morotai, *Indonesia*, 65 G3
Morpara, *Brazil*, 44 K2
Moscow, *Russia*, *national capital*, 84 D2
Moshi, *Tanzania*, 103 G4
Mosquitos, Gulf of, *North America*, 35 H5
Mossendjo, *Congo*, 102 B4
Mossoro, *Brazil*, 43 L5
Most, *Czech Republic*, 90 E1

Mostaganem, *Algeria*, 100 F1
Mostar, *Bosnia and Herzegovina*, 90 F3
Mosul, *Iraq*, 72 D4
Moulmein, *Burma*, 66 C4
Moundou, *Chad*, 102 C2
Mount Gambier, *Australia*, 54 H7
Mount Hagen, *Papua New Guinea*, 65 K5
Mount Isa, *Australia*, 54 G4
Mount Li, *China*, 68 G4
Moyale, *Ethiopia*, 103 G3
Moyobamba, *Peru*, 42 C5
Mozambique, *Africa*, *country*, 105 F3
Mozambique, *Mozambique*, 105 H3
Mozambique Channel, *Africa*, 105 G4
Mpika, *Zambia*, 104 F2
Mtwara, *Tanzania*, 103 H6
Mudanjiang, *China*, 69 L2
Mueda, *Mozambique*, 105 G2
Mufulira, *Zambia*, 104 E2
Multan, *Pakistan*, 70 B5
Mumbai, *India*, 71 C7
Mumbue, *Angola*, 104 C2
Munhango, *Angola*, 104 C2
Munich, *Germany*, 88 G4
Munster, *Germany*, 88 F4
Murcia, *Spain*, 89 D7
Murmansk, *Russia*, 86 K1
Murom, *Russia*, 84 E2
Murray, *Australia*, 54 G6
Murzuq, *Libya*, 98 D3
Muscat, *Oman*, *national capital*, 73 G7
Mutare, *Zimbabwe*, 105 F3
Mutoko, *Zimbabwe*, 104 F3
Mutsamudu, *Comoros*, 105 H2
Mutshatsha, *Democratic Republic of Congo*, 102 D6
Mwali, *Comoros*, 105 H2
Mwanza, *Tanzania*, 103 F4
Mwene-Ditu, *Democratic Republic of Congo*, 102 D5
Mweru, Lake, *Africa*, 104 E1
Mwinilunga, *Zambia*, 104 D2
Myanmar, *Asia*, *country*, 66 C3
Myitkyina, *Burma*, 66 C2
Mykolayiv, *Ukraine*, 84 C4
Mysore, *India*, 71 D8
Mzuzu, *Malawi*, 105 F2

n
Naberezhnyye Chelny, *Russia*, 85 G2
Nabeul, *Tunisia*, 90 D4
Nacala, *Mozambique*, 105 H2
Nador, *Morocco*, 89 D8
Naga, *Philippines*, 67 H5
Nagasaki, *Japan*, 69 L4
Nagoya, *Japan*, 69 N3
Nagpur, *India*, 71 D6
Nain, *Canada*, 31 N3
Nairobi, *Kenya*, *national capital*, 103 G4
Najran, *Saudi Arabia*, 73 D8
Nakhodka, *Russia*, 69 M2
Nakhon Ratchasima, *Thailand*, 66 D5
Nakhon Sawan, *Thailand*, 66 D4
Nakhon Si Thammarat, *Thailand*, 66 D6
Nakuru, *Kenya*, 103 G4
Nalchik, *Russia*, 72 D3
Namangan, *Uzbekistan*, 70 C2
Namib Desert, *Africa*, 104 B3
Namibe, *Angola*, 104 B3
Namibia, *Africa*, *country*, 104 C4
Nam Lake, *China*, 70 G4
Nampo, *North Korea*, 69 L3
Nampula, *Mozambique*, 105 G3
Namsos, *Norway*, 86 D2
Namur, *Belgium*, 88 F4
Nanaimo, *Canada*, 30 G4
Nanchang, *China*, 69 J5
Nancy, *France*, 88 F4
Nanded, *India*, 71 D7
Nanjing, *China*, 69 J4
Nanning, *China*, 68 G6
Nanping, *China*, 69 J5
Nantes, *France*, 89 D5
Napier, *New Zealand*, 55 Q7
Naples, *Italy*, 90 E3

Narmada, *India*, 71 C6
Narva, *Estonia*, 86 J4
Narvik, *Norway*, 86 F1
Nashik, *India*, 71 C6
Nashville, *U.S.A.*, *internal capital*, 33 J3
Nasi Lake, *Finland*, 86 G3
Nassau, *The Bahamas*, *national capital*, 33 L5
Nasser, Lake, *Egypt*, 99 H4
Natal, *Brazil*, 43 L5
Natitingou, *Benin*, 101 F6
Natuna Islands, *Indonesia*, 64 C3
Nauru, *Oceania*, *country*, 52 D5
Navapolatsk, *Belarus*, 87 J5
Navoiy, *Uzbekistan*, 70 B2
Nawabshah, *Pakistan*, 70 B5
Naxcivan, *Azerbaijan*, 72 E4
Nazca, *Peru*, 42 D6
Nazret, *Ethiopia*, 103 G2
Ndalatando, *Angola*, 104 B1
Ndele, *Central African Republic*, 102 D2
Ndjamena, *Chad*, *national capital*, 98 E6
Ndola, *Zambia*, 104 E2
Near Islands, *U.S.A.*, 31 A3
Nebraska, *U.S.A.*, *internal admin. area*, 32 F2
Necochea, *Argentina*, 45 G7
Negombo, *Sri Lanka*, 71 D9
Negro, *Brazil*, 42 F4
Negro, Cape, *Peru*, 42 B5
Negros, *Philippines*, 67 H6
Neiva, *Colombia*, 42 C3
Nekemte, *Ethiopia*, 103 G2
Nellore, *India*, 71 E8
Nelson, *New Zealand*, 55 P8
Nelspruit, *South Africa*, 104 F5
Nema, *Mauritania*, 101 D5
Neman, *Europe*, 87 G5
Nepal, *Asia*, *country*, 70 E5
Netherlands, *Europe*, *country*, 88 F3
Netherlands Antilles, *North America*, *dependency*, 35 L5
Nettilling Lake, *Canada*, 31 M2
Neuquen, *Argentina*, 45 E7
Nevada, *U.S.A.*, *internal admin. area*, 32 C3
Nevers, *France*, 89 E5
New Amsterdam, *Guyana*, 43 G2
Newark, *U.S.A.*, 33 M2
New Britain, *Papua New Guinea*, 65 M5
New Brunswick, *Canada*, *internal admin. area*, 31 N4
New Caledonia, *Oceania*, 55 M4
Newcastle, *Australia*, 55 K6
Newcastle upon Tyne, *United Kingdom*, 88 D3
New Delhi, *India*, *national capital*, 70 D5
Newfoundland, *Canada*, 31 P4
Newfoundland, *Canada*, *internal admin. area*, 31 N3
New Guinea, *Asia/Oceania*, 65 J4
New Hampshire, *U.S.A.*, *internal admin. area*, 33 M2
New Ireland, *Papua New Guinea*, 65 M4
New Jersey, *U.S.A.*, *internal admin. area*, 33 M3
New Mexico, *U.S.A.*, *internal admin. area*, 32 E4
New Orleans, *U.S.A.*, 33 J5
New Plymouth, *New Zealand*, 55 P7
Newport, *United Kingdom*, 88 D4
New Siberia Islands, *Russia*, 75 H2
New South Wales, *Australia*, *internal admin. area*, 54 H6
New York, *U.S.A.*, 33 M2
New York, *U.S.A.*, *internal admin. area*, 33 M2
New Zealand, *Australasia*, *country*, 55 Q8
Ngami, Lake, *Botswana*, 104 D4
Ngaoundere, *Cameroon*, 102 B2
Ngoma, *Zambia*, 104 E3
Nha Trang, *Vietnam*, 66 E5
Niagara Falls, *North America*, 31 M4
Niamey, *Niger*, *national capital*, 101 F6
Nias, *Indonesia*, 64 A3
Nicaragua, *North America*, *country*, 35 G5

Nicaragua, Lake, *Nicaragua*, 35 H5
Nice, *France*, 89 F6
Nicobar Islands, *India*, 71 G9
Nicosia, *Cyprus*, *national capital*, 91 K5
Nieuw Nickerie, *Surinam*, 43 G2
Niger, *Africa*, 101 G7
Niger, *Africa*, *country*, 98 D5
Niger Delta, *Nigeria*, 101 G8
Nigeria, *Africa*, *country*, 101 F7
Niigata, *Japan*, 69 N3
Nikopol, *Ukraine*, 84 C4
Niksic, *Yugoslavia*, 91 F3
Nile, *Africa*, 99 H3
Nile Delta, *Egypt*, 99 H2
Nimes, *France*, 89 F6
Ningbo, *China*, 69 K5
Niono, *Mali*, 101 D6
Nioro du Sahel, *Mali*, 101 D5
Nipigon, Lake, *Canada*, 31 L4
Nis, *Yugoslavia*, 91 G3
Nitra, *Slovakia*, 87 F6
Niue, *Oceania*, 52 G6
Nizhniy Novgorod, *Russia*, 84 E2
Nizhniy Tagil, *Russia*, 85 H2
Njazidja, *Comoros*, 105 H2
Njinjo, *Tanzania*, 103 G5
Nkongsamba, *Cameroon*, 102 A3
Nogales, *Mexico*, 34 B1
Nokaneng, *Botswana*, 104 D3
Norfolk Island, *Australia*, 55 N5
Norilsk, *Russia*, 74 E2
Norrkoping, *Sweden*, 86 F4
North America, 20
North Bay, *Canada*, 31 M4
North Cape, *New Zealand*, 55 P6
North Cape, *Norway*, 86 J1
North Carolina, *U.S.A.*, *internal admin. area*, 33 K3
North Dakota, *U.S.A.*, *internal admin. area*, 32 F1
Northern Ireland, *United Kingdom*, *internal admin. area*, 88 C3
Northern Mariana Islands, *Oceania*, 52 B3
Northern Territory, *Australia*, *internal admin. area*, 54 F3
North European Plain, *Russia*, 84 C2
North Frisian Islands, *Europe*, 88 F3
North Island, *New Zealand*, 55 Q7
North Korea, *Asia*, *country*, 69 L2
North Sea, *Europe*, 88 E2
North West Cape, *Australia*, 54 B4
Northwest Territories, *Canada*, *internal admin. area*, 30 G2
Norway, *Europe*, *country*, 86 D3
Norwegian Sea, *Europe*, 86 C2
Norwich, *United Kingdom*, 88 E3
Nosy Be, *Madagascar*, 105 J2
Nosy Boraha, *Madagascar*, 105 J3
Nottingham, *United Kingdom*, 88 D3
Nouadhibou, *Mauritania*, 100 B4
Nouakchott, *Mauritania*, *national capital*, 100 B5
Noumea, *New Caledonia*, 55 N4
Nova Iguacu, *Brazil*, 44 K4
Nova Mambone, *Mozambique*, 105 G4
Novara, *Italy*, 90 D2
Nova Scotia, *Canada*, *internal admin. area*, 31 N4
Novaya Zemlya, *Russia*, 74 C2
Novgorod, *Russia*, 86 J4
Novi Sad, *Yugoslavia*, 91 F2
Novocherkassk, *Russia*, 84 E4
Novo Mesto, *Slovenia*, 90 E2
Novorossiysk, *Russia*, 72 C3
Novosibirsk, *Russia*, 74 E3
Novyy Urengoy, *Russia*, 74 D2
Nubian Desert, *Africa*, 99 H4
Nueva Loja, *Ecuador*, 42 C3
Nukualofa, *Tonga*, *national capital*, 52 F7
Nukus, *Uzbekistan*, 72 G3
Nullarbor Plain, *Australia*, 54 E6
Nunavut, *Canada*, *internal admin. area*, 31 K2
Nungo, *Mozambique*, 105 G2
Nunivak Island, *U.S.A.*, 30 C3
Nuqui, *Colombia*, 42 C2

Prince of Wales Island, *Canada*, 31 K1
Prince Rupert, *Canada*, 30 F3
Principe, *Sao Tome and Principe*, 101 G8
Pripet, *Europe*, 87 J6
Pripet Marshes, *Europe*, 87 H5
Pristina, *Yugoslavia*, 91 G3
Providence, *Seychelles*, 105 K1
Providence, *U.S.A., internal capital*, 33 M2
Providence, Cape, *New Zealand*, 55 N9
Provo, *U.S.A.*, 32 D2
Prudhoe Bay, *U.S.A.*, 30 E1
Pskov, *Russia*, 87 J4
Pskov, Lake, *Europe*, 86 J4
Pucallpa, *Peru*, 42 D5
Puebla, *Mexico*, 34 E4
Pueblo, *U.S.A.*, 32 F3
Puerto Ayora, *Ecuador*, 42 N10
Puerto Cabezas, *Nicaragua*, 35 H5
Puerto Deseado, *Argentina*, 45 E9
Puerto Inirida, *Colombia*, 42 E3
Puerto Leguizamo, *Colombia*, 42 D4
Puerto Maldonado, *Peru*, 42 E6
Puerto Montt, *Chile*, 45 D8
Puerto Natales, *Chile*, 45 D10
Puerto Paez, *Venezuela*, 42 E2
Puerto Princesa, *Philippines*, 67 G6
Puerto Rico, *North America*, 34 L4
Puerto Suarez, *Bolivia*, 44 G3
Puerto Vallarta, *Mexico*, 34 C3
Pula, *Croatia*, 90 E2
Pulog, Mount, *Philippines*, 67 H4
Puncak Jaya, *Indonesia*, 65 J4
Pune, *India*, 71 C7
Puno, *Peru*, 42 D7
Punta Arenas, *Chile*, 45 D10
Puntarenas, *Costa Rica*, 35 H5
Purus, *Brazil*, 42 E5
Pusan, *South Korea*, 69 L3
Pushkin, *Russia*, 86 J4
Puula Lake, *Finland*, 86 H3
Pweto, *Democratic Republic of Congo*, 102 E5
Pya, Lake, *Russia*, 86 J2
Pye, *Burma*, 66 B4
Pyinmana, *Burma*, 66 C4
Pyongyang, *North Korea, national capital*, 69 L3
Pyramids of Giza, *Egypt*, 99 H3
Pyrenees, *Europe*, 89 D6
Pyrgos, *Greece*, 91 G4

q
Qaidam Basin, *China*, 70 G3
Qaraghandy, *Kazakhstan*, 74 D3
Qatar, *Asia, country*, 73 F6
Qattara Depression, *Egypt*, 99 G3
Qazvin, *Iran*, 72 E4
Qena, *Egypt*, 99 H3
Qingdao, *China*, 69 K3
Qinghai Lake, *China*, 68 F3
Qinhuangdao, *China*, 69 J3
Qiqihar, *China*, 69 K1
Qom, *Iran*, 72 F5
Qostanay, *Kazakhstan*, 85 J3
Quanzhou, *China*, 69 J6
Quebec, *Canada, internal admin. area*, 31 M3
Quebec, *Canada, internal capital*, 31 M4
Queen Charlotte Islands, *Canada*, 30 F3
Queen Elizabeth Islands, *Canada*, 30 H1
Queen Maud Land, *Antarctica*, 109 C3
Queensland, *Australia, internal admin. area*, 54 H4
Quelimane, *Mozambique*, 105 G3
Quellon, *Chile*, 45 D8
Quetta, *Pakistan*, 70 B4
Quevedo, *Ecuador*, 42 C4
Quezaltenango, *Guatemala*, 34 F4
Quezon City, *Philippines*, 67 H5
Quibdo, *Colombia*, 42 C2
Quillabamba, *Peru*, 42 D6
Quimper, *France*, 88 C5
Quincy, *U.S.A.*, 33 H3
Qui Nhon, *Vietnam*, 66 E5
Quirima, *Angola*, 104 C2

Quito, *Ecuador, national capital*, 42 C4
Qurghonteppa, *Tajikistan*, 70 B3
Qyzylorda, *Kazakhstan*, 72 J3

r
Raahe, *Finland*, 86 H2
Rabat, *Morocco, national capital*, 100 D2
Rabaul, *Papua New Guinea*, 65 M4
Rabnita, *Moldova*, 91 J2
Radisson, *Canada*, 31 M3
Radom, *Poland*, 87 G6
Ragusa, *Italy*, 90 E4
Rahimyar Khan, *Pakistan*, 70 C5
Raipur, *India*, 71 E6
Rajahmundry, *India*, 71 E7
Rajkot, *India*, 71 C6
Rajshahi, *Bangladesh*, 71 F6
Rakops, *Botswana*, 104 D4
Raleigh, *U.S.A., internal capital*, 33 L3
Ralik Islands, *Marshall Islands*, 52 D3
Ramnicu Valcea, *Romania*, 91 H2
Rancagua, *Chile*, 44 D6
Ranchi, *India*, 71 F6
Randers, *Denmark*, 87 D4
Rangoon, *Burma, national capital*, 66 C4
Rangpur, *Bangladesh*, 70 F5
Rapid City, *U.S.A.*, 32 F2
Ras Dashen, *Ethiopia*, 103 G1
Rasht, *Iran*, 72 E4
Ratak Islands, *Marshall Islands*, 52 E3
Rat Islands, *U.S.A.*, 31 A3
Rauma, *Finland*, 86 G3
Ravenna, *Italy*, 90 E2
Rawson, *Argentina*, 45 E8
Rechytsa, *Belarus*, 87 J5
Recife, *Brazil*, 43 M5
Reconquista, *Argentina*, 44 G5
Red, *Asia*, 68 F6
Red, *U.S.A.*, 33 G4
Red Deer, *Canada*, 30 H3
Redding, *U.S.A.*, 32 B2
Red Sea, *Africa/Asia*, 99 J4
Regensburg, *Germany*, 88 H4
Regina, *Canada, internal capital*, 30 J3
Regina, *French Guiana*, 43 H3
Rehoboth, *Namibia*, 104 C4
Reims, *France*, 88 F4
Reindeer Lake, *Canada*, 30 J3
Rennell Island, *Solomon Islands*, 55 M2
Rennes, *France*, 88 D4
Reno, *U.S.A.*, 32 C3
Reunion, *Indian Ocean*, 105 L4
Revelstoke, *Canada*, 30 H3
Revillagigedo Islands, *Mexico*, 34 B4
Reykjavik, *Iceland, national capital*, 86 N2
Rhine, *Europe*, 88 F4
Rhode Island, *U.S.A., internal admin. area*, 33 M2
Rhodes, *Greece*, 91 J4
Rhone, *Europe*, 89 F5
Riau Islands, *Indonesia*, 64 B3
Ribeirao Preto, *Brazil*, 44 J4
Riberalta, *Bolivia*, 44 E2
Richards Bay, *South Africa*, 104 F5
Richmond, *U.S.A., internal capital*, 33 L3
Riga, *Latvia, national capital*, 87 H4
Riga, Gulf of, *Europe*, 87 G4
Rijeka, *Croatia*, 90 E2
Rimini, *Italy*, 90 E2
Rio Branco, *Brazil*, 42 E5
Rio Cuarto, *Argentina*, 44 F6
Rio de Janeiro, *Brazil*, 44 K4
Rio Gallegos, *Argentina*, 45 E10
Rio Grande, *Argentina*, 45 E10
Rio Grande, *Brazil*, 44 H6
Rio Grande, *U.S.A.*, 32 F5
Riohacha, *Colombia*, 42 D1
Rivas, *Nicaragua*, 35 G5
Rivera, *Uruguay*, 44 G6
Riverside, *U.S.A.*, 32 C4
Rivne, *Ukraine*, 87 H6
Riyadh, *Saudi Arabia, national capital*, 73 E7
Roanoke, *U.S.A.*, 33 L3
Robson, Mount, *Canada*, 30 H3

Rochester, *U.S.A.*, 33 L2
Rockford, *U.S.A.*, 33 J2
Rockhampton, *Australia*, 55 K4
Rocky Mountains, *U.S.A.*, 32 D1
Romania, *Europe, country*, 91 G2
Rome, *Italy, national capital*, 90 E3
Rondonopolis, *Brazil*, 44 H3
Ronne, *Denmark*, 87 D4
Ronne Ice Shelf, *Antarctica*, 109 S3
Roraima, Mount, *South America*, 42 F2
Rosario, *Argentina*, 44 F6
Roseau, *Dominica, national capital*, 34 M4
Roslavl, *Russia*, 87 K5
Ross Ice Shelf, *Antarctica*, 109 M4
Rosso, *Mauritania*, 101 B5
Rostock, *Germany*, 88 H3
Rostov, *Russia*, 84 D4
Roti, *Indonesia*, 65 H6
Rotorua, *Australia*, 55 Q7
Rotterdam, *Netherlands*, 88 F4
Rouen, *France*, 88 E4
Rovaniemi, *Finland*, 86 H2
Roxas, *Philippines*, 67 H5
Rub al Khali, *Asia*, 73 E8
Rudnyy, *Kazakhstan*, 85 J3
Rufino, *Argentina*, 44 F6
Rufunsa, *Zambia*, 104 E3
Rukwa, Lake, *Tanzania*, 103 F5
Rundu, *Namibia*, 104 C3
Rurrenabaque, *Bolivia*, 44 E2
Ruse, *Bulgaria*, 91 H3
Russia, *Asia/Europe, country*, 74 E3
Ruvuma, *Africa*, 103 G6
Rwanda, *Africa, country*, 102 E4
Ryazan, *Russia*, 84 D3
Rybinsk, *Russia*, 84 D2
Rybinsk Reservoir, *Russia*, 84 D2
Rybnik, *Poland*, 87 F6
Ryukyu Islands, *Japan*, 69 L5
Rzeszow, *Poland*, 87 G6
Rzhev, *Russia*, 84 C2

s
Saarbrucken, *Germany*, 88 F4
Saarijarvi, *Finland*, 86 H3
Sabha, *Libya*, 98 D3
Sabzevar, *Iran*, 72 G4
Sacramento, *U.S.A., internal capital*, 32 B3
Sadah, *Yemen*, 73 E8
Safi, *Morocco*, 100 D2
Sahara, *Africa*, 98 C5
Saharanpur, *India*, 70 D5
Sahel, *Africa*, 98 C6
Sahiwal, *Pakistan*, 70 C4
Saida, *Algeria*, 100 F2
Saigon, *Vietnam*, 66 E5
Saimaa Lake, *Finland*, 86 H3
St. Andrew, Cape, *Madagascar*, 105 H3
St. Denis, *Reunion*, 105 L4
St. Etienne, *France*, 89 F5
St. Francis, Cape, *South Africa*, 104 D6
St. George, *U.S.A.*, 32 D3
St. George's, *Grenada, national capital*, 34 M5
St. Helier, *Channel Islands*, 88 D4
Saint John, *Canada*, 31 N4
St. John's, *Antigua and Barbuda, national capital*, 34 M4
St. John's, *Canada, internal capital*, 31 P4
St. Kitts and Nevis, *North America, country*, 34 M4
St. Lawrence, *Canada*, 31 M4
St. Lawrence, Gulf of, *Canada*, 31 N4
St. Lawrence Island, *U.S.A.*, 30 B2
St. Louis, *Senegal*, 101 B5
St. Louis, *U.S.A.*, 33 H3
St. Lucia, *North America, country*, 34 M5
St. Lucia, Cape, *South Africa*, 105 F5
St. Malo, *France*, 88 D4
St. Martha, Cape, *Angola*, 104 B2
St. Martin, *North America*, 34 M4
St. Mary, Cape, *Madagascar*, 105 J5
St. Paul, *U.S.A., internal capital*, 33 H1

St. Petersburg, *Russia*, 86 J4
St. Petersburg, *U.S.A.*, 33 K5
St. Pierre, *Seychelles*, 105 J1
St. Pierre and Miquelon, *North America*, 31 P4
St. Polten, *Austria*, 90 E1
St. Vincent and the Grenadines, *North America, country*, 34 M5
St. Vincent, Cape, *Portugal*, 89 B7
Sakhalin, *Russia*, 75 H3
Saki, *Azerbaijan*, 72 E3
Saki, *Nigeria*, 101 F7
Sakishima Islands, *Japan*, 69 K6
Sal, *Cape Verde*, 101 M11
Salado, *Argentina*, 44 F5
Salalah, *Oman*, 73 F8
Salamanca, *Spain*, 89 C6
Salem, *India*, 71 D8
Salem, *U.S.A., internal capital*, 32 B1
Salerno, *Italy*, 90 E4
Salihorsk, *Belarus*, 87 H5
Salinas, *U.S.A.*, 32 B3
Salta, *Argentina*, 44 E4
Saltillo, *Mexico*, 34 D2
Salt Lake City, *U.S.A., internal capital*, 32 D2
Salto, *Uruguay*, 44 G6
Salton Sea, *U.S.A.*, 32 C4
Salvador, *Brazil*, 43 L6
Salween, *Asia*, 66 C4
Salzburg, *Austria*, 90 E2
Samar, *Philippines*, 67 J5
Samara, *Russia*, 85 G3
Samarinda, *Indonesia*, 64 E4
Samarqand, *Uzbekistan*, 70 B3
Sambalpur, *India*, 71 E6
Samoa, *Oceania, country*, 52 F6
Sampwe, *Democratic Republic of Congo*, 102 E5
Sam Rayburn Reservoir, *U.S.A.*, 33 H4
Samsun, *Turkey*, 72 C3
San, *Mali*, 101 E6
Sana, *Yemen, national capital*, 73 D8
Sanandaj, *Iran*, 72 E4
San Andres Island, *Colombia*, 35 H5
San Antonio, *U.S.A.*, 32 G5
San Antonio, Cape, *Argentina*, 45 G7
San Antonio Oeste, *Argentina*, 45 F8
San Cristobal, *Ecuador*, 42 P10
San Cristobal, *Venezuela*, 42 D2
Sandakan, *Malaysia*, 65 E3
San Diego, *U.S.A.*, 32 C4
Sandoway, *Burma*, 66 B4
San Fernando, *Chile*, 44 D6
San Fernando de Apure, *Venezuela*, 42 E2
San Francisco, *Argentina*, 44 F6
San Francisco, *U.S.A.*, 32 B3
San Francisco, Cape, *Ecuador*, 42 B3
Sangihe Islands, *Indonesia*, 65 G3
San Jorge, Gulf of, *Argentina*, 45 E9
San Jose, *Costa Rica, national capital*, 35 H6
San Jose, *U.S.A.*, 32 B3
San Jose de Chiquitos, *Bolivia*, 44 F3
San Jose del Guaviare, *Colombia*, 42 D3
San Juan, *Argentina*, 44 E6
San Juan, *Puerto Rico*, 34 L4
San Julian, *Argentina*, 45 E9
Sanliurfa, *Turkey*, 72 C4
San Lucas, Cape, *Mexico*, 34 B3
San Luis, *Argentina*, 44 E6
San Luis Obispo, *U.S.A.*, 32 B3
San Luis Potosi, *Mexico*, 34 D3
San Marino, *Europe, country*, 90 E3
San Matias, Gulf of, *Argentina*, 45 F8
San Miguel de Tucuman, *Argentina*, 44 E5
San Nicolas de los Arroyos, *Argentina*, 44 F6
San Pedro, *Ivory Coast*, 101 D8
San Pedro de Atacama, *Chile*, 44 E4
San Rafael, *Argentina*, 44 E6
San Remo, *Italy*, 90 C3
San Salvador, *Ecuador*, 42 N10
San Salvador, *El Salvador, national capital*, 34 G5

Tabriz, *Iran*, 72 E4
Tabuk, *Saudi Arabia*, 73 C6
Tacloban, *Philippines*, 67 J5
Tacna, *Peru*, 42 D7
Tacoma, *U.S.A.*, 32 B1
Tacuarembo, *Uruguay*, 44 G6
Tademait Plateau, *Algeria*, 100 F3
Tadmur, *Syria*, 72 C5
Taegu, *South Korea*, 69 L3
Taejon, *South Korea*, 69 L3
Tagus, *Europe*, 89 B7
Tahat, Mount, *Algeria*, 100 G4
Tahiti, *French Polynesia*, 53 J6
Tahoua, *Niger*, 98 C6
Taian, *China*, 69 J3
Taichung, *Taiwan*, 69 K6
Tai Lake, *China*, 69 J4
Taimyr Peninsula, *Russia*, 75 F2
Tainan, *Taiwan*, 69 K6
Taipei, *Taiwan, national capital*, 69 K5
Taiping, *Malaysia*, 64 B3
Taiwan, *Asia, country*, 69 K6
Taiwan Strait, *Asia*, 69 J6
Taiyuan, *China*, 68 H3
Taizz, *Yemen*, 73 D9
Tajikistan, *Asia, country*, 70 B3
Taj Mahal, *India*, 70 D5
Tajumulco, *Guatemala*, 34 F4
Taklimakan Desert, *China*, 70 E3
Talara, *Peru*, 42 B4
Talaud Islands, *Indonesia*, 65 G3
Talca, *Chile*, 45 D7
Taldyqorghan, *Kazakhstan*, 70 D1
Tallahassee, *U.S.A., internal capital*, 33 K4
Tallinn, *Estonia, national capital*, 86 H4
Taltal, *Chile*, 44 D5
Tamale, *Ghana*, 101 E7
Tamanrasset, *Algeria*, 100 G4
Tambacounda, *Senegal*, 101 C6
Tambov, *Russia*, 84 E3
Tampa, *U.S.A.*, 33 K5
Tampere, *Finland*, 86 G3
Tampico, *Mexico*, 34 E3
Tana, Lake, *Ethiopia*, 103 G1
Tandil, *Argentina*, 45 G7
Tanga, *Tanzania*, 103 G5
Tanganyika, Lake, *Africa*, 102 E5
Tangier, *Morocco*, 100 D1
Tangshan, *China*, 69 J3
Tanimbar Islands, *Indonesia*, 65 H5
Tanjungkarang-Telukbetung, *Indonesia*, 64 C5
Tanjungredeb, *Indonesia*, 64 E3
Tanta, *Egypt*, 99 H2
Tan-Tan, *Morocco*, 100 C3
Tanzania, *Africa, country*, 103 F5
Tapachula, *Mexico*, 34 F5
Tapajos, *Brazil*, 43 G5
Tarakan, *Indonesia*, 64 E3
Taranto, *Italy*, 90 F3
Taraz, *Kazakhstan*, 70 C2
Targu Mures, *Romania*, 91 H2
Tarija, *Bolivia*, 44 F4
Tarim Basin, *China*, 70 E3
Tarkwa, *Ghana*, 101 E7
Tarnow, *Poland*, 87 G6
Tarragona, *Spain*, 89 E6
Tartagal, *Argentina*, 44 F4
Tartu, *Estonia*, 86 H4
Tartus, *Syria*, 72 C5
Tashkent, *Uzbekistan, national capital*, 70 B2
Tasmania, *Australia, internal admin. area*, 55 J8
Tasman Sea, *Australasia*, 55 L7
Tataouine, *Tunisia*, 98 D2
Taunggyi, *Burma*, 66 C3
Taupo, Lake, *New Zealand*, 55 Q7
Taurus Mountains, *Turkey*, 91 J4
Tavoy, *Burma*, 66 C5
Tawau, *Malaysia*, 65 E3
Taytay, *Philippines*, 67 G5
Taza, *Morocco*, 100 E2
Tbilisi, *Georgia, national capital*, 72 D3
Tchibanga, *Gabon*, 102 B4
Tebessa, *Algeria*, 100 G1

Tegal, *Indonesia*, 64 C5
Tegucigalpa, *Honduras, national capital*, 35 G5
Tehran, *Iran, national capital*, 72 F4
Tehuacan, *Mexico*, 34 E4
Tehuantepec, Gulf of, *Mexico*, 34 E4
Tehuantepec, Isthmus of, *Mexico*, 34 E4
Tekirdag, *Turkey*, 91 H3
Tel Aviv-Yafo, *Israel*, 73 B5
Teller, *U.S.A.*, 30 C2
Temuco, *Chile*, 45 D7
Ten Degree Channel, *India*, 71 G9
Tenerife, *Canary Islands*, 100 B3
Tenkodogo, *Burkina Faso*, 101 E6
Tennessee, *U.S.A.*, 33 J3
Tennessee, *U.S.A., internal admin. area*, 33 J3
Teofilo Otoni, *Brazil*, 44 K3
Teotihuacan, *Mexico*, 34 E4
Terceira, *Azores*, 100 K10
Teresina, *Brazil*, 43 K4
Ternate, *Indonesia*, 65 G3
Terni, *Italy*, 90 E3
Ternopil, *Ukraine*, 87 H6
Terracotta Army, *China*, 68 G4
Terra Firma, *South Africa*, 104 D5
Teseney, *Eritrea*, 99 J5
Tete, *Mozambique*, 105 F3
Tetouan, *Morocco*, 100 D1
Tetovo, *Macedonia*, 91 G3
Texarkana, *U.S.A.*, 33 H4
Texas, *U.S.A., internal admin. area*, 32 G4
Thailand, *Asia, country*, 66 D4
Thailand, Gulf of, *Asia*, 66 D6
Thai Nguyen, *Vietnam*, 66 E3
Thanh Hoa, *Vietnam*, 66 E4
Thar Desert, *Asia*, 70 B5
Thasos, *Greece*, 91 H3
Thaton, *Burma*, 66 C4
Thessaloniki, *Greece*, 91 G3
Thies, *Senegal*, 101 B6
Thika, *Kenya*, 103 G4
Thimphu, *Bhutan, national capital*, 70 F5
Thompson, *Canada*, 31 K3
Three Points, Cape, *Africa*, 101 E8
Thunder Bay, *Canada*, 31 L4
Tianjin, *China*, 69 J3
Tibesti Mountains, *Africa*, 98 E4
Tibet, *China*, 70 F4
Tibet, Plateau of, *China*, 70 F4
Tidjikja, *Mauritania*, 100 C5
Tien Shan, *Asia*, 70 D2
Tierra del Fuego, *South America*, 45 E10
Tighina, *Moldova*, 91 J2
Tigris, *Asia*, 73 E5
Tijuana, *Mexico*, 34 A1
Tikal, *Guatemala*, 34 G4
Tikhvin, *Russia*, 86 K4
Tillaberi, *Niger*, 101 F6
Timbuktu, *Mali*, 101 E5
Timisoara, *Romania*, 91 G2
Timor, *Asia*, 65 F5
Timor Sea, *Asia/Australasia*, 65 G6
Tindouf, *Algeria*, 100 D3
Tirana, *Albania, national capital*, 91 F3
Tiraspol, *Moldova*, 91 J2
Tiruchchirappalli, *India*, 71 D8
Titicaca, Lake, *South America*, 42 E7
Tlemcen, *Algeria*, 100 E2
Toamasina, *Madagascar*, 105 J3
Tobago, *Trinidad and Tobago*, 34 M5
Toba, Lake, *Indonesia*, 64 A3
Tobol, *Asia*, 85 K2
Tobolsk, *Russia*, 85 K2
Tobyl, *Kazakhstan*, 85 J3
Tocantins, *Brazil*, 43 J4
Togo, *Africa, country*, 101 F7
Tokelau, *Oceania*, 52 F5
Tokyo, *Japan, national capital*, 69 N3
Tolanaro, *Madagascar*, 105 J5
Toledo, *Spain*, 89 D7
Toledo, *U.S.A.*, 33 K2
Toledo Bend Reservoir, *U.S.A.*, 33 H4

Toliara, *Madagascar*, 105 H4
Tolyatti, *Russia*, 85 F3
Tolybay, *Kazakhstan*, 85 J3
Tomakomai, *Japan*, 69 P2
Tombouctou, *Mali*, 101 E5
Tomsk, *Russia*, 74 E3
Tonga, *Oceania, country*, 52 F6
Tongliao, *China*, 69 K2
Tonkin, Gulf of, *Asia*, 66 E4
Tonle Sap, *Cambodia*, 66 D5
Toowoomba, *Australia*, 55 K5
Topeka, *U.S.A., internal capital*, 33 G3
Top, Lake, *Russia*, 86 K2
Topoli, *Kazakhstan*, 85 G4
Torghay, *Kazakhstan*, 85 J4
Tornio, *Finland*, 86 H2
Toronto, *Canada, internal capital*, 31 M4
Torrens, Lake, *Australia*, 54 G6
Torreon, *Mexico*, 34 D2
Torres Strait, *Australasia*, 54 H2
Tortuga Island, *Venezuela*, 42 E1
Toubkal, *Morocco*, 100 D2
Tougan, *Burkina Faso*, 101 E6
Touggourt, *Algeria*, 100 G2
Toulon, *France*, 89 F6
Toulouse, *France*, 89 E6
Tours, *France*, 88 E5
Townsville, *Australia*, 54 J3
Toyama, *Japan*, 69 N3
Tozeur, *Tunisia*, 98 C2
Trabzon, *Turkey*, 72 C3
Tralee, *Ireland*, 88 B3
Transantarctic Mountains, *Antarctica*, 109 S4
Transylvanian Alps, *Romania*, 91 G2
Trapani, *Italy*, 90 E4
Trento, *Italy*, 90 D2
Trenton, *U.S.A., internal capital*, 33 M2
Tres Arroyos, *Argentina*, 45 F7
Tres Marias Reservoir, *Brazil*, 44 J3
Tres Puntas, Cape, *Argentina*, 45 E9
Trieste, *Italy*, 90 E2
Trincomalee, *Sri Lanka*, 71 E9
Trinidad, *Bolivia*, 44 F2
Trinidad, *Trinidad and Tobago*, 34 M5
Trinidad and Tobago, *North America, country*, 34 M5
Tripoli, *Lebanon*, 72 C5
Tripoli, *Libya, national capital*, 98 D2
Trivandrum, *India*, 71 D9
Trnava, *Slovakia*, 87 F6
Trois-Rivieres, *Canada*, 31 M4
Tromso, *Norway*, 86 F1
Trondheim, *Norway*, 86 D3
Troyes, *France*, 88 F4
Trujillo, *Peru*, 42 C5
Tsau, *Botswana*, 104 D4
Tses, *Namibia*, 104 C5
Tshabong, *Botswana*, 104 D5
Tshane, *Botswana*, 104 D4
Tshikapa, *Democratic Republic of Congo*, 102 D5
Tshwane, *Botswana*, 104 D4
Tsimlyansk Reservoir, *Russia*, 84 E4
Tsiroanomandidy, *Madagascar*, 105 J3
Tsumeb, *Namibia*, 104 C3
Tuamotu Archipelago, *French Polynesia*, 53 K6
Tubmanburg, *Liberia*, 101 C7
Tubruq, *Libya*, 98 F2
Tucson, *U.S.A.*, 32 D4
Tucupita, *Venezuela*, 42 F2
Tucurui Reservoir, *Brazil*, 43 J4
Tugela Falls, *South Africa*, 104 E5
Tuguegarao, *Philippines*, 67 H4
Tula, *Russia*, 84 D3
Tulcea, *Romania*, 91 J2
Tulsa, *U.S.A.*, 33 G3
Tumaco, *Colombia*, 42 C3
Tumbes, *Peru*, 42 B4
Tunduma, *Tanzania*, 103 F5
Tunduru, *Tanzania*, 103 G6
Tunis, *Tunisia, national capital*, 98 D1
Tunisia, *Africa, country*, 98 C2
Tunja, *Colombia*, 42 D2

Tupelo, *U.S.A.*, 33 J4
Tupiza, *Bolivia*, 44 E4
Turbat, *Pakistan*, 73 H6
Turbo, *Colombia*, 42 C2
Turin, *Italy*, 90 C2
Turkana, Lake, *Africa*, 103 G3
Turkey, *Asia, country*, 72 C4
Turkistan, *Kazakhstan*, 70 B2
Turkmenabat, *Turkmenistan*, 72 H4
Turkmenbasy, *Turkmenistan*, 72 F3
Turkmenistan, *Asia, country*, 72 G4
Turks and Caicos Islands, *North America*, 35 K3
Turku, *Finland*, 86 G3
Turpan, *China*, 70 F2
Turpan Depression, *China*, 70 G2
Tuscaloosa, *U.S.A.*, 33 J4
Tuvalu, *Oceania, country*, 52 E5
Tuxtla Gutierrez, *Mexico*, 34 F4
Tuzla, *Bosnia and Herzegovina*, 91 F2
Tuz, Lake, *Turkey*, 91 K4
Tver, *Russia*, 84 D2
Twin Falls, *U.S.A.*, 32 D2
Tynda, *Russia*, 75 G3
Tyrrhenian Sea, *Europe*, 90 D3
Tyumen, *Russia*, 85 K2

U

Ubangi, *Africa*, 102 C3
Uberaba, *Brazil*, 44 J3
Uberlandia, *Brazil*, 44 J3
Ubon Ratchathani, *Thailand*, 66 D4
Ucayali, *Peru*, 42 D5
Udaipur, *India*, 71 C6
Uddevalla, *Sweden*, 86 D4
Udon Thani, *Thailand*, 66 D4
Uele, *Democratic Republic of Congo*, 102 D3
Ufa, *Russia*, 85 H3
Uganda, *Africa, country*, 103 F3
Uitenhage, *South Africa*, 104 E6
Ujung Pandang, *Indonesia*, 65 E5
Ukhta, *Russia*, 74 C2
Ukraine, *Europe, country*, 84 C4
Ulan Bator, *Mongolia, national capital*, 68 G1
Ulanhot, *China*, 69 K1
Ulan Ude, *Russia*, 75 F3
Ulm, *Germany*, 88 G4
Uluru, *Australia*, 54 F5
Ulyanovsk, *Russia*, 85 F3
Uman, *Ukraine*, 87 J6
Ume, *Sweden*, 86 F2
Umea, *Sweden*, 86 G3
Umnak Island, *U.S.A.*, 31 C3
Umtata, *South Africa*, 104 E6
Unalaska Island, *U.S.A.*, 31 C3
Ungava Bay, *Canada*, 31 N3
Ungava Peninsula, *Canada*, 31 M2
Unimak Island, *U.S.A.*, 31 C3
United Arab Emirates, *Asia, country*, 73 F7
United Kingdom, *Europe, country*, 88 D3
United States of America, *North America, country*, 32 F3
Upington, *South Africa*, 104 D5
Uppsala, *Sweden*, 86 F4
Ural, *Asia*, 85 G4
Ural Mountains, *Russia*, 85 H2
Uray, *Russia*, 85 J1
Urganch, *Uzbekistan*, 70 A2
Urmia, *Iran*, 72 E4
Uruapan, *Mexico*, 34 D4
Urucui, *Brazil*, 43 K5
Uruguaiana, *Brazil*, 44 G5
Uruguay, *South America, country*, 44 G6
Urumqi, *China*, 70 F2
Usak, *Turkey*, 91 J4
Ushuaia, *Argentina*, 45 E10
Uskemen, *Kazakhstan*, 74 E3
Utah, *U.S.A., internal admin. area*, 32 D3
Utsjoki, *Finland*, 86 H1
Utsunomiya, *Japan*, 69 N3
Uy, *Asia*, 85 J3
Uyuni, *Bolivia*, 44 E4
Uzbekistan, *Asia, country*, 74 D3

ACKNOWLEDGEMENTS

Every effort has been made to trace the copyright holders of the material in this book. If any rights have been omitted, the publishers offer to rectify this in any subsequent edition, following notification. The publishers are grateful to the following organizations and individuals for their contributions and permission to reproduce material (t=top, m=middle, b=bottom, l=left, r=right):

Cover © Jacques Descloitres, MODIS Land Science Team; (globe) © Digital Vision; **Endpapers** © Ric Ergenbright/CORBIS; **p1** © Jim Zuckerman/CORBIS; **p2–3** © Art Wolfe/Science Photo Library; **p4–5** Stephen Moncrieff, Digital Vision; **p4** (tr) © Geospace/Science Photo Library; **p6** (bl) © CNES, 1988 Distribution SPOT Image/Science Photo Library; (mr) Stephen Moncrieff; **p7** (tm & tr) European Map Graphics Ltd; (b) © Paul A. Souders/CORBIS; **p8–9** (background) © Digital Vision; **p8** (mr) PHOTO ESA; **p9** (tl) © NERC Satellite Station, University of Dundee www.sat.dundee.ac.html; (br) Science Photo Library/European Space Agency; **p10** (b) Stephen Moncrieff; (tr) © Dan Guravich/CORBIS; **p11** (bl) European Map Graphics Ltd; (tr) © W. Perry Conway/CORBIS; **p12** (b) © Christopher Cormack/CORBIS; **p13** Stephen Moncrieff, Craig Asquith; **p14** (tr) © Bill Ross/CORBIS; (b) Craig Asquith; **p15** Craig Asquith; **p16–17** European Map Graphics Ltd; **p22–23** © Richard Cummins/CORBIS; **p23** (br) © W. Perry Conway/CORBIS; **p24** (tr) © Worldsat International/Science Photo Library; (m) © NASA/JSC; (b) © Raymond Gehman/CORBIS; **p25** © NASA/CORBIS; **p26–27** (b) © Richard Cummins/CORBIS; **p26** (t) © Dave G. Houser/CORBIS; **p27** (tr) © Joe McDonald/CORBIS; **p28** (l) © Angelo Hornak/CORBIS; (tr) © Carl & Ann Purcell/CORBIS; **p29** (tl) © Schafer & Hill/GettyImages; (br) © Michael & Patricia Fogden/CORBIS; **p36–37** © Galen Rowell/CORBIS; **p37** (tr) © Eye Ubiquitous/CORBIS; **p38** (m) © Julian Baum & David Angus/Science Photo Library; (bl) © Yann Arthus-Bertrand/CORBIS; (mr) © NASA/JSC; **p39** (r) © CNES, 1986 Distribution SPOT Image/Science Photo Library; (bl) © CNES, Distribution SPOT Image/Science Photo Library; **p40–41** (b) © Robert Frerck/GettyImages; **p40** (tr) Claus Meyer/GettyImages; **p41** (tl) Walter Bibikow/GettyImages; (tr) Peter Oxford/BBC Wild; **p46–47** © Still Pictures/Pascal Kobeh; **p47** (br) © Bates Littlehales/CORBIS; **p48–49** (b) © Amos Nachoum/CORBIS; **p48** (ml) © 1995, Worldsat International and J. Knighton/Science Photo Library; (tr) © NASA/JSC; **p49** (tr) © CNES, Distribution SPOT Image/Science Photo Library; (ml) © CORBIS; **p50** © Yoshio Tomii/Bruce Coleman; **p51** (tr) © Klein/Hubert/Still Pictures; (bl) © Zefa visual media; **p56–57** © Michael S. Yamashita/CORBIS; **p57** (br) © Keren Su/CORBIS; **p58** (tr) © Worldsat International/Science Photo Library; (m) © CNES, 1986 Distribution SPOT Image/Science Photo Library; (b) © Liu Liqun/CORBIS; **p59** (t) © NASA JPL; (br) © CNES, 1987 Distribution SPOT Image/Science Photo Library; **p60** (l) © Keren Su/CORBIS; (tr) © Keren Su/China Span/Alamy; **p61** (tl) © www.pictor.com; (b) © Papilio/CORBIS; **p62** (tr) © Richard T. Nowitz/CORBIS; (b) © Archivo Iconografico, S.A./CORBIS; **p63** (ml) © www.pictor.com; (tr) © Wolfgang Kaehler/CORBIS; (b) © Brian & Cherry Alexander Photography; **p76–77** © Digital Vision; **p77** (br) Agripicture/© Peter Dean; **p78–79** (b) © Peter Adams/GettyImages; **p78** (tr) NASA/GSFC/MITI/ERSDAC/JAROS, & U.S./Japan ASTER Science Team; (ml) © NASA GSFC Scientific Visualization Studio; **p79** (tr) © CNES, 1994 Distribution SPOT Image/Science Photo Library; (m) © German Remote Sensing Data Center; **p80** (tr) © The Art Archive/Historiska Muséet Stockholm/Dagli Orti; (bl) © Enzo & Paolo Ragazzini/CORBIS; **p81** (t) © Zefa visual media; (br) © Frans Lanting/Minden Pictures; **p82** © Paul Hardy/corbisstockmarket.com; **p83** (t) © Bob Krist/CORBIS; (b) © Araldo de Luca/CORBIS; **p92–93** © Tom Brakefield/CORBIS; **p93** (br) © Gallo Images/CORBIS; **p94** (tr) © Worldsat International/Science Photo Library; (bl) © Yann Arthus-Bertrand/CORBIS; (br) © NASA JPL; **p95** (r) © Jacques Descloitres, MODIS Land Science Team; (bl) © NASA/JSC; **p96** © Roger Wood/CORBIS; **p97** (ml) © Charles O'Rear/CORBIS; (tr) © Wolfgang Kaehler/CORBIS; (b) © Karl Ammann/CORBIS; **p106** (tr) © Worldsat International/Science Photo Library; (m) © Jan Jordan; **p107** (t) © NRSC Ltd/Science Photo Library; (b) © Digital Vision; **p110–111** (b) © Paul A. Souders/CORBIS; **p110** (tl) © Peter M. Wilson/CORBIS; (tm) © Joe McDonald/CORBIS; (ml) © Charles O'Rear/CORBIS; (mr) © Vanni Archive/CORBIS; **p111** (br) Galen Rowell/CORBIS; **p112–125** (background) © Digital Vision; (Afghanistan, Bahrain, Comoros, Rwanda, Turkmenistan and East Timor flags) © Shipmate Flags, Vlaardingen, The Netherlands; (all other flags) © Flag Enterprises Ltd; **p125** (b) AFP Photos/Henry Ray Abrams; **p126** (b) Craig Asquith.

Managing editor: Gillian Doherty
Managing designer: Mary Cartwright
Cover design by Zöe Wray
With thanks to Ruth King